WE MEAN BUSINESS

An elementary course in business English

Susan Norman

Longman Group UK Limited
Longman House, Burnt Mill
Harlow, Essex CM20 2JE, England
and Associated Companies throughout the world.

© Longman Group UK Limited 1982, 1993
All rights reserved; no part of this publication may be
reproduced, stored in a retrieval system, or transmitted
in any form or by any means, electronic, mechanical,
photocopying, recording, or otherwise, without
the prior written permission of the Publishers.

First published 1982
Updated edition 1993

ISBN 0 582 216044

Printed in Malaysia by TCP

Illustrated by Kathy Baxendale, Paul Sullivan
and Taurus Graphics

CONTENTS

INTRODUCTION – Course Content		Page x
	Methodology	Page xvi

UNIT ONE — A VISITOR TO BOS — Page 1

Business Content: Organisation chart
Structures: The verb *to be*
Possessive adjectives
Genitive ('s)
Question words: *What? Where? Who?*
Functions: Introductions; greetings; giving personal information; registering at a hotel
Lexis: Jobs, countries, nationalities, titles

Language drills tapescript — Page 8
Workbook answers — Page 11
Workbook contents:
- Exercise 1 Overseas sales staff (genitive 's)
- Exercise 2 Countries (and nationalities and *to be*)
- Exercise 3 Greetings and introductions
- Exercise 4 A/an

UNIT TWO — A NEWCOMER — Page 12

Business content: Telephone conversations; business letter format
Structures: Demonstrative pronouns: *this/that/these/those*
There is/there are
Prepositions: *on, in, above, below, under, between, next to, to the left/right of, on the right/left*
Question words: *How many?*
Function: Describing location
Lexis: Office furniture, equipment, stationery, cardinal numbers, business letter terminology

Language drills tapescript — Page 20
Workbook answers — Page 23
Workbook contents:
- Exercise 5 Word puzzle (office furniture)
- Exercise 6 Calculations (numbers)
- Exercise 7 Jumbled words (describing location)
- Exercise 8 Business letters (headings and endings)

UNIT THREE — THE BOS BUILDING — Page 25

Business content: A memorandum; telephone conversations; company names
Structures: Present progressive tense
Imperatives
Prepositions (*continued*)
Question word: *Which?*
Functions: Discussing activities; giving directions; giving commands

CONTENTS

Lexis:	Ordinal numbers, parts of a building, some office activities

Language drills tapescript — Page 30

Workbook answers — Page 34

Workbook contents:	Exercise 9 Ordinal numbers
	Exercise 10 Office plan
	Exercise 11 What are you doing? (present progressive)
	Exercise 12 A memo (punctuation and capital letters)

UNIT FOUR — OFFICE ROUTINE — Page 35

Business content:	A survey; a block chart
Structures:	Present simple tense
	Adverbs used with the present simple
	Question words: *How? How long? How often? What time? When?*
Functions:	Discussing routine actions and timetables; telling the time; writing a personal letter
Pronunciation:	Final -*s*
Lexis:	Travel/means of transport, time, some verbs of office routine

Language drills tapescript — Page 42

Workbook answers — Page 47

Workbook contents:	Exercise 13 Times
	Exercise 14 Transport puzzle
	Exercise 15 A timetable (reading comprehension)
	Exercise 16 Present simple and progressive tenses
	Exercise 17 A personal letter

UNIT FIVE — ORDERING STATIONERY — Page 49

Business content:	An order; a business letter (reply to a request)
Structures:	Count and mass nouns
	Plurals
	Adjectives
	Need
	Have got
Function:	Expressing need
Lexis:	Stationery, adjectives to describe stationery, party food, numerical expressions

Language drills tapescript — Page 59

Workbook answers — Page 62

Workbook contents:	Exercise 18 Plurals pronunciation (final -*s*)
	Exercise 19 Word puzzle (stationery)
	Exercise 20 Questions
	Exercise 21 Adjectives puzzle
	Exercise 22 Numbers crossword

CONTENTS

CONSOLIDATION UNIT A
YOUR NEWS AND NEWS EXTRACTS   Page 63

Workbook answers Test A   Page 67

Workbook contents: Test A   1 Plurals
2 Prepositions
3 Times
4 Question formation
5 Ordinal numbers
6 Pronouns

UNIT SIX   JOY'S LEAVING PARTY   Page 69

Structures: *Would like* (*to* + infinitive)
Articles: *a/the/one*
Let's + infinitive

Functions: Describing people; ordering a meal; invitations; suggestions

Pronunciation: Word stress

Lexis: Days of the week, adjectives to describe personal appearance, entertainment, a menu

Language drills tapescript   Page 75

Workbook answers   Page 78

Workbook contents: Exercise 23 Offers (short answers)
Exercise 24 Description puzzle (personal description)
Exercise 25 An invitation
Exercise 26 One (to replace nouns)

UNIT SEVEN   THE IDEAL SECRETARY   Page 79

Business content: A survey; a memo; job advertisements; letters of recommendation

Structures: *Can* + infinitive
Was/were
Prepositions (*revision*)

Function: Giving opinions

Lexis: Adjectives to describe personal qualities, *to give*

Language drills tapescript   Page 86

Workbook answers   Page 89

Workbook contents: Exercise 27 Short answers
Exercise 28 Hidden word puzzle (adjectives/qualities)
Exercise 29 A description (of an office)
Exercise 30 Jumbled words (describing a secretary)
Exercise 31 The alphabet
Exercise 32 Can you do it? (numbers puzzle)

v

CONTENTS

UNIT EIGHT — APPOINTMENTS — Page 90

Business content: Making appointments; business letters
Structures: Present progressive with future reference
Must/have to/have got to
Imperatives (*revision*)
Functions: Giving directions; expressing obligation
Lexis: Dates, expressions of time, months

Language drills tapescript — Page 96

Workbook answers — Page 100

Workbook contents:
Exercise 33 Days and months
Exercise 34 Vocabulary (categories)
Exercise 35 Appointments (present progressive future)
Exercise 36 Prepositions (with time expressions)

UNIT NINE — JOB SATISFACTION — Page 102

Business content: Pie chart; report; petty cash; time and motion study
Structures: Verbs and expressions of liking + *ing*
Should/why don't . . .?
Present simple tense (*revision*)
Function: Suggestions
Lexis: Fractions, jobs, report and petty cash vocabulary; numbers (*revision*)

Language drills tapescript — Page 109

Workbook answers — Page 113

Workbook contents:
Exercise 37 Figures
Exercise 38 Question tags
Exercise 39 Jobs
Exercise 40 Word stress
Exercise 41 Would like to do/like doing
Exercise 42 Fractions

UNIT TEN — JOB APPLICATIONS — Page 114

Business content: Curriculum vitae; job interviews; letters of application
Structures: Past simple tense
Question words: *Who saw . . .? Who did . . . see?*
Functions: Describing past actions; discussing biographical information
Pronunciation: Final *-d*
Lexis: Regular and irregular verbs

Language drills tapescript — Page 120

Workbook answers — Page 124

Workbook contents:
Exercise 43 Odd-man-out
Exercise 44 They're/their/there

CONTENTS

        Exercise 45 Categories puzzle
        Exercise 46 Curriculum vitae (reading comprehension)
        Exercise 47 Experience (writing a paragraph)

CONSOLIDATION UNIT B
YOUR NEWS AND NEWS EXTRACTS   Page 126

Workbook answers Test B   Page 129

Workbook contents: Test B 1 Structure formation
                            2 Dates
                            3 Short answers
                            4 Question formation
                            5 Prepositions (with expressions of time)
                            6 Tenses

UNIT ELEVEN   A MEETING   Page 131

Business content: Job experience; letters of enquiry; interviews
Structures: Present perfect tense
                Adverbs used with the present perfect
                Could/would you . . . ?
                Will future
                Possessive pronouns
                Capital letters and punctuation
                Question words: *Whose? Who's?*
Function: Polite requests

Language drills tapescript   Page 137

Workbook answers   Page 142

Workbook contents: Exercise 48 Contractions
                                Exercise 49 Pronouns
                                Exercise 50 Remembering (past simple/present perfect)
                                Exercise 51 Word trail (punctuation marks)
                                Exercise 52 Punctuation (in a letter)

UNIT TWELVE   BOS IS THE BEST   Page 144

Business content: Advertising circulars; reprographics; a survey
Structures: Comparatives and superlatives
                Short answers (*So can I/I can't*)
Functions: Comparing objects, processes and situations
Lexis: Adjectives, abbreviations

Language drills tapescript   Page 149

Workbook answers   Page 152

Workbook contents: Exercise 53 Comparisons (of two offices)
                                Exercise 54 It's/its
                                Exercise 55 Comparing situations

CONTENTS

UNIT THIRTEEN COMPLAINTS   Page 153

Business content: Post room procedures; telexes; a letter of complaint
Structures: The passive
                    Short answers (*Nor do I/I do*)
Functions: Comparing situations; discussing procedures; complaining
Lexis: Numbers (*revision*), world exports

Language drills tapescript   Page 158

Workbook answers   Page 162

Workbook contents: Exercise 56 News article (cloze test in the passive)
                    Exercise 57 Post room puzzle
                    Exercise 58 Comparing situations
                    Exercise 59 Problems

UNIT FOURTEEN TELEPHONE MESSAGES   Page 164

Business content: Telephone messages
Structures: Reported (indirect) speech
                    Could/might be . . .
                    Look like . . .
                    Too + adjectives
Function: Hypothesising
Pronunciation: Homophones
Lexis: Office equipment and stationery (*revision*)

Language drills tapescript   Page 169

Workbook answers   Page 173

Workbook contents: Exercise 60 To do/doing
                    Exercise 61 Rhyming words
                    Exercise 62 Word puzzle
                    Exercise 63 Reported speech

UNIT FIFTEEN PLANS   Page 174

Business content: Meetings, minutes and agenda
Structures: *Going to* future
                    Reported speech (*continued*)
Function: Discussing plans
Lexis: Meetings

Language drills tapescript   Page 177

Workbook answers   Page 179

Workbook contents: Exercise 64 Short responses
                    Exercise 65 Going to/present progressive
                    Exercise 66 Word stress
                    Exercise 67 The news (vocabulary)
                    Exercise 68 A worker's quiz

CONSOLIDATION UNIT C
YOUR NEWS AND NEWS EXTRACTS   Page 181

Workbook answers Tests C and D   Page 184

Workbook contents: Test C   1   Question formation
                                                              2   Reported speech
                                                              3   Past participles
                                                              4   Short responses
                                                              5   Figures
                                                              6   Comparatives
                       Test D   1   Multiple choice sentence completion
                                                             2   Multiple choice sentence completion

INTRODUCTION

COURSE CONTENT

We Mean Business is an elementary business English course consisting of:

Students' Book (SB)

Teacher's Book (TB)

Workbook (WB)

Cassette of listening exercises

Two cassettes of language drills (LD)

Other abbreviations used in the TB to save space are:

language drills tapescript (in TB)

h/w	– homework	
T	– teacher	T–S
TT	– teachers	S–S
S	– student	SS–SS
SS	– students	

T–S, S–S, SS–SS: see note on pairwork, TB page xvii

The course is aimed at SS embarking on study for a business career. They may have little or no knowledge of English, or in fact business, but the course progresses at a fairly rapid pace which makes it particularly suitable for 'false' beginners or anyone needing a complete revision of basic structures. The course is designed to provide work for between 60 and 90 contact hours, plus h/w, although the amount of time it takes to cover the material will vary greatly from class to class and will depend to a large extent on whether or not the additional activities and optional material are used. TT might also 'dip into' the material and use individual exercises to augment other courses at low language levels and all TT are recommended to use only as much or as little of the material as is relevant to their own SS. Exercises which are omitted may be used at a later date for revision.

Language content

The overall grading of the language content is structural, each structure being contextualised in a specific situation and expressing a specific language function. The practice of question forms (which are often neglected in T–S interaction) is greatly increased by the emphasis throughout the course on pairwork. SS are also expected to give short natural answers to questions, rather than 'full sentences' for the sake of extra structure practice which would be highly unnatural. The structural approach is simplified by the introduction of *only one* main concept at a time for any structure and the emphasis throughout is on the acquisition of relevant and useful language practised in a meaningful context.

INTRODUCTION

Much of the classwork is designed to improve SS' communicative ability, fluency and oral mastery of the language. However, throughout the course, there are also exercises which highlight the skills of reading, writing, listening and pronunciation. The aim within each unit has been to provide a variety of interesting exercises which lend themselves to stimulating classroom exploitation, but which are flexible enough to be used in a variety of teaching systems. Suggestions for presentation and exploitation of the material, for suitable h/w activities and for further activities are given in the TB. The contents list sets out the language content of the course in detail and the aim of each exercise is stated in the TB.

Business content

Specific business content in the course is deliberately limited, but many aspects of office life, business correspondence and simple business skills and procedures are introduced as a means of practising language and there is a systematic approach to the teaching of business letters. The aim has been to lay the groundwork for more detailed business or commercial studies SS might undertake at a later date at a higher language level, such as with *We're In Business* by the same author. Where it has proved impossible to be neutral, business practice relates to Britain unless otherwise stated.

Please remember also that business procedures, politics and social habits change with time. This updated edition of *We Mean Business* is accurate at the time of going to press, but be aware of things which might change or date (we have tried to keep these to a minimum). View such things positively by asking SS to update them.

Some of the vocabulary relating to business lies outside that normally considered relevant at an elementary level of language learning. Although it is obviously relevant in the context of this course, some of the business vocabulary, particularly that in the consolidation units, is presented for recognition only, to be activated in the course of SS' subsequent studies.

Some business documents and forms are presented in the book, partly to introduce them to inexperienced learners, but also because form-filling is a valid language exercise, particularly in a business context. If SS are to be discouraged from writing in their books, they could be asked to copy out the forms before they do the relevant exercises. A more satisfactory approach, however, in terms of making the activity more realistic, would be for the T to provide printed or photocopied forms, memo sheets etc for SS to fill in.

For business content at a higher language level see the companion volume to this course, *We're In Business* by the same author.

We Mean Business: Students' Book

The SB contains 15 main units, three consolidation units and the listening cassette tapescript. The exercises are numbered consecutively throughout the book, partly for ease of reference, but also to give SS additional number practice. The contents list reproduced in both SB and TB details the language and business content of each unit.

Main units Each main unit begins with an introductory exercise which contains much of the language exploited more fully in the rest of the unit. The introductory exercises are in the form of dialogues presented with photos which are also recorded on the listening cassette. They can be exploited for reading or listening comprehension before or after SS study the rest of the unit. SS are only expected to give short answers to the comprehension questions (preferably orally) as full answers sometimes require the use of structures which have not been presented. Excerpts from the dialogues can also be used to present or practise structures, vocabulary or pronunciation.

The main language points are summarised in the language notes at the end of each unit. SS can be directed to the language notes to learn selected items before they are presented or practised in class or they can be studied after the classwork (where the emphasis is on communicative oral work) to help SS grasp the grammatical 'rules' and patterns in the language. These notes only reflect language presented in each unit and frequently simplify the grammatical content to make it more accessible to elementary SS, so they are not comprehensive or an alternative to a grammar book.

Consolidation units These three units are based on 'news items' taken from the 'radio' (on cassette) and 'newspaper cuttings'. They revise and consolidate structures and lexis presented in previous units in the context of world and local news. No new structures are presented in these units, but SS are exposed to a wider business context and a greater range of vocabulary.

The focus in these units is on the receptive listening and reading skills, as a contrast to the oral emphasis in the main units. Many of the exercises can be done as tests, or equally be adapted for pairwork, groupwork or whole class activities.

Newspapers and radio news programmes are a rich source of business language frequently available to foreign learners in their own countries, yet both are difficult to understand without help. The consolidation units provide a graded introduction to the news media and many of the exercises in these units could be adapted to exploit real programmes and articles.

Cassette tapescript SS should be discouraged from reading the tapescript until after they have done the relevant listening exercises. Scripts are printed in full only if they are not included in the body of the SB (the introductory exercises for each unit, for example, are not printed again in the tapescript).

We Mean Business: Recordings

Listening cassette 🖭 The listening cassette is an integral part of the course, as throughout there is a systematic approach to improving the listening skill. To improve SS' ability to cope with the spoken English they are likely to encounter in real life, some of the characters speak with a slight regional or foreign accent, but none of these is strong enough to interfere with understanding. On the cassette are recorded the introductory exercise in each unit plus all other listening exercises marked in the SB and TB with the symbol 🖭.

Language drills cassettes The LDs can be used in a laboratory where SS can record their responses on tape, but they can also be used in a listening laboratory or in the classroom. The drills are three-phase: prompt, space for SS' response, correct response. The pace of the drills varies, but all the sentences are spoken at a natural speed for native speakers. This may seem fast to foreign learners at first, but they are more likely to achieve natural intonation patterns if they try to imitate the models exactly. All the drills are spoken in a standard southern educated English accent, although different male and female voices are used for variety.

Drills have the same number as the exercise they refer to. Not all exercises are exploited with a drill and some exercises have more than one drill (numbered A, B, C etc). There are no drills relating to the consolidation unit exercises. The LDT is in the TB and the recorded examples for each drill are printed in the SB immediately after the related exercise. Some of the drills are comprehension exercises relating to the SB and SS are sometimes referred to prompts in the exercises, in which case SS need to refer to the SB. However, since the drills are to improve oral/aural competence, whenever possible (and this is marked in the LDT) SS should do the drills with their books closed.

Although the drills are an optional part of the course, they are recommended for use with SS or classes who benefit from individual reinforcement of language. The drills allow SS to concentrate on oral precision, especially where the emphasis in classwork is on communication. Not all classes will need to do every drill and the T is recommended to choose those drills most relevant to his/her own SS. Different SS could well do different drills according to their particular needs and problems.

The purpose and format of the drills is varied, the aim being to keep SS mentally alert and to prevent the mechanical repetition which can inhibit rather than promote language learning. Although all the drills are designed to improve pronunciation and fluency (SS should strive to reproduce exactly the sounds, stress, intonation and speed of the models) different drills focus on different language skills (the aim of each drill is stated in the LDT). Drills can be done before or after classroom practice, but the structures and vocabulary they contain should be presented before they are attempted.

TT should refer to the LDT in the TB before SS do the drills as they do not always follow the same format as the classroom exercises and may need particular preparation. Some of the drills practise aspects of the language which are not fully covered in the classwork and TT are directed to them for use in class if the drills are not being used regularly in a laboratory. TT might also use the LD cassettes in class as a model for intonation patterns, the pronunciation of names etc.

To save space, examples (which are repeated on the cassettes) are not written out again in the LDT. Nor are dialogues written out in full in the LDT if they appear in the SB. However, although not all dialogues are recorded on the listening cassette, those which are exploited with a drill are recorded in full first so that they can be used for presentation in class if required.

We Mean Business: Workbook

The WB is an optional course component and may be used by the whole class or by individual SS for additional practice or revision. The T might also choose to use specific exercises in class or for h/w.

The WB contains 15 units to correspond to and practise language from the main units in the SB. Many of the exercises are in the form of games or puzzles for motivation; a complete list of the WB exercises is contained in the TB contents list. Certain exercises extend the language learnt in class rather than simply practising it and where further preparation is needed there is a note in the TB.

The WB also contains three tests to correspond to the consolidation units in the SB, plus an extra test at the end of the book. The tests cover structural items in previous units and may be used either to check attainment after the course of study or to diagnose areas of weakness.

INTRODUCTION

We Mean Business: Teacher's Book

The TB contains:
Course contents list
Introduction: Course content
          Notes on methodology and contents

18 units to correspond to the 18 units in the SB and WB, each containing:
- Contents list for the unit
- Answers and teaching notes
- Suggested additional activities
- LDT and notes on LD (except for consolidation units)
- WB answers and notes

For ease of reference, answers are written immediately after each exercise heading. Where the exercise follows the same format as the LD, the T is referred to the LDT for answers, but sample answers to freer writing exercises such as letters and reports are intended as a guide only. The aim of each exercise is stated before any teaching suggestions and where exercises may not in themselves be sufficient presentation of new language, a method of presentation is suggested. Although the teaching suggestions reflect how the course was intended to be used, TT should exploit the material in any way appropriate to their SS.

Language explanations are given as a guide to the level of explanation necessary for elementary SS. They are simplified and necessarily incomplete, so TT are recommended to use a grammar book such as *Longman English Grammar* by L.G. Alexander (Longman) or *A Communicative Grammar of English* by Geoffrey Leech and Jan Svartvik (Longman) for further reference.

Although the medium of instruction is intended to be English, there are places in the course where certain vocabulary items are most simply explained by translation. With multi-national classes, SS should be allowed to use native-language English dictionaries at this point. From about Unit 6, however, all SS should be referred to a simplified English-English dictionary such as the *Longman New Pocket English Dictionary*. The T is recommended to spend some time familiarising the SS (perhaps with the help of the accompanying booklet) with this invaluable source of self-help.

INTRODUCTION

METHODOLOGY

The following notes explain some of the ideas underlying the material in this course and give suggestions on exploiting the material to the best advantage. The suggestions, exercises and additional activities can frequently be adapted for teaching and practising other language items either in this or other courses.

The medium of instruction

The medium of instruction in the SB is English and the course was designed to be taught in English. SS quickly become used to responding to English instructions and to using the language themselves in class, particularly if they are not over-corrected. On the other hand, if the only time SS are asked to use English is in the course of a drill when they are under pressure to produce perfect sentences on which they will be judged, the effect can be very demotivating and undermine their confidence.

Where SS are unused to being taught in English, the T can gradually introduce phrases of greeting and farewell and classroom management (taking the register, simple instructions such as *Please open your books at* ... etc) and then extend this to general social chat until the whole course is being conducted in English. Obviously there are cases where there is a direct relationship between structures or vocabulary in English and the native language when the easiest teaching method is translation (some of the WB exercises ask SS for translations into their own language). It is also a good idea to train SS to use dictionaries, both native language-English and English-English. The dangers of translation though, are that SS become dependent on it, come to rely on the T translating and so do not put in the effort to understand the English. Also the class can become a discussion about English in the native language rather than practice of, and in, English.

Lesson-planning/timetabling

The exercises in the SB are in a logical order for the presentation of the material they contain. The notes in the TB follow this order and also include suggestions for presentation or further practice activities. However, it is recognised that the constraints of the timetable and examinations, availability of language laboratories, planning-in of h/w etc might mean that it is impractical to work through the exercises as suggested, and frequently this is reflected in the TB where alternative approaches are given. The recommended procedure for planning this course therefore is:

– Estimate the amount of time available to spend on this book.
– Plan-in the essential material and language items that SS must have covered by the end of that time, making allow-

INTRODUCTION

ance for class time, time spent in language laboratories and home study.
- Make a note of additional areas of study from this course (or using supplementary material) which are of particular relevance to your SS and which you will do if you have time.

When it comes to the day-to-day business of teaching, you are recommended to read through the whole unit in the TB even if you are not planning to use all the material in that unit. Since the exercises in each unit are fairly closely interrelated, you may find that there are certain items which you will have to explain (albeit briefly) before SS can successfully complete the exercises you have chosen to do. You might also find suggestions that will make your lessons more lively and interesting for you and the SS.

Stages of language learning

The main stages in teaching new language are:

- *presentation*: this is either self-evident from the SB exercises or suggestions are given in the TB
- *drilling*: possibly chorus drilling, then individual drilling (T–S) leading to pairwork (S–S and SS–SS)
- *further practice*: further exercises and drills which bring in the language in new contexts
- *creative or 'free' stage*: where SS have the chance to use a variety of language items in a less-controlled context. Many of the suggested additional activities in the TB come into this category, as does roleplay (TB page xxvi)
- *revision*: the consolidation units revise structures presented in previous units and some language items are revised in later units of the book.

It is generally accepted that language learning is a cyclical process and that knowledge builds up over a period of time. Once SS have a grasp of a language item therefore, move on to the next one. You can always come back to exercises which are omitted and use them for further practice or revision at a later date.

Pairwork

Many of the exercises in this course are marked to be done in pairs. Some of the reasons for this are:

- When practising structures, a stimulus and response more closely resembles a conversation than the series of unconnected utterances in most drills. SS are helped to retain the meaning of a structure when it is in context (even such a minimal context). This feeling is enhanced by giving SS a choice of response wherever possible (eg Exercises 92–3).

- Two SS working together are more likely to arrive at correct utterances or the solution to a task than individual SS work-

INTRODUCTION

ing alone (as the English saying goes: Two heads are better than one).
- SS can frequently learn as well from one another as from the teacher.
- If SS work together you remove the testing element (with possible failure in front of classmates) that always exists when SS are asked to work alone. This usually has a good effect on SS' confidence and thereby on their linguistic performance. (SS are still required to work individually and produce correct written work for h/w.)
- The whole class gets the chance to practise new structures several times in a short space of time rather than the common T–S situation where a maximum of six SS say sentences while the rest of the class loses interest.
- The focus of the lesson is moved away from the T, which is good not only for the sake of variety, but also because it puts the responsibility for learning more obviously where it belongs – on the SS.
- The T is free to move around the class helping SS with learning difficulties.

In order to achieve this happy state, there are several simple rules to follow. Everyone must know the form and meaning of the structure they are practising, so this must have been presented beforehand (suggestions are given in the TB) or must be evident from the exercise itself. SS must also understand the exact form of the exercise and what they are expected to do, so the stages of setting up pairwork must make this clear:

- Indicate the exercise in the book.
- Give the first stimulus and elicit the correct response from a S (T–S). Give the second stimulus and elicit the response from another S.
- Indicate two other SS (who are not sitting next to one another) to give the next stimulus and response (S–S, also called 'open pairs'). Indicate two other SS sitting apart to do further stimuli-responses.

Up to this stage it is important that everyone hears and pays attention to what is said and that the T corrects SS who make mistakes with the form of the drill or with the structure.

- Indicate that SS work in pairs with the person sitting next to them (SS–SS, or 'closed pairs'). Make sure that SS know to take turns so that both get a chance to say the stimuli and both to say the responses.

It is not necessary to work through the whole exercise before SS work in closed pairs. Once a couple of examples have been done, SS should be able to work out further examples for themselves. Occasionally move SS round so that they are working with a different partner (a) for variety (b) so that stronger and weaker SS can help or learn from one another. A possible format for Exercise 5 then would be:

T to S1: *What does Fred do?*
    S1: *He's a managing director.*
T to S2: *Luisa* (T indicates S3 who is some distance away)
    S2: *What does Luisa do?*
    S3: *She's a receptionist.*
T (indicating SS 4 and 5 who are sitting apart): *Simon*
    S4: *What does Simon do?*
    S5: *She's a ...*
T (interrupting to correct): *Is Simon a woman?*
    S5: *He's a sales assistant.*
T indicates SS–SS.

Where the drills are prompted by a series of pictures or single words these can be printed on cards and used to initiate an 'action chain' (see TB page 36).

Groupwork

Groupwork is suggested in the TB for many different kinds of activity:

- *problem-solving* (eg TB page 104)
- *writing* (eg TB page 64)
- *marking h/w* (on the same principle as the writing on TB page 64)
- *games* (eg Fish TB page 57)
- *roleplay* (eg Exercise 107)
- *projects* (eg Exercise 142, 206)
- *reading comprehension* (eg Exercise 126)
- *listening comprehension* (eg Exercise 89)

If groups need to use a cassette recorder for an activity and only one is available, groupwork has the advantage that different groups can be working on different activities (Exercises 87, 88, 89) as long as the T plans the lesson so that groups move round in time to do each activity (unless SS have been grouped to work on an area in which they need specific practice).

Groupwork shares many of the advantages of pairwork and, as with pairwork, it is important to give each group a clearly-defined task which is motivating in itself so that groups can work without supervision (although again the T is free to circulate and help individuals or groups with problems). Emphasise that each S is responsible for the whole group carrying out the task, although you might also appoint a group leader whose job it is to make a note of and possibly report on the group's responses or decisions.

Factors to consider when setting up groupwork are (a) the size

INTRODUCTION

of each group, and (b) which SS to put together in a group. In general the ideal size for most of the groupwork in this book (apart from the pyramid activity on TB page 81) is between four and seven SS. Sometimes it is a good idea to put SS of the same level of ability to work together on specific tasks, sometimes one can deliberately mix SS of different abilities so that stronger SS help weaker ones. One might also take into account whether to put friends together or whether sometimes to separate them and on some occasions one can arrange random groups.

To arrange random groups, decide how many groups you want (eg 5 groups of 6 SS). Ask SS to number off round the class from 1 to 5, 1 to 5 etc until everyone has a number between one and five. Then tell all the number ones to get together as a group, all the number twos to be another group, etc. (If you later want these groups to form new groups, eg 10 groups of three SS, ask them to number off again from 1 to 10, 1 to 10 etc group by group. SS then move to their new groups with people of the same number.)

Whole class activities

These activities are an extension of pairwork and groupwork and involve all the SS moving around the classroom to come into contact with as many other SS as possible with whom to practise specific language in a short time (a maximum time for this kind of activity is 10 minutes). The technique can be used occasionally as an alternative to SS–SS pairwork for intensive practice of newly-presented language (TB page 50) or SS can practise short dialogues in this way (eg Exercises 8 & 9), particularly where several alternatives are possible within the framework of the dialogue (Exercise 130, TB page xxv). In general though, it is important that there is a specific task for SS to complete, eg *doing a survey* (Exercises 13, 103, 142, 192), *finding information or solving a problem* (Jobs, TB page 7; shopping, TB page 56; appointments, TB page 94) or *finding a partner according to specific language requirements* (TB page 156). Although the SS' main interest (the motivating factor) lies in the task itself, there is always a language point which is practised in the course of the activity. It is essential that this language point has been pre-taught (pairwork, groupwork and whole class activities are essentially for *practice* of known language) and, of course, that the task has been clearly explained *before* the SS stand up. The essence of these activities is that there is an *information-gap*: each S has information that other SS require and requires information from those other SS. This is the basis of communication. The greatest advantage of this kind of activity is that SS seem content to repeat phrases again and again in order to complete the task where they would be bored by saying the same phases three or four times in a more conventional drill. Whole class activities can also have an extremely revitalising effect on a class which has been sitting still for a long period of time.

The two problems which TT frequently mention in connection with pairwork, groupwork and whole class activities are noise and discipline. All language TT can differentiate between 'productive sound' and 'unproductive noise' and so step in to help SS who do not appear to be working on the task in hand. Given that it is generally accepted that SS need a great deal of practice if they are to learn a language effectively, the problem is mainly one of convincing colleagues that these activities are the most effective and efficient ways of giving large numbers of SS maximum practice in minimum time. Colleagues rarely question the efficacy of chorus-drilling, which, while it is not a technique to be ignored, is not as effective as these other three. Similarly, there will always be some discipline problems whatever teaching techniques you employ. In order to minimise the disruptive effect on the rest of the class, SS who will not join in with these activities can be given extra written work to do alone while the other SS carry on with their tasks. The SS being disciplined still have the chance to practise language (in a different way) and perhaps they will decide that the other activities look more fun and so opt to join in productively on subsequent occasions.

The receptive skills (reading and listening)

Working on the assumption that SS should be able to understand more than they can write or say (they can to some extent control and simplify the language they produce, but they have no control over the complexity of written and oral material they are likely to come across), most of the listening material and some of the reading texts in the course are graded at a higher level than the language SS are expected to produce. To counterbalance this and to make the language more accessible, the exploitation exercises are deliberately simple.

Many of the exercises (particularly related to the listening material) are designed to encourage SS to skim for general meaning or to scan/listen for specific information. In both cases, SS should not worry about words and expressions they do not understand as long as this does not interfere with the task they have to do. Essential vocabulary that SS need to know (and which may have to be pre-taught) in order to carry out the task is stated in the relevant TB notes. Because of this emphasis on picking out essential information and known words from an unfamiliar context, TT should not translate the text. However, the texts are available for more detailed study at a later date when SS know more language if they are required (eg you could listen again in detail to the description of parts of a business letter in Exercise 23 or to the language Simon and Anne use at dinner in Exercise 94). It will be de-

INTRODUCTION

trimental to the learning process to do this too soon after doing the listening comprehension as described in the TB.

With the reading and listening materials, the exploitation exercises tend to be of an active variety, getting away from the notion that reading and listening are 'passive' skills. SS should 'listen and do' or 'read and do' rather than simply listening or reading.

There is at least one listening activity in each unit besides the taped introductory dialogue. Most of them belong to one of these main types:

- *Listen and match* (Exercises 3, 23, 30, 46, 89, 94, 122, 164, 173, 178, 202, 227). SS have to link words or names with words, pictures etc according to information they can gather from the tape.
- *Listen and complete* (Exercises 10, 72, 111, 149, 189, 220). SS have to extract specific information from a listening text in order to fill in a form or chart.
- *Listening for numbers* (Exercises 19, 35, 65, 78, 136, 160, 201). Throughout the course there has been an attempt to familiarise SS with numbers – an essential part of all business life.

With every listening activity, it is up to the T how often the tape should be played (or up to the SS if they are in charge of the cassette recorder, perhaps doing groupwork). The criteria is to play it the minimum number of times necessary to complete the listening task satisfactorily (ideally once).

SS with specific listening difficulties should be encouraged to do the listening activities which are exploited as LD (or some of the class listening activities) in a language/listening laboratory. All too often, SS who have not actually heard something on the tape can pick up the meaning from their classmates so that their own listening skill never improves.

Some additional listening activities, 'listen and differentiate', are suggested in the TB (*personal/personnel*, TB page 3; *How/What do you do?*, TB page 7, *What day/date is it?*, TB page 92). The method is described on TB page 3. The aim in these short (five minute) exercises is to sensitise SS to minimal differences in short utterances. If they can hear the difference, they are more likely to be able to produce it.

There are fewer specific reading exercises as so much of the book has to be read even while practising other skills. However, most of the reading passages are fairly authentic representations of things SS would read in the course of their everyday (working) lives: *newspaper extracts* (Consolidation units, Exercise 105), *business letters* (see TB page xxix), *reports, memos, job advertisements* (Exercise 112) etc. Where it is natural

INTRODUCTION

to do so (notes, personal letters etc) some of the reading texts are handwritten to give SS exposure to this form of writing.

Suggested exploitation for reading texts (eg introductory exercises): *Asking questions* (a) The standard procedure where SS read the text and the T asks questions of individual SS (who should give *short* answers as this is to check comprehension not ability to manipulate structure) (b) The T gives the questions before SS read the passage and SS are only given a limited amount of time for reading (c) The T gives the answers to questions about the passage and SS make up the questions (Exercises 105 & 193) (d) SS make up questions for each other to answer. These four procedures can also be used with listening texts.

Cutting-up (Exercise 126, TB page 93). SS have to understand the connection between sentences/words/phrases in order to put the lines in the right order. With something like an introductory exercise, you could photocopy, cut up and mix up the six pictures or lines of dialogue for SS to put in the right order. With a long text (possibly one giving information about commercial practice) you could cut it up line by line, every two lines, or paragraph by paragraph (this last helps SS become aware of the form of longer texts, how to present information, how to link paragraphs etc).

Journalist approach (TB page 8). This also involves communication skills in groupwork activities.

The productive skills (speaking and writing)

Much of the classwork throughout the course is oral, but this does not mean that the other skills are neglected. There are many written exercises which challenge the SS to be more precise in their use of vocabulary and structure (the emphasis in the oral classwork is on fluency and communication) and further written work to be done in class or as h/w is suggested in the TB.

The course is aimed at SS who are already familiar with roman script. For SS who are not, extra work will need to be integrated into the early units of the book.

Pronunciation

The aim of the course is not that SS should acquire the accent of a native speaker, but that they should be readily understood by other speakers of English. There is not time in a course of this nature to cover in detail all aspects of pronunciation, but this book does try to awaken an awareness of those aspects of pronunciation which prove the greatest barrier to communication. The aim has been to integrate the teaching of pronunciation with other aspects of language and it will help SS if each new structure is presented with a definite stress and intonation (the LD cassettes can be used to provide a model). The emphasis should be first that SS can hear and identify aspects of pronunciation and then that they try to imitate them. The model provided on the LD cassettes is an educated southern English accent. Phonetic script is not introduced into the course, but TT might wish SS to understand the phonetic script used in their dictionaries. In this case, the T introduces the script gradually as work is done on individual sounds.

Some pronunciation exercises are written into the SB:

- *word stress* (Exercise 96–99, WB Exercises 40 & 66)
- *sentence stress* (Exercise 148)
- *sounds* (final *s*, Exercise 49, WB Exercise 18; final *d*, Exercise 144)

Others are suggested in the TB:
- *word stress* (TB pages 3, 7)
- *sounds* (*work/walk*, TB page 42; *d/t*, TB page 115; *th*, TB page 92; *won't/want*, TB page 132)

An attempt is also made to help SS link sounds and spelling (homophones, Exercises 215–6; rhyming words, WB Exercise 61).

As with other areas of the course, TT are recommended to omit items which are not a problem for their SS and to introduce other areas with which their SS are having difficulties.

One approach to the teaching of sounds is to isolate 'minimal pairs' (words which differ by one sound only, eg *ship – sheep*, *hat – had*; The different sounds are the ones which are practised). A possible presentation is to represent the two words on the board using pictures and numbers. If we are contrasting the sounds /ɪ/ and /iː/ with the words *ship* and *sheep*, these might be:

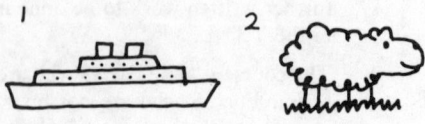

Give a model of both sounds while pointing at the appropriate picture. Say (or play from a prepared tape) one of the words and ask SS to call out the appropriate number to show they have recognised the sound. Do this several times with individual SS. If you are saying the words, continue in the same way, but cover your mouth or turn away so that SS cannot see the shape of your lips. Then try saying the words in pairs or groups of three:

eg T: *ship — ship*   S1: *one — one*
   T: *sheep — ship*   S2: *two — one*
   T: *ship — ship — sheep* S3: *one — one — two*

Next ask individual SS to say words (singly or in pairs) for you to identify (if you cannot identify them correctly, it is presumably a fault in the SS' pronunciation). Then let SS practise in pairs. Next suggest other words containing these sounds for SS to identify them. Try to get a variety of spellings, eg *shield*, *sing*, *she*, *dear*, *businesswomen* etc. Finally ask SS to suggest other words to add to the two lists.

A final note on pronunciation: ask your SS to aim for *clarity* not *speed*. Talking more quickly makes understanding more difficult when pronunciation is not perfect.

Presenting dialogues

There are some simple rules to follow if you want SS to be able to reproduce a short dialogue (eg Exercises 8, 9, 26, 27, 28, 50, 95, 214) and use it naturally. Taking one of the dialogues in Exercise 130 as an example, a suggested procedure might be:

- Mime having a headache (hold your head and moan) to elicit *What's the matter?* Even if SS do not know this phrase, they will attempt something like it and you can introduce the exact wording.
- Practise the question round the class: T–S, S–S. Encourage SS to mime headaches as a prompt for the enquiry.
- Mime again to elicit the answer: *I've got a headache*.
- Practise the two lines (with the gesture/mime) T–S, S–S, SS–SS.
- Bring the attention back to yourself and ask for suggestions for what you can do about your headache. Elicit (again supplying words SS do not know): *Why don't you take an aspirin?*
- Practise the three lines T–S–T, S1–S2–S1. Be careful to keep the dialogue between two people and do not be tempted to practise the three lines with three different people.
- Introduce the final line: *That's a good idea!*
- Practise the whole dialogue T–S, S–S, SS–SS.

When SS are familiar with the dialogue, you can introduce substitutions so that SS can exercise a degree of choice within the main framework. In this case you could introduce other ailments eg headache, stomach ache, toothache etc (with appropriate grimaces), or further suggestions eg *Why don't you lie down?*, or an alternative structure: *You should take an aspirin*.

These stages can be used to introduce any short dialogue (you might choose to exploit one of the introductory dialogues in

INTRODUCTION

this way). You do not always have to elicit the lines. You can present the whole dialogue using a cassette (or taking both parts yourself) before teaching it line by line as suggested. If you encourage SS to use appropriate gestures and exaggerated intonation patterns and to stand up while they are practising the whole dialogue (possibly with different partners or as a whole class activity) their increased enthusiasm is likely to have a beneficial effect on their pronunciation.

An alternative presentation is to give one half of the dialogue to half the class to learn and prepare and the other half to the rest of the SS (you will need to work with both groups at this initial learning stage). SS then mingle (as in a whole class activity) and say the dialogue with SS from the other group until they have heard it often enough to have learnt the other half. You can move around the class and help out with obvious difficulties. SS can then try saying the half of the dialogue they did not learn originally until all the SS can take either part.

One way of extending a short dialogue is to work out ways in which it can be varied. Taking Exercise 214 as an example, introduce the first line: *What a lovely coat!*

Elicit alternative responses from the SS and gradually build up a chart like this one on the board:

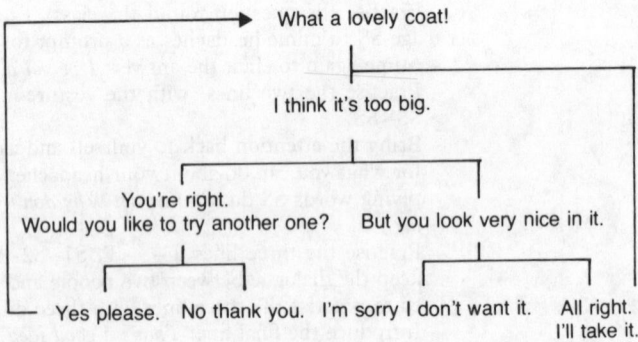

SS can then practise the dialogue again (possibly with other items of clothing) choosing a different outcome each time.

Roleplay exercises

The aim of roleplay is to put SS in a context which is guided enough to limit the language they will use, but which is also free enough to allow them a choice of appropriate language. Roleplay encourages fluency and communication which excessive correction or T-intervention will inhibit. The basic steps in organising roleplay exercises therefore are:

- divide SS into the suggested group numbers
- set up the task clearly (with or without reference to the book)
- with a class unused to groupwork or roleplay, ask one group to start the activity as a demonstration while the others watch
- give SS an idea of the time restriction (about 8 minutes is the maximum amount of time that should be spent on any stage of the roleplay exercises in this book)
- ask the SS to begin
- go quickly round the class to make sure that everyone has understood the task and that they have begun the roleplay (inexperienced groups often sit and discuss the task instead of actually doing it)
- in the remaining time, listen out for errors and possible problems, but only intervene where SS are not carrying out the task
- stop the activity at the appointed time or earlier (it is better to stop while they are still enjoying it than to go on until everyone gets bored)

After the roleplay task, you could bring up a couple of language mistakes which are being made by a lot of SS, but SS will often make 'performance' mistakes while they are speaking freely (just as native speakers do) and will resent intensive criticism of their attempts and correction of language items which they produce correctly when not under stress. It is often better therefore to note areas where SS seem to have a genuine weakness and use this as the basis of future lessons. When SS are used to the idea of roleplay, you could arrange for individual groups to carry out a roleplay task in front of video cameras or tape their conversation on cassette. This can be a useful basis for a session of 'error analysis', but again it can be very disspiriting to stop at every error (particularly when it is clear that SS are aware of them) and it is perhaps more important to praise ideas and strategies SS have used or language which is particularly appropriate or which SS have only recently learnt.

The types of roleplay exercise in this book are:

Completing a dialogue (Exercises 117, 150) SS should work in pairs and be given a few minutes to think about the missing responses. SS then take a role each and go straight through the dialogue with one S supplying the missing part. It is important that the S reading the given part should try to make it as natural as possible. In their pairs, SS can then discuss their performance and decide on improvements. The T can initiate a brief class discussion on problem areas. SS can then do the dialogue again taking the other part (and possibly working with different partners so that each person has the benefit of four people's ideas). Each S then writes up what he/she considers to be the best version for h/w.

Guided roleplay (Exercises 70–1, 152, 221) This is very similar to completing a dialogue in that SS are working from prompt material but neither part is scripted and SS are free to react to one another. The way of operating is the same.

Three/four-stage roleplay (Exercises 175, 222) The mode of operation is the same as above, except that SS get several opportunities to try out the same kind of language in similar dialogues, but they have a slightly different situation each time to add variety. With this kind of activity, the time limit at each stage needs to be strictly controlled so that SS move on fairly swiftly to each new stage. Between each dialogue spend a few minutes discussing with the whole class (a) any language difficulties (keep this short) (b) a few of the ideas SS have expressed in their dialogues (this gives others ideas to incorporate in their own dialogues).

Free roleplay project (radio programme, Exercise 107) It is essential to give enough preparation time for SS to come up with ideas and try out what they are going to say. Encourage them to work from notes to produce lively reporting rather than reading prepared scripts which can sound rather 'dead'.

Variations: Once SS are used to doing roleplay exercises you could introduce adaptations to the basic format.

(1) Set up the situation as normal, but tell SS that you will clap your hands during the conversation. Whenever you clap your hands they must swap roles and continue the conversation from the point they were at (they should not start again from the beginning). Give them a chance to get the conversation established before you clap for the first time and do not clap more than four times in a five-minute session. This approach encourages SS to listen carefully to what the other person is saying rather than simply concentrating on their own contribution. It is also fun, which reduces the pressure of trying to speak a foreign language perfectly.

(2) Set up the situation as normal, except that SS work in groups of four, two SS to each role (two SS take role A and two take role B). One S from each role begins the dialogue (A1 + B1) while the other two listen but say nothing. When you clap your hands and say 'A' student A2 takes over the conversation from A1 (A2 + B1). When you clap your hands and say 'B', student B2 takes over from B1 (A2 + B2). Again do not clap your hands too often during the activity and say clearly 'A', 'B' or 'both' after you have clapped. The conversations should all continue without a break from the point they had reached. Again SS are encouraged to listen closely to

INTRODUCTION

what their partners and their 'opponents' say, but they are also given time within the structure of the activity to think of new ideas or language they want to introduce.

Business letters

Most people in business have at some stage to be able to write, understand or process business letters, so SS are made aware of the component parts of a good business letter:

- *grammatical structure* (throughout the course)
- *vocabulary and business practice* (throughout the course)
- *business letter phraseology* (Exercises 73–4, 114, 128, 154, 180–1, 196, 209)
- *format/layout* (TB pages 16, 41; Exercises 23–4, 58)
- *headings and endings* (WB Exercise 8)
- *use of titles* (SB page 14, TB page 2 and 17)
- *UK addresses* (TB page 85)
- *punctuation and use of capitals* (Exercise 113, WB Exercise 52)

Business letters are also used as the vehicle to teach or practise other aspects of language so that SS become more familiar with them:

- *reading comprehension* (Exercises 126–7)
- *verb forms* (Exercise 153)
- *listening comprehension/dictation* (Exercises 113, 180)

If SS wish to learn to write good business letters, they are more likely to make an effort if they are asked to write on blank A4 paper in block style leaving a line between paragraphs and possibly inventing or copying a company letterhead for authenticity. It can also be motivating to write real letters to British or American companies requesting information or brochures (you or the SS can find addresses in newspapers or from tourist agencies). An additional advantage is that the genuine replies can also be exploited in class.

UNIT ONE
A VISITOR TO BOS

1

Business content:	Organisation chart
Structures:	The verb *to be*
	Possessive adjectives
	Genitive ('s)
	Question words: *What? Where? Who?*
Functions:	Introductions; greetings; giving personal information; registering at a hotel
Lexis:	Jobs, countries, nationalities, titles

TEACHING NOTES

Introductions

It is a good idea to start with games in which people introduce themselves even if SS already know one another. They create a good class spirit and SS use English from the beginning.

NB I use first names in class, but all these games can be done using surnames and titles (in which case you might have to teach titles first – see Exercise 2). SS might like to take an English name for these lessons.

1 Ask SS to arrange themselves in alphabetical order in a circle. Everybody then says his/her name in turn: *Hello, I'm Susan. Hello, I'm . . .*

2 Ask SS to shake hands with everyone else in the room and say: *How do you do. I'm . . .* Only allow 30 seconds for them to do this.

3 Stand in circles of about 8. The aim is to learn the names of the people in your group and practise the verb *to be*. Play like this with each person adding his/her own name:
S1: *I'm Susan.*
S2: *She's Susan. I'm David.*
S3: *She's Susan. He's David. I'm John.*
The last person in each group has to remember everyone else's name.

NB If you play this game later with SS in different groups, try to make sure that someone who was at the beginning of the circle at the first attempt is near the end the second time. A variation on the game, although it cannot be played with absolute beginners, is that each person thinks of a job or profession which begins with the same letter as his/her name, eg. *I'm Susan. I'm a surgeon. David's a director. John's a journalist etc.* Apart from possibly learning new vocabulary, SS may need to be reminded to use the indefinite article with jobs.

4 Teach the question *'What's your name?'* Ask everyone to check the names of anyone in the class whose name they do not know or have not remembered.

UNIT ONE

    5   The whole class stands in a circle. Each person has to introduce the people on either side of him/her, eg. *This is Mary and this is John*.
(See also WB Exercise 3)

By presenting the phrases clearly before SS carry out each activity, you will have covered the initial presentation of many of the language items in this unit. Complete this session by writing on the board:

This is . . .	*This is . . .*
How do you do.	*He is Fred./He's Fred*
I am Susan./I'm Susan	*She is Mary./She's Mary*

At this stage you could go on to teach the remainder of the present tense of *to be* (*you/they/we/are*) with the contracted forms. Remind the SS that *you* can be singular or plural.
NB Since the emphasis throughout this book is on the oral presentation and practice of structures, contracted forms are used and preferred in most exercises. Full verb forms are used in written exchanges.

Exercise 1   Comprehension

Answers: *1 George Passas (Mr Passas)* *2 Greece* *3 No*
4 He is a sales representative *5 Yes*
Do not do this exercise until you have taught all the structures in this unit (see TB page xii for notes on the presentation of these introductory exercises). On the tape George Passas has a slight Greek accent, Mary Mackie has a slight Scottish accent and Fred McLean has a slight northern accent.

The BOS motto, *We Mean Business*, is a pun on the word 'business'. It means we seriously intend to do something.

Exercise 2   Are they married? (LD)

Answers: *See LDT*

Aim: To teach titles, pronunciation of names and *I don't know*.

Practise the names of the BOS staff from the book, possibly with the aid of the LD cassette. Teach the titles *Mr* /mɪstə^r/, *Mrs*/mɪsɪz/, *Miss* /mɪs/, *Ms* /məz/. Practise the names like this:
T: *Fred*   SS: *Mr McLean*
SS can also practise titles with their own names. Many women prefer the title 'Ms' as the equivalent of 'Mr' because it does not show their marital status.
Teach the question: *Is Fred married?* and the short answers: *Yes he is./No he isn't*. Teach *I don't know* as an idiomatic phrase. Do not mention the present simple tense at this stage. SS can talk about the BOS staff as indicated in Exercise 2. For h/w they can write sentences about the female staff, eg *Luisa is married. She is Mrs Middle. Mary is single/not married*. etc.

A VISITOR TO BOS

To teach the numbers 1 to 8 and the letters a to h

SS should first be able to recognise the numbers. You say a number and they hold up the right number of fingers. Then you hold up your fingers and they say the correct numbers. Check that SS know the letters *a* to *h* in a similar way by pointing to the letters on the board. NB See notes on teaching and practising the alphabet on TB page 7.

Exercise 3 What do they do?

Answers: *1–b 2–e 3–h 4–a 5–g 6–d 7–c 8–f*

Aim: Linking sounds with their written equivalents.

Teach the list of jobs in this exercise (let SS look the words up in foreign-language/English dictionaries if necessary). Practise the pronunciation of the jobs – you say the reference letter, the SS say the job. Play the tape for Exercise 3. The editor of the BOS magazine is a woman. Let SS work in pairs to link each name with the right job. Play the tape as often as necessary. SS do not have to understand anything else in the conversation. Check answers using reference numbers and letters.

Pronunciation/Listening practice: You might want to help SS differentiate between the word stress patterns of *personal* and *personnel*. Point out the difference, then when you say personal (O o o), they reply *secretary*. When you say *personnel* (o o O), they reply *manager*. Keep up a fast pace. The activity should not last for more than five minutes.

Exercise 4 Writing about jobs

Answers: *2 Luisa Middle is a receptionist. 3 Simon Young is a sales assistant. 4 Sheila Baker is a sales manager. 5 Mary Mackie is a personal secretary. 6 Paul Johnson is a sales representative. 7 Joy Bradley is a secretary. 8 Howard Spencer is a personnel manager.*

Aim: Written back-up of classwork.

This exercise can be done for h/w or in class for a change of pace. Point out the written conventions: (a) capital letters for names and at the beginning of a sentence; (b) full stop at the end of the sentence; (c) full verb forms, not contractions.

Exercise 5 Talking about jobs (LD A & B)

Answers: *See LDT*

Aim: Oral practice of job vocabulary; question *What does . . . do?*

Teach the question *What does Fred do?* as if it were an idiom or set phrase. Do not introduce the present simple at this stage. If necessary, explain *etc* in the note in the SB. It is short for *etcetera*/etsetərə/ and means *and so on*.

UNIT ONE

Exercise 6   Talking about BOS staff (LD)

Answers: *See LDT*

Aim: To teach the question form and short answers of *to be*.

Show how the question is formed:
Luisa is a receptionist.
√ *Luisa* ⓘⓢ *a receptionist.* ⟨?⟩
Is Luisa a receptionist?

Teach the question intonation, possibly using the LD cassette as a model. Point out the formation of the short answers (*yes* and *no* are also acceptable answers). SS can do the exercise as directed and they can also write eight questions for h/w. Remind SS to write a question mark instead of a full stop.

Exercise 7   Organisation chart (LD A & B)

Answers: *See LDT*

Aim: To teach genitive *'s* in a business context.

This exercise introduces a standard organisation chart (also called an *organigram*) which might have to be explained to some SS. It shows the hierarchy within the company.

The exercise should be done orally in pairs. SS should only make the sentences indicated and not try making up their own. They could also write sentences from this exercise for h/w. Remind them to write the apostrophe before the *-s*. (See also WB Exercise 1)

Exercise 8   Introducing people

Aim: Practising names and introductions using *this is*; building group identity.

You have already taught this exercise in the introduction games (number 5). You could now do the exercise as directed in the book for revision. NB George and Mary's voices have an RP accent on the LD cassette, in this and all other drills, as SS might want to use the cassette as a model for their pronunciation. Point out the commas which separate the name of the person you are talking to from the rest of the sentence.

Exercise 9   Greeting people (LD A & B)

Aim: Practising names and greetings; building group identity.

Introduce this dialogue in one of the ways suggested on TB page xxv, possibly using the LD tape. When the SS have learnt the dialogue, let them stand up and practise it with a lot of different people for a few minutes. Exercises 8 and 9 would be a good way of starting your second lesson if a new class needs reminding of each other's names.

A VISITOR TO BOS

Exercise 10   Registering at a hotel

Answers:

Aim: Listening comprehension (selective dictation).

SS need only understand enough of the dialogue to complete the task. Paul has a slight French accent and Mary has a slight American accent. The names are spelt out on the cassette so check that SS know the English alphabet (see notes on TB page 7) and the expression *double m*. You may also have to pre-teach the nationalities *French* and *American*.

Exercise 11   Word puzzle

Answers: 1 *Greece*   2 *Egypt*   3 *Italy*   4 *Japanese*
5 *British*   6 *Brazil*   7 *Spanish*   8 *French*
Hidden word: *Egyptian*

Aim: To teach countries and nationalities:

Use the map in the SB (or a world map on the wall) to teach the countries and appropriate nationalities in this exercise. You might also include the countries and nationalities of the SS in the class, but do not try to teach more than a dozen at one time. SS can do the word puzzle for h/w or in pairs in class. (See also WB Exercise 2). If you think your SS could do it, you could teach the question tag question with nationalities: *You're Italian, aren't you?* See TB page 105 for a way of practising it. You can hear the intonation pattern on the listening cassette, Exercise 3, in the sentence *You're the personnel manager, aren't you?*
NB England is one of the four countries which make up the United Kingdom of Great Britain and Northern Ireland. The other three countries are Scotland, Wales and Northern Ireland (Southern Ireland or Eire is a separate state). English people

UNIT ONE

frequently use the terms 'English' and 'British' interchangeably, but the Welsh, Scots and Irish tend to make a distinction between English, British, Scottish, Irish and Welsh. (*Scotch* is an adjective used to describe things, eg Scotch whisky, Scotch eggs, Scotch broth.

Exercise 12 Personal information (LD A & B)

Answers: *See LDT*

Aim: Question practice.

SS should be able to work out the meanings of the questions from the sample answers. Point out how the question is made with *to be* and a question word:
1 *He is from France.* 2 √ *He is from France.?*
3 √ *Is he from France?* 4 *Where is he from?*

Introduce the questions in the present simple as semi-idiomatic phrases, explaining that they will be dealt with more fully in Unit 4. Do not start teaching the present simple tense at this stage. You will also have to teach the *you/your* form of the questions (which you will do anyway for Exercise 13) before SS can do LD 12B. Start by asking questions about Jacques and Maria (you will have to teach *she/her*) which the SS answer. Then let them ask you questions about the representatives, before they practise in pairs. Encourage the use of short answers (*What's his surname? – de la Plaine* etc) except where you wish to add more information (*Is he married? – Yes. He's married to an Egyptian girl.*)

SS could write a few sentences about the representatives for h/w. Alternatively they could each write six questions about the representatives to be answered by another S.

NB Point out that although names in Britain are normally written with a capital letter, foreign names are sometimes different, eg de la Plaine, van Ek, von Stroheim.

You might also use the pictures of the representatives to teach the words *family, wife, husband, child/children, son, daughter.* If so, SS could include some of these words in any written work they do about the representatives (perhaps for revision in a later lesson), or more simply they could refer back to Exercise 2 and write sentences such as: *Fred's wife is Mrs McLean. Luisa's husband is Mr Middle.* (Fred, Howard and Paul are married. Simon is not.)

Exercise 13 Questionnaire

Aim: Question practice in a freer context.

With a multi-national adult class the real facts about them will probably provide enough variety to make the exercise interesting. Younger SS might prefer to make up facts about themselves (or they could pretend to be famous people). If you did not teach the *you* forms of the questions for LD 12B, elicit them now. Pre-teach the important requests: *Can you say that again please?* and *Can you spell that please? Can you . . .?* is the form used throughout the early units of this book for polite requests. Teach it here as an idiom, but revise these phrases when you next meet the *Can you . . .?* form.

For h/w SS could write a few lines about the people in the survey eg *Luisa Middle is Spanish. She is a receptionist and she is married.* Teach the word *and* for joining two (and only two at this stage) short sentences.

Additional activities

Listening practice   See if SS can distinguish between the question *What do you do?* and *How do you do* Say the phrases quickly to individual SS. They must reply *I'm a student* to the first and *How do you do* to the second.

Who am I? This gives extra practice of job vocabulary. Write the 8 jobs in Exercise 3 on pieces of card – one job on each card and enough cards for each S to have one plus a few more (each job will appear on more than one piece of card). SS take a piece of card, but do not look at it. They hold the card in front of their foreheads so that everyone else can see it, but they cannot. They then try to find out their own job by asking eg *Am I a sales manager?* Other SS answer *Yes you are* or *No you're not.* Each S can only ask and answer one question of another S before they both move on to another partner. SS who find out what their job is quickly can be given another job. The card they hand in can be handed out to the next S who finishes, and so on. Play the game for about 5 minutes.

The alphabet   If SS do not know the pronunciation of the alphabet, you can practise it with them in the first two or three lessons. The letters are written out at the end of SB Unit 1, but the following presentation may help SS remember the pronunciation:

Pronunciation of letters

/ei/	/i:/	/ɛ/	/ai/	/au/	/a:/	/u:/
a	b(bee)	f(ef)	i(eye)	o	r	q(queue)
h(aitch)	c	l	y(why)			u(you)
j(jay)	d	m				w(double you)
k(kay)	e	n				
	g	s				
	p	x				
	t					
	v					
	z (US; UK pronounced: *zed*)					

UNIT ONE

NB There is no provision in this course for teaching the roman alphabet. SS are presumed to know its written form.

To practise the alphabet, point to individual SS and ask them to say the letters of the alphabet in order, one letter each. If someone makes a mistake, they have to begin again at the letter *a*, the next person has to say *b* etc. As a final check, either at this stage or in the next lesson, repeat the process, but start at the end of the alphabet and work backwards (z, y, x, w, v . . . etc). This exercise can also be done in small groups. (See also WB Exercise 31)

The Letter Game This is a game for 3 to 8 players. Each player *secretly* writes down 10 letters on a piece of paper (eg A F G H L M S T X Y). In turn each player says one of the letters on his/her piece of paper. Everyone who has that letter on his/her paper (including the person who says the letter) crosses it out. The winner is the first person to cross out all his/her letters.

Spelling Ask SS to arrange themselves alphabetically in a circle (to show awareness of the order of the alphabet – very necessary for many forms of reference and research). In turn you can ask them to spell items of vocabulary, their names or other people's names. You can also give spot spelling tests (orally) at spare moments in class.

LANGUAGE DRILLS TAPESCRIPT

Drill 2 Look at the pictures of the BOS staff and answer these questions, like this:

P: Is Luisa married?
R: *Yes. She's Mrs Middle.*
P: Is Mary married?
R: *No. She's Miss Mackie.*

P: Is Fred married?
R: *I don't know.*

Now you try. (First repeat examples)
P: Is Sheila married?
R: *Yes. She's Mrs Baker.*
P: Is Howard married?
R: *I don't know.*
P: Is Simon married?
R: *I don't know.*

P: Is Paul married?
R: *I don't know.*
P: Is Joy married?
R: *No. She's Miss Bradley.*

Aim: Comprehension; practice of names, titles and *I don't know*.

Drill 5A Ask questions about the BOS staff, like this:

P: Fred
R: *What does Fred do?*

Now you try.
P: Luisa
R: *What does Luisa do?*

P: Simon
R: *What does Simon do?*

A VISITOR TO BOS

P: Sheila
R: *What does Sheila do?*
P: Mary
R: *What does Mary do?*

P: Paul
R: *What does Paul do?*

Aim: Question practice (SS can do this drill with their books closed).

Drill 5B Do Exercises 3 and 4 before you do this drill. Answer these questions about the BOS staff, like this:

P: What does Fred do?
R: *He's a managing director.*

P: What does Luisa do?
R: *She's a receptionist.*

Now you try.
P: What does Simon do?
R: *He's a sales assistant.*
P: What does Sheila do?
R: *She's a sales manager.*
P: What does Mary do?
R: *She's a personal secretary.*

P: What does Paul do?
R: *He's a sales representative.*
P: What does Joy do?
R: *She's a secretary.*
P: What does Howard do?
R: *He's a personnel manager.*

Aim: Comprehension; practice of job vocabulary.

Drill 6 Take your information from Exercises 3 and 4 and give short answers to these questions, like this:

P: Is Luisa a receptionist?
R: *Yes she is.*

P: Is Paul a secretary?
R: *No he isn't.*

Now you try.
P: Is Sheila a sales manager?
R: *Yes she is.*
P: Is Mary a personnel manager?
R: *No she isn't.*
P: Is Fred a managing director?
R: *Yes he is.*

P: Is Simon a sales assistant?
R: *Yes he is.*
P: Is Joy a sales representative?
R: *No she isn't.*
P: Is Howard a personal secretary?
R: *No he isn't.*

Aim: Comprehension; practice of short answers and personal pronouns.

Drill 7A Look at the organisation chart and answer these questions, like this:

P: Who's Mary's boss?
R: Fred.

Now you try.
P: Who's Paul's boss?
R: *Sheila.*
P: Who's Sheila's boss?
R: *Fred.*
P: Who's Sheila's assistant?
R: *Simon.*

P: Who's Fred's personal secretary?
R: *Mary.*
P: Who's Simon's boss?
R: *Sheila.*
P: Who's Sheila's secretary?
R: *Joy.*

UNIT ONE

P: Who's Howard's boss?
R: *Fred*

Aim: Comprehension.

Drill 7B Ask questions about the BOS staff, like this:

P: Mary – boss
R: *Who's Mary's boss?*

Now you try.
P: Paul – boss
R: *Who's Paul's boss?*
P: Sheila – boss
R: *Who's Sheila's boss?*
P: Sheila – assistant
R: *Who's Sheila's assistant?*
P: Fred – personal secretary
R: *Who's Fred's personal secretary?*
P: Simon – boss
R: *Who's Simon's boss?*

P: Sheila – secretary
R: *Who's Sheila's secretary?*
P: Howard – boss
R: *Who's Howard's boss?*

Aim: Question practice (SS can do this drill with their books closed).

Drill 9A and 9B

See dialogue in SB.

Aim: Dialogue practice (SS should say the dialogue a second time with their books closed).
NB The whole dialogue is recorded before SS take parts so it can be used for presentation in class.

Drill 12A Ask these questions about a woman, like this:

P: What's his first name?
R: *What's her first name?*

Now you try.
P: What's his surname?
R: *What's her surname?*
P: What's his nationality?
R: *What's her nationality?*
P: Where is he from?
R: *Where is she from?*

P: What does he do?
R: *What does she do?*
P: Is he married?
R: *Is she married?*

Aim: Practice of questions and personal pronouns (SS can do this drill with their books closed).

Drill 12B Ask someone these questions, like this:

P: What's his first name?
R: *What's your first name?*

Now you try.
P: What's his surname?
R: *What's your surname?*

A VISITOR TO BOS

> P: What's his nationality?
> R: *What's your nationality?*
> P: Where is he from?
> R: *Where are you from?*
> P: What does he do?
> R: *What do you do?*
> P: Is he married?
> R: *Are you married?*

> Aim: Practice of questions in the *you* form (SS can do this drill with their books closed).

WORKBOOK ANSWERS

Exercise 1 Overseas sales staff

> *2 Jacques is Marie-Jo's boss. 3 Jacques is Chantal's boss. 4 Chantal is Jacques's/Jacques' secretary.* (The next four sentences can be in any order.) *5 Lorenzo is Marisa's boss. 6 Marisa is Lorenzo's assistant. 7 Lorenzo is Francesca's boss. 8 Francesca is Lorenzo's secretary.*

Exercise 2 Countries

> *2 I am Austrian. I'm from Austria. 3 She is Belgian. She's from Belgium. 4 They are Brazilian. They're from Brazil. 5 You are Chinese. You're from China. 6 We are Egyptian. We're from Egypt. 7 He is English. He's from England. 8 You are Finnish. You're from Finland. 9 We are French. We're from France. 10 I am German. I'm from Germany. 11 She is Greek. She's from Greece. 12 They are Indian. They're from India. 13 He is Italian. He's from Italy. 14 You are Japanese. You're from Japan. 15 We are Spanish. We're from Spain. 16 I am Swedish. I'm from Sweden. 17 She is Swiss. She's from Switzerland. 18 He is American. He's from the USA.*

> Although several of these countries have not been previously taught, SS should (with the help of the wordsquare) be able to work out the names of the countries. You can check that they know which countries the names refer to afterwards.

> NB USA stands for United States of America. You can also say *He's from America* or *He's from the United States (the US).*

Exercise 3 Greetings and introductions

> *1–B 2–F 3–C 4–G 5–E 6–A 7–D*

Exercise 4 A/an

> *2 an 3 an 4 a 5 an 6 an 7 a 8 a*

> This exercise highlights the difference between *a* (before nouns beginning with a consonant) and *an* (before vowels). You will have to point out this difference in class before SS can do the exercise.
> NB Introduce 'irregularities' (eg *an hour, a university, a European* etc) as they occur, not at this initial stage.

UNIT TWO
A NEWCOMER
2

> *Business content*: Telephone conversations; business letter format
> *Structures*: Demonstrative pronouns: *this/that/these/those*
> *There is/there are*
> Prepositions: *on, in, above, below, under, between, next to, to the left/right of, on the right/left*
> Question words: *How many*?
> *Function*: Describing location
> *Lexis*: Office furniture, equipment, stationery, cardinal numbers, business letter terminology

TEACHING NOTES

Exercise 14 Comprehension

Answers: *1 Simon Young   2 One   3 On Anne's desk   4 On the bottom shelf*

Do not do this exercise until SS have learnt the office vocabulary, prepositions and numbers. Do not teach '*former* secretary' unless SS question its meaning.

Exercise 15 Office furniture (LD A & B)

Answers: *See LDT*

Aim: Revision of structures (Unit 1) with new vocabulary.

Teach the eight items of vocabulary in this exercise while SS look at the pictures of the BOS staff on SB page 2, so that they cannot see the words. Introduce the exercise bit by bit, still referring to the pictures on SB page 2. Practise each phase with the pictures before going on to the next phase.

Phase 1 T: *Picture A.*   S1: *What's this?*   S2: *It's a notice board.*
Phase 2 Introduce the possessive sentence:
            T: *Notice board*   S: *It's Fred's notice board*
Phase 3 Remind SS of the question form and short answers.
            T: *Is it Fred's notice board?*   S: *Yes it is.*
            T: *Picture A*   S1: *Is it Fred's notice board?*
            S2: *Yes it is*
Phase 4 Run through the complete 4 lines of the drill and let SS practise in pairs as indicated in Exercise 15.

A NEWCOMER

When SS look at the words in Exercise 15, ask them how they think *ph* is pronounced in English. They should be able to work out that it is /f/ since you have already introduced the pronunciation of *graph* and *telephone*. The sound also appears in *photocopier* in Exercise 16.
NB The short forms of *telephone* are *phone* (spoken) and *Tel* (written).

SS could write eight sentences based on this exercise for h/w.

Exercise 16 Office equipment (LD A & B)

Answers: *See LDT*

Aim: To practise office vocabulary.

Give SS a few minutes in pairs to decide on the right word for each picture. They have a choice of two and already know some words, so they should get many of them right. Introduce the drill in two parts and let the SS practise in pairs. The only new concept is that of choice, indicated by the use of *or*.

Exercise 17 Mixed-up words

Answers: *1 wastepaper bin   2 desk   3 shelf   4 drawer   5 notice board   6 telephone   7 filing cabinet   8 books   9 photocopier   10 graph   11 letter   12 word processor*

Aim: Reinforcement of office vocabulary.

This exercise can be done for h/w or as a game in class, preferably with SS working in pairs. You can make up this kind of activity yourself to practise related vocabulary terms (see also WB Exercise 5).

Exercise 18 Hidden word puzzle

Answers: *1 above   2 next   3 to   4 below   5 left   6 under   7 on*   Hidden word: *between*
Sample sentence: *X is between v and y.*

Aim: To introduce some prepositions.

Ask SS to work out the answers to the word puzzle for h/w by referring to the picture showing prepositions on SB page 17. You can reinforce this self-study learning by practising or testing prepositions in class in a subsequent lesson.

One way of revising prepositions when SS know more vocabulary is for them to sit back-to-back in pairs. Each pair has the same collection of small items eg book, pen, pencil, rubber, ruler etc. One S arranges the items in clear relationship to one another (the ruler to the right of the pencil, the rubber on the book etc) and explains the arrangement to his/her partner. The partner can ask questions, but neither SS may look at the other's arrangement until they are both sure their arrangements are identical.

UNIT TWO

Exercise 19 Numbers

> Answers: *See SB tapescript*
>
> Aim: Listening comprehension for number recognition.
>
> SS have already learnt the numbers from 1 to 8. Now teach (or previously have asked SS to learn for h/w) the numbers up to 20. Even if you teach the numbers in class, SS should still learn the spelling for h/w.
>
> SS can work alone or in pairs to do this exercise. Play the tape as many times as you think necessary. SS have only to write down the number they hear. They do not have to understand the rest of the sentences. When you have checked their answers, SS can do the second part of the exercise in class under test conditions (to see if they have learnt the spelling of the numbers) or for h/w. (See also WB Exercise 6)
>
> NB See TB page 154 for the difference between *a* and *one* (cf Sentence 15). Note also that there used to be a difference between a UK and US billion. Now the same terminology is used in US and UK (see SB Language notes).

To introduce plurals

> Show the basic way of forming the plural by adding *s* to the singular. Let SS practise as you call out words eg T: *book*, S – *books*; T: *desk*, S – *desks* etc. Notice that *coffee pots*, *pot plants*, *filing cabinets*, *word processors* and *notice boards* all form the plural in the normal way. The only irregular plural SS need to learn now is *shelf* – shelves.

To introduce demonstratives

> Revise *this* and teach *that* using SS' names: *This is Helga* (exaggerate the fact that you are very close) and *That's Jacques* (exaggerate the distance). Let SS practise talking about one another in this way. Start by giving them cues:
>
> T: *Marcia – this.*   Marcia: *This is Pierre.*
> T: *Paul – that.*   Paul: *That's Jean.*
>
> Take four items which are available in the plural in the classroom (eg books, shelves, chairs, desks, tables, drawers, etc). Elicit from the SS *This is* and *That's* referring to one of each of the items. Group several of them together in different parts of the classroom and illustrate *These are* and *Those are*. First let individual SS move around the classroom making statements about individual and plural objects in this way, and then let the whole class move about the room talking about objects and people to each other.

Exercise 20 Showing someone where things are (LD)

> Answers: *See LDT*
>
> Aim: To practise demonstratives and plurals.

A NEWCOMER

SS can do this exercise in pairs and write the twelve sentences for h/w. When Joy says 'your', she means that the object belongs specifically to Anne. When she says 'the', she is referring to an object which belongs in the office, but is shared by more than one person.

Exercise 21 Anne's office

Answers *3 True. 4 False.   There is a pot plant on a filing cabinet. 5 False. The notice board is next to the graph/above the table/next to the filing cabinets. 6 True. 7 False. There is a coffee pot on the bottom shelf./There are six books on the top shelf. 8 False.   There are three filing cabinets. 9 True. 10 True. 11 False.   The coffee pot is on the bottom shelf./ There are six books on the top shelf. 12 False. There are three trays on Anne's desk./There is a photocopier on the table. 13 False.   There is a calculator on Simon's desk. 14 True. 15 False.   There is one typewriter in the room.* (These are suggested corrections. Other sentences are possible.)

Aim: Written practice of office vocabulary and prepositions.

If necessary revise these prepositions with physical objects in the classroom or with pictures on the board: *on, in, next to, between, under, above*.
NB *Under* a physical object, but *below* on a flat surface in a two-dimensional presentation eg *on the wall* below *the picture, in the letter* below *the signature*.

SS can do Exercise 21 in pairs or under test conditions in class or for h/w. They could also describe Anne and Simon's office orally or in written form for h/w using *There is/are*. For revision you could ask SS to describe their classroom, or you or the SS could make up True/False statements about the office picture or the classroom.
NB English people sometimes use *There is* plus a plural noun (as *il y a* is used in French). Despite this, it is better to teach SS to differentiate between the singular and the plural forms which are still considered grammatically correct by educated speakers.

Exercise 22 Where is it?

Aim: Question practice with office vocabulary.

This is really a drill disguised as a guessing game which SS can do in pairs. There are no 'correct' sentences or answers, although the T should move around the classroom to make sure SS understand what to do and to correct them as necessary.

Exercise 23 Business letter format

Answers: *1 letterhead   2 reader's name and address   3 date   4 references   5 opening salutation   6 body of the letter*

UNIT TWO

7 closing salutation   8 signature   9 *writer's name*
10 *writer's position in the company*   11 *enclosures*

Aim: To introduce the format of a business letter; listening comprehension.

SS can recognise the names of the parts of the letter (for ease of reference later) by listening to their positions in the letter and linking up the names with the reference numbers. SS are not expected to understand every word of the tape or learn all the terms by heart. At this stage SS do not have to understand the content of the letter either, although you could refer back to it later for comprehension. Before SS do this exercise you will need to teach and practise the prepositions referring to two dimensions: *at the top/bottom, on the right/left, in the middle, above, below* (see also picture dictation on TB page 18). You should also practise the pronunciation of the names of the parts of the letter before SS listen to the tape (See TB page 41 note on Exercise 58.)

Exercise 24   Parts of a letter

Aim: To practise prepositions and parts of a letter.

SS can do this exercise in pairs as indicated in the SB.

Notes on business letter format

The business letter is in block style, as are all the other letters in this book, because it is the most commonly used in offices today (the typist does not have to waste time indenting the beginning of each paragraph). Other styles are possible, but only one is introduced in this book to avoid confusion.

Other terms can also be used to refer to different parts of the letter (eg the *reader* can be called the *addressee*, the *closing salutation* can be called the *complimentary close* etc). It is better to use only one form at this introductory stage, although later you will teach the terms used in the SS' next textbook.

It is important at some stage to explain (or elicit) why a business letter is arranged as it is. You might prefer to do this when a business letter is compared with a personal letter in Unit 4, but a suggested approach is given here: Build up the letter on the board by explaining that BOS Ltd want to write to Simple Stationers Ltd. A company always has its address at the top of each letter so that the reader knows where to reply. This address is often printed on the paper and called a letterhead (it is at the *head* of the *letter*). Companies keep a copy of each letter for future reference so the reader's name and address is also written on the letter (as it appears on the envelope). The date (which can be on the left or right) is important; it helps you follow a sequence of letters and can be a useful reference for either the writer or the reader (*Thank you for your letter of 29 December...In my letter of 20 December, I referred to...*). In

A NEWCOMER

modern business letters the cardinal number is commonly used. (Dates are dealt with more fully in Unit 8). The references are also useful for helping the writer and reader trace the letter, or decide what it is about. The references are often the initials of the writer and the person who typed the letter (here Simon Young and Joy Bradley), but they can also be an order or invoice number, the name of a department, etc.

In your opening salutation, it is polite to use the reader's name if you know it. The first paragraph of a letter usually refers to any previous contact or correspondence and states the writer's intentions. The final paragraph is usually a polite formula. The rules for using *Yours faithfully* and *Yours sincerely* are given in the SB. The writer of the letter signs it and the name of the writer is typed underneath (it is often difficult to read a signature). It is particularly important to put a full title and name in international business where names of other nationalities are not always familiar. The rules for titles are given on SB page 14. A woman should write her title (*Mrs*, *Ms* or *Miss*) in brackets before her name. The writer's position in the company is typed under the name, so the reader knows who he/she is dealing with. If anything is enclosed with the letter, you write *Encl.* at the bottom, partly to remind the writer to put in the enclosures, but also so that the reader will know immediately if anything has been left out.

NB Although there are some special formulae and conventions, the language of modern business letters is very similar to that of polite conversation. Old-fashioned expressions (eg *Thanking you for yours of 15th ult*) are avoided and structures are kept as simple as possible. (See also WB Exercise 8)

Exercise 25 Telephoning (LD A, B & C)

Answers: *See LDT*

Aim: Number practice.

Do this exercise in pairs in class. Point out the different ways of saying numbers for room, telephone and extension numbers (perhaps using the LD cassette as a model). Notice in the telephone numbers that there is a slight pause between the area code and the personal number. Notice also the use of '*double two*' for two numbers the same (just as we say '*double m*' when spelling the name Simmons). For further numbers practice see the Fizz-buzz game on TB page 18.

Exercises 26, 27, 28 (LD A & B × 3)

Aim: Number practice in a business context.

You might use these dialogues at different times with a different presentation for each (see TB page xxv). SS should substitute other names and numbers from the BOS list. Pre-teach the meaning of the switch-board girl's lines in Exercise 28.

UNIT TWO

When SS have practised the three dialogues separately, ask them to build up slightly longer dialogues using the same basic forms.

NB The word *phone* is written in Exercise 26 as an abbreviation for *telephone*. *Phone* is commonly used as a noun or a verb and is very occasionally written with an apostrophe (*'phone*).

Additional activities

Picture dictation To practise prepositions (referring to two dimensions) and office furniture. SS need a blank piece of paper each. Say where things are in an office and they draw them (the quality of the drawing is not important). Start by telling them to draw a desk in the middle of the paper. Draw a desk in the middle of the board to check that they know what they are supposed to do. Then give them other instructions in relation to the desk eg *To the right of the desk there's a filing cabinet. On the filing cabinet there's a coffee pot. On the desk there are two telephones* etc. Only give each instruction once to encourage SS to listen carefully.

When you have given 10 to 12 instructions, check their pictures (and ask them to look at each other's pictures) and then ask them individually to give you back the instructions you gave them. This stage of active production is more difficult than understanding the instructions and it gives you a chance to correct mistakes. This activity can also be effective at higher levels to practise *in the top right-hand corner* etc.

Fizz-buzz This is a game to practise numbers. In order to play this game effectively SS really need to know the numbers from 1 to 100. It should therefore not be played until SS have had the chance to learn and practise these numbers (see SB page 17). Fizz-buzz/fizbʌz/ is a game for three to seven people (a large class should split into smaller groups). The players sit in a circle. In turn they count in English. (S1 says *one*, S2 says *two*, S3 says *three* . . . etc). When a number with a five in is reached (5, 15, 50, 51, 52 etc) or a number which can be divided by 5 (5, 10, 15, 20 etc) *FIZZ* must be said instead of the number. When a number with a seven in it is reached (7, 17 . . . 70, 71 etc) or a number which can be divided by seven (7, 14, 21, 28 etc) *BUZZ* must be said. The sequence begins therefore: 1, 2, 3, 4, fizz, 6, buzz, 8, 9, fizz, 11, 12, 13, buzz, fizz, 16, buzz, 18, 19, fizz, buzz, 22 etc . . .

NB 35 = fizz-buzz (5 × 7); 55 = fizz-fizz (it has two fives in it) etc. Players must count as quickly as they can. When SS make a mistake, either with the English numbers or with saying *fizz* or *buzz*, they must start from the beginning again with *one*. This ensures maximum practice of the more commonly used lower numbers.

A NEWCOMER

Pronunciation For practice in differentiating the *-teen* and *-ty* numbers (*thirteen/thirty, fourteen/forty* etc), give a dictation of a selection of these numbers. The correct stress is: *nineteen* (O O), *ninety* (O o). See also *Telephoning* below.

Telephoning SS might know this game as *Battleships* in their own language. In this business version there are fewer squares to reduce the length of the game and the figures practise the *-ty/-teen* numbers and those letters of the alphabet which are most often confused. SS play in pairs and each S makes two charts like this:

	A	E	G	H	I	J
13						
30						
14						
40						
15						
50						

	A	E	G	H	I	J
13						
30						
14						
40						
15						
50						

On the first chart each S marks four people in the company *in secret*: 4 squares next to each other in a straight line marked with the letter B are the *boss*; 3 squares next to each other in a straight line marked with the letter M are the sales manager; 2 squares next to each other in a straight line marked with the letter R are the receptionist; 1 square marked with the letter S is the secretary.

For example:

	A	E	G	H	I	J
13						
30		B	B	B	B	
14						
40	M					S
15	M		R	R		
50	M					

The staff can be marked anywhere in the square, but each person must be in a straight line vertically or horizontally on adjacent squares. The aim of the game is to speak on the phone to all the people in the other person's square before your opponent speaks to all the people in your square.

UNIT TWO

You have spoken to someone on the phone when you have located all the squares on which their letters are written. To play:

- S1 calls out a square using its reference number and letter (eg A40, H15 etc).
  If S2 has a letter on this square, he/she says *'You're through'*. S1 marks a cross (X) in that square on his/her second chart. Note that the caller does not know which person has been located.
  If S2 does not have a letter on that square, he/she says, *I'm afraid he/she's busy*. S1 marks the square with a dot (.) on his/her second chart.
- S2 now tries to locate S1's staff in the same way.
  S1 and S2 take turns to call out squares. The first chart shows where a S's staff are hidden. The second chart is used to show where the opponent's staff are and which squares have been called.

LANGUAGE DRILLS TAPESCRIPT

Drill 15A Look at the words and pictures and answer these questions, like this:

P: Picture 1 What's this?
R: *It's a notice board*.

Now you try.
P: Picture 2 What's this?
R: *It's a desk*.
P: Picture 3 What's this?
R: *It's a telephone*.
P: Picture 4 What's this?
R: *It's a chair*.
P: Picture 5 What's this?
R: *It's a typewriter*.

P: Picture 6 What's this?
R: *It's a wastepaper bin*.
P: Picture 7 What's this?
R: *It's a graph*.
P: Picture 8 What's this?
R: *It's a filing cabinet*.

Aim: Practice of office vocabulary.

Drill 15B Look at the words and pictures and answer these questions, like this:

P: Picture 1 Is it Fred's notice board?
R: *Yes it is*.

P: Picture 2 Is it Sheila's desk?
R: *No it isn't. It's Simon's desk*.

Now you try.
P: Picture 3 Is it Luisa's telephone?
R: *Yes it is*.
P: Picture 4 Is it Joy's chair?
R: *No it isn't. It's Sheila's chair*.
P: Picture 5 Is it Mary's typewriter?
R: *Yes it is*.

P: Picture 6 Is it Fred's wastepaper bin?
R: *No it isn't. It's Howard's wastepaper bin*.
P: Picture 7 Is it Paul's graph?
R: *Yes it is*.

P: Picture 8 Is it Luisa's filing cabinet?
R: *No it isn't. It's Joy's filing cabinet.*

Aim: Comprehension; practice of short answers (NB The sentence stress is on the names).

Drill 16A

Look at the pictures and answer these questions, like this:

P: Picture 1 What's this? Is it a desk or a table?
R: *It's a desk.*

Now you try.
P: Picture 2 What's this. Is it a wastepaper bin or a chair?
R: *It's a chair.*
P: Picture 3 What's this? Is it a photocopier or a telephone?
R: *It's a photocopier.*
P: Picture 4 What's this? Is it a filing cabinet or an in-tray?
R: *It's a filing cabinet.*
P: Picture 5 What's this? Is it a typewriter or a calculator?
R: *It's a calculator.*

P: Picture 6 What's this? Is it a letter or a book?
R: *It's a book.*
P: Picture 7 What's this? Is it a drawer or a shelf?
R: *It's a drawer.*
P: Picture 8 What's this? Is it a pot plant or a coffee pot?
R: *It's a pot plant.*
P: Picture 9 What's this? Is it a notice board or a graph?
R: *It's a graph.*

Aim: Practice of office vocabulary.

Drill 16B

Ask questions, like this:

P: Desk or table
R: *What's this? Is it a desk or a table?*

Now you try.
P: Wastepaper bin or chair
R: *What's this? Is it a wastepaper bin or a chair?*
P: Photocopier or telephone
R: *What's this? Is it a photocopier or a telephone?*
P: Filing cabinet or in-tray
R: *What's this? Is it a filing cabinet or an in-tray?*
P: Typewriter or calculator
R: *What's this? Is it a typewriter or a calculator?*

P: Letter or book
R: *What's this? Is it a letter or a book?*
P: Drawer or shelf
R: *What's this? Is it a drawer or a shelf?*
P: Pot plant or coffee pot
R: *What's this? Is it a pot plant or a coffee pot?*
P: Notice board or graph
R: *What's this? Is it a notice board or a graph?*

Aim: Question practice with office vocabulary (SS can do this drill with their books closed).

Drill 20

Look at the pictures and answer the questions, like this:

P: Picture 1 What's this?
R: *This is your desk.*
P: Picture 2 What are these?
R: *These are your trays.*

UNIT TWO

P: Picture 7 What's that?
R: *That's the notice board.*

P: Picture 8 What are those?
R: *Those are the books.*

Now you try.
P: Picture 3 What are these?
R: *These are your telephones.*
P: Picture 4 What's this?
R: *This is your in-tray.*
P: Picture 5 What are these?
R: *These are your drawers.*
P: Picture 6 What's this?
R: *This is your typewriter.*
P: Picture 9 What's that?
R: *That's the coffee pot.*

P: Picture 10 What are those?
R: *Those are the shelves.*
P: Picture 11 What are those?
R: *Those are the filing cabinets.*
P: Picture 12 What's that?
R: *That's the photocopier.*

(*Pictures 7 and 8: see examples*)

Aim: Practice of demonstratives and office vocabulary.

Drill 25A

Look at the list of room numbers and answer the questions, like this:

P: What's Sheila's room number?
R: *One-oh-three*

Now you try.
P: What's Joy's room number?
R: *One-oh-two*
P: What's Paul's room number?
R: *One-oh-one*
P: What's Mary's room number?
R: *Two-oh-seven*

P: What's Fred's room number?
R: *Two-oh-five*
P: What's Howard's room number?
R: *Two-oh-six*
P: What's Simon's room number?
R: *One-oh-two*

Aim: Number practice.

Drill 25B

Look at the list of extension numbers and answer these questions, like this:

P: What's Sheila's extension number?
R: *Sixty-two*

Now you try.
P: What's Joy's extension number?
R: *Sixty-seven*
P: What's Paul's extension number?
R: *Fifty-eight*
P: What's Mary's extension number?
R: *Fifty-five*
P: What's Fred's extension number?
R: *Fifty-seven*

P: What's Luisa's extension number?
R: *Eighty-one*
P: What's Howard's extension number?
R: *Sixty*
P: What's Simon's extension number?
R: *Seventy*

A NEWCOMER

Aim: Number practice.

Drill 25C Look at the home telephone numbers and answer these questions, like this:

P: What's Sheila's home number?
R: *Seven-three-nine-double two-oh-two*

Now you try.

P: What's Joy's home number?
R: *Six-two-seven-five-one-eight-three*
P: What's Paul's home number?
R: *Four-five-nine-eight-double one-six*
P: What's Mary's home number?
R: *Four-eight-six-seven-oh-three-one*

P: What's Howard's home number?
R: *Two-four-two-seven-nine-five-one*
P: What's Simon's home number?
R: *Three-two-eight-double six-five-nine*

Aim: Number practice with telephone numbers.

Drills 26A & B, 27A & B, 28A & B

See dialogues in SB.

Aim: Telephone dialogue practice; number practice (SS should say the drills a second time with their books closed).
NB The dialogues are recorded in full before SS take parts so that they can be used for presentation in class if preferred.

WORKBOOK ANSWERS

Exercise 5 Word puzzle

The words are: *chair   wastepaper bin   filing cabinet   typewriter   notice board*

The question is: *Who is Fred's secretary?* The answer is *Mary (Mackie)*

Exercise 6 Calculations

2 *five*   3 *fourteen*   4 *nineteen*   5 *three*   6 *two*   7 *five*   8 *eight*

Exercise 7 Jumbled words

Sample sentences: *What is in the office? Is the telephone on the books? Are these your books? Is the desk in your office? This is the office. What is that on the desk? Is that your telephone? Those books are on the desk in your office. What is that on the desk under the telephone?* etc (Other variations are possible.) This exercise allows SS a degree of creativity in a controlled context where

UNIT TWO

they can learn the limitations of the language (eg they cannot say *What this is?* or *This is office.*) as well as perhaps combining words in new ways to produce acceptable sentences.

Exercise 8 Business letters

1–d   2–e   3–i   4–g   5–k   6–c   7–f   8–a   9–j   10–b   11–l   12–h This exercise tests whether SS have understood the conventions governing the use of openings and endings of business letters.

UNIT THREE
THE BOS BUILDING

3

Business content:	A memorandum; telephone conversations; company names
Structures:	Present progressive tense Imperatives Prepositions (*continued*) Question word: *Which*?
Functions:	Discussing activities; giving directions; giving commands
Lexis:	Ordinal numbers, parts of a building, some office activities

TEACHING NOTES

Exercise 29   Comprehension

Answers: *1 It is upstairs on the second floor.   2 No. He is having lunch. (He is at lunch)   3 Canteen and post room.   4 He is visiting a customer.   5 Helen.*

SS might be able to work out the answers to this exercise without understanding them, but it is better if you do it after you have introduced the present progressive (also called the present continuous) and ordinal numbers.
NB   The word stress on *magazine* is usually ooO in Britain, but influence from the USA means that Ooo is also heard.

To introduce the present progressive

Introduce 5 verbs in the present progressive with pictures from magazines, stick figures drawn on the board and/or mimes or video. Possible verbs are: *She's typing. He's talking. He's reading. She's writing. He's eating.* Stress that this is what all these people are doing NOW. If you establish the mime for each action, you can teach the mimes to the SS for them to elicit the sentences from each other as they practise in pairs. Teach the question *What are you doing?* and the form *I'm . . .* for extra practice with the same verbs. Write up on the board the infinitive of the verbs and show how the *–ing* form is made:
to eat: eat + ing = eating
to type: typ¢ + ing = typing (see SB page 25)
Then ask SS to write out a full pattern of one verb eg

I am eating	*He is eating*	*We are eating*
You are eating	*She is eating*	*They are eating*

They should be able to do this from their knowledge of *to be*. You might find 'time lines' a useful way of reinforcing the concept of tenses (although you might not introduce this one until you contrast the present progressive with the present simple. The present progressive time line is:

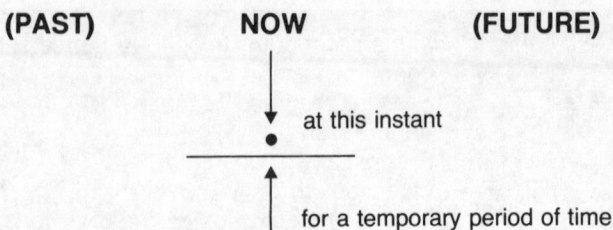

Exercise 30 Listening comprehension

Answers: 2–g 3–f 4–e 5–d 6–i 7–h 8–c 9–a

Aim: Listening comprehension; deducing the meaning of vocabulary.

By listening to the tape as often as necessary and using the names, pictures and notes SS should be able to work out for themselves the meanings of all the verbs.

Exercise 31 What are they doing now? (LD)

Answers: *See LDT*

Check that SS can say each of the verbs in the present progressive and then let them practise the verbs and phrases in pairs. SS can write 9 sentences about what the staff are doing for h/w. (See also WB Exercise 11)

Exercise 32 Checking what people are doing (LD)

Answers: *See LDT*

Aim: Oral practice of questions and short answers in the present progressive.

SS should be able to work out the question form and the short answers from their knowledge of *to be* in Units 1 and 2. Elicit it from them before they do this exercise in pairs.

Exercise 33 Telephoning   (LD A & B)

Answers: *See LDT*

Aim: Practising the present progressive in a business situation.

The *can* form is re-introduced for a polite request here, and you will also have to teach the short polite refusal *I'm afraid not*.
NB SS should only ask for the five people indicated. It would be unnatural to use the present progressive about any of the other people (you would probably say, *I'm afraid he/she's busy at the moment*).

THE BOS BUILDING

Exercise 34   Present progressive

Answers: *1 He is thinking. 2 They are visiting customers. 3 We are eating our lunch. 4 Luisa is greeting a visitor. 5 Mary is taking shorthand. 6 You are having lunch. 7 You are writing a letter. 8 Sheila is interviewing someone. 9 I am speaking on the phone. 10 Helen is sitting in her office. 11 The salesman is selling stationery. 12 He is reading a report. 13 I am putting these books on the table. 14 She is getting on the bus.*

Aim: To practise spelling of present participle.

This written exercise can be done in class or for h/w. See irregular verb list on SB page 139 for the spelling of participles with some irregular verbs.

Exercise 35   Ordinal numbers

Answers: *See SB tapescript*

Aim: Number recognition.

SS have to recognise only the ordinal numbers from *first* to *twentieth* which they should have learnt previously (for practice you can say the cardinal number and they reply with the ordinal number). Play the tape as many times as you think necessary. SS do not have to understand the meaning of each sentence.
NB   *Henry the* eighth *had* six *wives. Eighth* is the *ordinal* number. (Incidentally his first wife was Catherine of Aragon, his second was Anne Boleyn, his third Jane Seymour, his fourth Anne of Cleves, his fifth Catherine Howard and his sixth was Catherine Parr.)

SS can write the numbers out in full, either in class under test conditions, or for h/w. (See also WB Exercise 9)

Exercise 36   Which floor?

Answers: Ground – *BOS Ltd reception*; Basement, Ground floor, 1st and 2nd floor – *BOS Ltd*; 7th floor – *JLN Co Ltd*; 5th floor – *Moore & Moore*; 3rd floor – *Roach Bros*; 4th floor – *Messrs Smith & Co*; 6th floor – *Williams Designs*.

Aim: Teaching business abbreviations.

Teach some of the abbreviations which occur in company names: *Ltd* = *limited*, *Co* = *company*, *Bros* = *brothers*, *Messrs* comes from the French *messieurs* and is pronounced /mesəz/. The names are said: Roach *Brothers*, JLN *Company Limited*, *Messrs* Smith *and Co*. Although you may not want to talk about the types of company with SS at this stage, you might find the following information useful: *Bros* implies that a company was started by brothers sharing the same name (even though the founders of the company may be long dead and the owners now

27

UNIT THREE

have a different name). *Messrs* (now not very common) implies that men with different names started the company. Both these types of company are probably 'partnerships' and the partner-owners have full personal liability for debts to creditors, ie they may have to pay creditors with their private funds if the business fails. There are certain regulations governing the formation of a *limited* company, but essentially the directors' liability to creditors is limited to the assets of the company. They do not have to pay creditors from their private funds if the company goes into liquidation. *Ltd* signifies a 'private limited company', while *plc* stands for 'public limited company'.

SS can do this exercise for h/w or quickly in class. Remind SS that we say *on* a floor but *in* the basement.
NB In many countries what we in Britain call the ground floor is called the 1st floor, the 1st floor is the 2nd floor etc. The basement can also be called the lower ground floor.

Exercise 37 Company location (LD A & B)

Answers: *See LDT*

Aim: To practise ordinal numbers and questions with *Which*.

The meaning of the question *Which?* (a choice from a limited number) should be clear from the context.

Exercise 38 Commands

Sample sentences (other sentences are possible): *Sit down. Put your book on the floor. Touch your desk. Sit on your desk. Stand on your hands.* (SS can put their hands under their feet rather than doing a handstand.) *Put your book on your head. Put your hands on your head. Touch your head. Stand on your chair. Put your chair on your desk. Turn right.*

Aim: To teach and practise imperatives.

Teach the nouns in this exercise by pointing to the objects and the verbs by acting them. As soon as possible, have the SS responding to your commands taken from the list of words in the SB. Start with *Stand up* and *Sit down* to get them used to the idea of moving. Make sure they are really listening by putting in a false instruction (tell them to stand up when they are already standing up and see how many people sit down). Introduce the new verb *Touch* and use it with all the nouns and, finally, introduce *Put*. When SS understand the words, let them tell you the instruction and you do the instructions, correcting their sentences if necessary. When they have a clear grasp of all the words, they can practise in pairs as suggested in the SB. On this or another occasion you could also introduce the negative imperative *Don't do (something)*.

Additional activity

The Boss Says Give instructions to the class, but they only

THE BOS BUILDING

obey if you say *The boss says* before the instructions eg *The boss says put your hands on your head* – the SS obey. *Touch your desk* – the SS do not obey. Once the SS have got the idea, it is essential to keep up a fast pace. Give each S three 'lives'. Every time a S makes a mistake, s/he loses a life. Anyone who is 'dead' goes to the back of the class, but continues to follow the instructions till the end of the game.

If you find it difficult to get some of the SS out, you can 'cheat' by pretending that the game is over and telling them all to sit down. If they do, you can point out that you did not say *The boss says*, so they are all out!

Exercise 39   The BOS Building (LD)

Aim: To teach room names and practise prepositions.

Introduce the names of the rooms (SS can look them up in foreign-language/English dictionaries if necessary). *Opposite* is the only new preposition. SS work in pairs asking each other where each room is. (See also WB Exercise 10) The LD tests comprehension rather than the SS' active repertoire but it can be used as a guide to sample answers to the exercise.

Exercise 40   Directions from reception (LD)

Answers: *See LDT for Exercises 39, 40 and 41.*

Aim: To practise asking and telling the way politely.

The two new words are *upstairs* and *downstairs*. See TB page xxv for ways of introducing dialogues with variations.

Exercise 41   Directions in the BOS building (LD)

Answers: *See LDT for Exercises 39, 40 and 41.*

This is another way of telling someone the way. Present this dialogue in a different way (see TB page xxv) and at a different time from the one in Exercise 40 for revision.

Exercise 42   Word puzzle

Answers: *1* door   *2* ground   *3* downstairs   *4* of   *5* out   *6* up   *7* opposite   *8* in   *9* lift   *10* basement   *11* on   *12* floor

Aim: To reinforce vocabulary learned in this unit.

The exercise can be done individually or in pairs, in class or for h/w.

Exercise 43   A memorandum

Answer: (see page 30)

Aim: To introduce the format of a memo.

The exercise involves a simple substitution of information. Discuss with the SS which information in the original memo is

UNIT THREE

BRIGHTER OFFICE SUPPLIES LIMITED

MEMORANDUM

LIMITED

```
TO:       All staff
FROM:     Jane Seymour, company nurse
DATE:     30 November 1992
Subject:  Medical room hours
```

I am available to see staff on Tuesday and Thursday between 10.30 and 3.30am in the medical room. I can also see staff by appointment.

The medical room is room 203 on the second floor. Come out of the lift and take the corridor on the left. The medical room is on the left.

---

being substituted. They can write the memo with the new information for h/w.

SS should be encouraged to write out the full heading so that the memo looks authentic, although it would be better if you could obtain a blank memo for them to fill in.

Since a memo (or memorandum) is used for communication within a company there is no need for addresses to be shown, but the names, departments, date and subject heading are very important for reference. Mention the format of the date briefly (dates are dealt with more fully in Unit 8) and introduce the days of the week: *Monday, Tuesday, Wednesday, Thursday* (they are consolidated in Unit 6).

People write memos (a) when they want to communicate the same information to a number of people in the company, (b) when they want a written record of the information, (c) to summarise or confirm decisions taken orally. (See also WB Exercise 12)

LANGUAGE DRILLS TAPESCRIPT

Drill 31

Look at the pictures and notes and answer these questions, like this:

P: What's Luisa doing?
R: *She's welcoming a visitor.*

Now you try.
P: What's Anne doing?
R: *She's typing a letter.*
P: What's Howard doing?
R: *He's interviewing someone.*
P: What's Joy doing?
R: *She's taking shorthand.*
P: What's Fred doing?
R: *He's visiting a customer.*

P: What's Simon doing?
R: *He's talking on the phone.*
P: What's Mary doing?
R: *She's sending a telex.*
P: What's Helen doing?
R: *She's reading a magazine.*
P: What's Paul doing?
R: *He's having lunch.*

THE BOS BUILDING

Drill 32

Aim: Practice of present progressive.

Look at the pictures and notes. Give short answers to these questions about what people are doing, like this:

P: Is Luisa welcoming a visitor?
R: *Yes she is.*

P: Are Simon and Joy having lunch?
R: *No they're not.*

Now you try.
P: Is Mary sending a telex?
R: *Yes she is.*
P: Is Simon talking on the phone?
R: *Yes he is.*

P: Is Fred visiting a customer?
R: *Yes he is.*
P: Is Howard interviewing someone?
R: *Yes he is.*

Aim: Comprehension; practice of short answers.

Drill 33A

Look at the pictures and notes. Answer these people on the phone, like this:

P: Can I speak to Howard Spencer please?
R: *I'm afraid not. He's interviewing someone.*

Now you try.
P: Can I speak to Joy Bradley please?
R: *I'm afraid not. She's taking shorthand.*
P: Can I speak to Fred McLean please?
R: *I'm afraid not. He's visiting a customer.*

P: Can I speak to Simon Young please?
R: *I'm afraid not. He's talking on the phone.*
P: Can I speak to Paul Johnson please?
R: *I'm afraid not. He's having lunch.*

Aim: Comprehension; practice of the present progressive in a business context.

Drill 33B

Ask to speak to these people on the phone, like this:

P: Fred McLean
R: *Can I speak to Fred McLean please?*

Now you try.
P: Howard Spencer
R: *Can I speak to Howard Spencer please?*
P: Simon
R: *Can I speak to Simon please?*
P: Mrs Baker
R: *Can I speak to Mrs Baker please?*

P: Mary Mackie
R: *Can I speak to Mary Mackie please?*
P: Mr Johnson
R: *Can I speak to Mr Johnson please?*

Aim: Practice of polite request in a business context (SS can do this drill with their books closed).

UNIT THREE

Drill 37A Look at the diagram of the floors of the BOS building. Answer these questions, like this:

P: Which floor is Roach Brothers on?
R: *It's on the third floor.*

Now you try.
P: Which floor is BOS reception on?
R: *It's on the ground floor.*
P: Which floor is JLN Company Limited on?
R: *It's on the seventh floor.*
P: Which floor is Moore and Moore on?
R: *It's on the fifth floor.*

P: Which floor is Messrs Smith and Co on?
R: *It's on the fourth floor.*
P: Which floor is Williams Designs on?
R: *It's on the sixth floor.*

Aim: Comprehension; practice of ordinal numbers.

Drill 37B Ask questions about which company is on which floor, like this:

P: Seventh
R: *Which company is on the seventh floor?*

Now you try.
P: Fifth
R: *Which company is on the fifth floor?*
P: Third
R: *Which company is on the third floor?*
P: First
R: *Which company is on the first floor?*

P: Ground
R: *Which company is on the ground floor?*
P: Basement
R: *Which company is in the basement?*

Aim: Question practice referring to an office building (SS can do this drill with their books closed).

Drill 39 Look at the plan of the BOS building and answer these questions, like this:

P: Which room is opposite the stationery store?
R: *The store room*

Now you try.
P: Which room is opposite the store room?
R: *The stationery store*
P: Which room is between G1 and G3?
R: *G2*
P: Which room is above the telex room?
R: *G6*

P: What's above the switchboard?
R: *Reception*
P: Which room is between room one-oh-two and room one-oh-six?
R: *Room one-oh-four*
P: Which room is below G4?
R: *The post room*

THE BOS BUILDING

P: Which room is between the stationery store and the switchboard?
R: *The telex room*

P: Which room is opposite G5?
R: *G7*

Aim: Comprehension
NB The example is not repeated in this drill.

Drill 40   Ask your way to places in the BOS building, like this:

P: The canteen
R: *Excuse me. Where's the canteen please?*

Now you try.
P: Room four oh five
R: *Excuse me. Where's room four oh five please?*
P: The telex room
R: *Excuse me. Where's the telex room please?*
P: The post room
R: *Excuse me. Where's the post room please?*

P: Room G6
R: *Excuse me. Where's room G6 please?*
P: Reception
R: *Excuse me. Where's reception please?*

Aim: Practice in asking for directions (SS can do this drill with their books closed).

Drill 41   Look at the layout of the BOS building. Listen to these instructions and say which room you come to, like this:

P: Come out of the lift on the fourth floor and take the corridor on the right. It's on the right.
R: *Room 406 or 407*

Now you try.
P: Come out of the lift on the fourth floor and take the corridor on the right. It's on the left.
R: *Room 405*
P: Come out of the lift in the basement. It's on the left.
R: *The canteen*
P: Come into the building on the ground floor. Take the corridor on the right. It's on the left.
R: *Room G5*
P: Come out of the lift in the basement. Take the corridor on the right. It's on the right.
R: *The stationery store or the telex room*

P: Come out of the lift on the fifth floor. Take the corridor on the left. It's on the right.
R: *Room 504*
P: Come out of the lift in the basement. Take the corridor on the right. It's on the left.
R: *The store room or the post room*

UNIT THREE

Aim: Comprehension of instructions.
NB The example is not repeated in this drill.

WORKBOOK ANSWERS

Exercise 9 Ordinal numbers

2 21st   3 2nd   4 4th   5 6th   6 3rd   7 5th   8 20th

SS have only to recognise the ordinal numbers in these sentences. They do not need to understand the rest of the sentences.

Exercise 10 Office plan

*1 office manager's office   2 typing pool   3 post room
4 reception   5 personnel manager's office   6 sales office
7 managing director's office   8 sales manager's office*

Exercise 11 What are you doing?

2 I am taking shorthand.   3 I am typing a letter.   4 I am talking on the phone/telephone.   5 I am reading a memo.   6 I am sending a telex. These sentences can be in any order.

Exercise 12 A memo

```
BRIGHTER OFFICE SUPPLIES LIMITED

            MEMORANDUM

    TO:       All staff
    FROM:     Howard Spencer,
              Personnel department
    DATE:     30 October 1992
    Subject:  Appointment system

I am not available to see staff on Monday and Wednesday this
week because I am interviewing new staff. I can still see
staff by appointment.
```

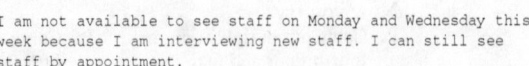

This exercise gives practice in laying out a memo correctly. You have already introduced most of the aspects of punctuation and capitalisation that occur in this memo and SS can use the memo in the SB as a model.

UNIT FOUR
OFFICE ROUTINE

4

> *Business content*: A survey; a block chart
> *Structures*: Present simple tense
> Adverbs used with the present simple
> Question words: *How? How long? How often? What time? When?*
> *Functions*: Discussing routine actions and timetables; telling the time; writing a personal letter
> *Pronunciation*: Final *-s*
> *Lexis*: Travel/means of transport, time, some verbs of office routine

TEACHING NOTES

Exercise 44 Comprehension

Answers: *1 By tube and train   2 About 11 o'clock   3 Between 1.15 and 1.30   4 An hour   5 Between 2.15 and 2.30*

SS might be able to work out the answers to this exercise before they start this unit, but you could wait until you have taught the present simple tense and telling the time. SS will have to work out the answer to question 5 as it is not specifically stated. You might teach and practise the colloquial expression *on the dot* (meaning *exactly*). You can remind SS to be on time for their next lesson which starts at.... *on the dot*.
NB The *tube* refers only to the London Underground system; in many other cities it is called a *metro*.

Exercise 45 Telling the time (LD)

Answers: *See LDT*

If possible, make a clock with movable hands to teach the time. Start by teaching the *o'clock* times, then the *quarter to* and *past* and *half past* times. Then teach all the '*five minute*' times. That is all SS need in order to do this exercise.

If you also teach the word *about*, meaning *approximately*, in expressions such as *It's about five past three*, SS will be able to tell the time for most everyday purposes. The word is introduced in Exercise 44. You can teach the question form *What's the time?* before you teach the polite form in the exercise. The LD uses a variety of forms the SS might hear, but they only have to produce the *Can you...?* form (the form previously introduced for polite requests).
NB We also say *a quarter to...* and *a quarter past...*, although it is better not to confuse SS with the two forms.

UNIT FOUR

Exercise 46 Joy's routine (LD)

Answers: *See LDT Also:* b 9.35 – A open the post – picture 6; c 10.00 – F take shorthand – picture 7; d 11.00 – H make coffee – picture 1; e 11.30 – E type letters – picture 10; f 1.30 – G have lunch – picture 8; g 2.35 – I send telexes – picture 4; h 4.00 – D make tea – picture 9; i 4.30 – J do the filing – picture 3; j 5.30 – C go home – picture 5

Aim: Listening comprehension and recognition of written forms.

Teach the verbs by linking them with the pictures and saying what Joy is doing, using the present progressive tense. It is not necessary to introduce the present simple before SS do this exercise as they only have to match up the time, notes and pictures, but you might point out that we use a different present tense for things people do regularly (again and again).
Give SS enough time to process the information. Pause the tape as necessary or let SS operate the cassette player.

To introduce the present simple tense

Mime four actions and elicit sentences from SS in the present progressive; eg *You're getting up/eating breakfast/driving to work/opening the post*
Establish that you do these things every day and introduce/elicit sentences such as *You get up every day at 8 o'clock*. You can then transpose the sentences to the third person singular: *Anne gets up at 8 o'clock every day* etc. The form will not be totally unfamiliar since SS have already met the infinitive as an imperative in the *Language notes* to Unit 3. The main point to emphasise to SS is the addition of *-s* in the third person singular. The time lines for the present simple are:

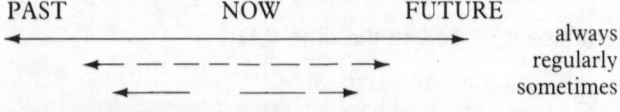

Encourage SS to pick out time expressions which are frequently used with the present simple (*regularly, every day* etc).

You could establish a substitution drill for further practice:

T: *I drive to work every day.*   S1: *I drive to work every day.*
T: *You*   S2: *You drive to work every day.*
T: *At 9 o'clock*   S3: *You drive to work at 9 o'clock.*
T: *Anne*   S4: *Anne drives to work at 9 o'clock.*
T: *opens the post*   S5: *Anne opens the post at 9 o'clock. etc*

NB You could also do this kind of substitution drill as an *action chain*. SS sit in circles of about eight. S1 says the sentence. You give him/her a card with the first substitution on it which s/he incorporates into the sentence (as above). S1 then turns to S2 who follows the same procedure. S2 turns to S3 and so on. Meanwhile S1 has been given the second substitution. The chain continues until all SS have incorporated all the substitutions. With a large class you will have several groups going at once.

Exercise 47 Writing about routine

Answers: *Joy starts work at 9.30. First she opens the post. Then she takes shorthand. She makes coffee at 11 o'clock. In the morning she also types letters. She has lunch at half past one. In the afternoon she sends telexes and does the filing. She makes tea at four o'clock. She goes home at 5.30.* (These sentences can be varied slightly.)

Aim: Written practice of the present simple.

This exercise can be written in class or for h/w. SS should be able to understand the questions without necessarily being able to produce them (they do not need to) particularly as they have previously met questions in the present simple in Exercises 5 and 12. When SS have written the paragraph, point out to them the use of the words *first, then* and *also* for connecting a sequence of actions into a paragraph.

See WB Exercise 16 for a comparison between the present simple and the present progressive.

Exercise 48 Questions and answers (LD)

Answers: *See LDT*

Aim: To introduce questions and short answers in the present simple.

Teach the question form: *They start work at 9 o'clock.*

They start work at 9 o'clock. (with *Do* inserted at start and *?* at end)
Do they start work at 9 o'clock?
Do they start work ~~at 9 o'clock~~? (with *When* substituted)
When do they start work?

Remind SS that in the third person singular *do* becomes *does*. Write a few sentences in the present simple on the board and ask SS to make questions from them, perhaps with different question words. The short answer is the same for all main verbs: *Yes I do/No I don't.*

This exercise should be done orally in class, in pairs.

Exercise 49 Spelling and pronunciation (LD)

Answers: *See LDT*

Aim: Pronunciation practice of the present simple third person singular.

UNIT FOUR

Play the first three examples on the tape to point out the three different sounds to the SS. Then play the tape as often as you feel is necessary for the SS to complete the exercise. SS can do the written part of the exercise before or after listening to the tape (possibly for h/w). It is not important for them to understand the meaning of every verb. The spelling rule is straightforward.

The pronunciation rule is as follows:
/ɪz/ after the sounds: /s/ /z/ /ʃ/ /ʒ/ /tʃ/ /dʒ/
/s/ after all other voiceless sounds: /p/ /t/ /k/ /f/ /θ/
/z/ after all other voiced sounds: /d/ /b/ /v/ /g/ /ð/ /l/ /n/ /m/ /ŋ/ /w/ /r/ and all vowel sounds

These rules also apply to the pronunciation of the plural and genitive 's. Teach SS the rule for the /ɪz/ sounds, but only introduce other sounds as you meet them.

Exercise 50   Timetables (LD A, B & C)

Answers: *See LDT*

Aim: To practise saying the time.

This exercise introduces the 24-hour clock which is frequently used in business and is also becoming more common in everyday speech (see SB page 33). We say these times by dividing the numbers into two parts eg 16 30 – *sixteen thirty*; 06 18 – *six eighteen*.
(NB 2400 = *twenty-four hundred*; 0600 = *oh six hundred*). The drill practises (a) asking about the departure times of public transport (NB notice the use of the present simple with timetables); (b) talking about the 24-hour clock; (c) converting times from the 24-hour clock (see also WB Exercise 13).

Point out that we insert the word *minute(s)* when we talk about 'non-five minute' times.

See the notes on presenting dialogues on TB page xxv before you do this exercise. You might like to break down the drill into parts before you do the full dialogue, as is done in the LD. Other means of transport are introduced on the LD: *coach*, *boat* and *plane*. They are further practised in WB Exercise 14. Note that *plane* (sometimes written with an apostrophe: *'plane*) is short for *aeroplane* (*airplane* in the USA). The *tube* can also be called the *metro*, *underground* or *subway*. *Bus* was originally short for *omnibus*, although the longer form is very rarely heard nowadays.

You should also teach the words: *morning*, *afternoon*, *evening*, *midday*, *noon*, *midnight* and *hour* (NB *an* hour); and possibly the associated formal greetings *Good morning*, *Good afternoon*, *Good evening* (and *Goodbye*?).

OFFICE ROUTINE

Exercise 51 Journeys (LD)

Answers: *See LDT*. Also: The times in minutes between stations are:
train: CC to W – 2; CC to LB – 12; W to LB – 10.
tube: CC to W – 3; CC to LB – 20; W to LB – 17.
bus: CC to W – 10; CC to LB – 25; W to LB – 15.

Aim: Fluency; to practise *How long?* and *to take*.

The verb *to take* is introduced in the sense of a journey or an activity taking a certain amount of time. Notice the other use of this verb: *It takes me 20 minutes to drive to work.* Only introduce the form in the book at this stage.

Exercise 52 Travelling to work (LD)

Answers: *See LDT*

Aim: Further practice of the present simple with routine actions.

Pre-teach the means of transport using the pictures (or magazine pictures). (See also WB Exercise 14) Note that you can also say '*She goes* by *car*', 'by *bicycle*', but 'on *foot*'.

Exercise 53 Wordsquare

Answers: 1 *midday*   2 *midnight*   3 *noon*   4 *minutes*
5 *hour*   6 *drives*   7 *walks*   8 *work*   9 *tube*   10 *bus*
11 *car*   12 *from*   13 *to*   14 *travel*   15 *leaves*
16 *regularly*   17 *every*   18 *day*   19 *never*   20 *come*
21 *by*   22 *her*   23 *room*   24 *or*   25 *filing*   26 *on*

Aim: Vocabulary consolidation.

This exercise can be done individually or in pairs in class or for h/w. Pre-teach the words *horizontal(ly)*, *diagonal(ly)* and *vertical(ly)* for recognition.

Exercise 54 A survey (LD A & B)

Answers: *See LDT*

Aim: To practise adverbs and present simple word order.

SS take their information from a survey – a common business activity. Make sure SS understand the convention of counting in fives, thus ̷H̷H̷. With inexperienced SS, ask them to write several numbers in this way.

Note that the question is still '*How many people . . .*' (not *person*) even when the answer is one.

Exercise 55 A block chart

Answers: See SB page 40.

NB The '*occasionally*' figure should be added to the '*always*' figure to find the position of the top line.

UNIT FOUR

Aim: Improving a business skill to incorporate with language practice.

Encourage SS to work together to draw the chart (possibly with only one partner having access to the figures) to encourage further language practice.

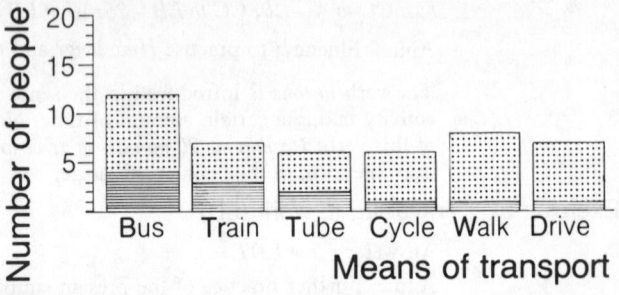

Exercise 56 A report

Answers: *There are twenty people in the survey. Four people always travel to work by bus, eight people occasionally travel by bus and eight people never travel by bus. Three people always travel by train, four people occasionally travel by train and thirteen people never travel by train. Two people always travel by tube, four people occasionally travel by tube and fourteen people never travel by tube. One person always cycles to work, five people occasionally cycle and fourteen people never cycle. One person occasionally walks to work, seven people occasionally walk and twelve people never walk. One person always drives to work, six people occasionally drive and thirteen people never drive.*

Aim: Written practice of the present simple.

The exercise can be written in class or done for h/w.

Point out to SS the use of commas in lists of things (in this case where three short sentences are joined to make one sentence). There is no comma before *and* (*and* is instead of a comma).

Reinforce the note in the SB that the singular of *people* is *person*. NB (You might occasionally meet the plural *persons* but this is only used in very specific circumstances such as in grammatical references or formal notices.)

Additional activity

For further practice set up a class survey to find out how people travel to school/work. Everybody in the class asks everyone else: *How do you usually travel to school/work?* to which each person may give one means of transport. The results could be presented in a block chart and as a short report.

Exercise 57 A personal letter

Answers: *1 Janet   2 Joy   3 In London (5 Essex Road,*

London SW12 5JL)   4 *In Bournemouth*   5 *Nothing./She is sitting in her office with nothing to do./She is writing to Janet./She is waiting for 5 o'clock.*   6 *She gets up.*   7 *By tube and train*   8 *In the canteen*   9 *To the cinema*   10 *Every month/once a month*   11 *Next week*   12 *Next month/in November*

Aim: Reading comprehension.

SS ought to be able to write short answers to the questions without help. Do not pre-teach vocabulary; if SS find words difficult help them understand them from the context (eg *Is a 'boring' job good or bad?* The precise meaning often does not matter.) Either ask the questions orally, or ask SS to write the answers in class or for h/w. (See also WB Exercise 17)

Exercise 58   Personal and business letters

Answers: *The overall style of personal letters is less formal than business letters. Personal letters are often handwritten, not typed. You do not write the reader's name and address on a personal letter. You often do not write the year in the date. There are no references. You can use contractions (I'm, it's etc) in a personal letter. You do not have a formal ending in a personal letter.*
(NB Other endings for personal letters are: Best wishes, Love, with love from for family and close friends). *The writer often only writes his/her first name and not his/her full signature. The writer does not print his/her name and job at the bottom of the page. The style is usually indented, not block.*
NB   Although some people have their private address printed at the top of their writing paper, other people frequently do not write their full address when they are writing to family or close friends who are familiar with their address.

Aim: To reinforce the style and format of a business letter.

Ask SS to try to work out the reasons for each part of a business letter if you did not explain it in Unit 2 (see TB page 16). They could listen again to the tape for Exercise 23 and try to decipher more of the information it contains. This exercise can be done in the SS' L1 with a monolingual class.

Additional activities

Asking the time   Ask SS the time occasionally throughout this and subsequent lessons for quick practice (people's watches often show different times and this can be exploited by asking for the *exact* time. NB In this context it might be useful to teach *My watch is (probably/usually) slow/fast.*

Time dictation   Read out sentences containing a time and SS write down the time (like Exercises 19 and 35) eg:
He's coming at half past five this afternoon. (5.30)
The bus always arrives at exactly twenty-two minutes past seven. (7.22)
The time is exactly nineteen nineteen. (19.19) etc . . .

UNIT FOUR

SS can make up their own time dictation: Ten SS each say a time from the 24-hour clock (eg 2034) which everyone writes down. For h/w they all write the times out in full as we normally refer to them (eg 07.34: *twenty-six minutes to eight*).

Pronunciation A possible pronunciation point arising in this unit is the contrast between the sounds /ɔː/ as in *walk* and /ɜː/ as in *work*. (See TB page xxiv) Other minimal pairs containing these sounds are: *short – shirt; form – firm; board/bored – bird; born – burn*.

Jumbled words A further exercise which encourages SS to use the language in this unit more creatively (see WB Exercise 7 and TB note, page 23) is to write the following words on the board:
in – it – he – by – from – to – past – is – take – -s – train – the – work – Victoria – Harlow – minute – o'clock – five – eight – quarter.

Ask SS in pairs or small groups to make up as many sentences as possible in a restricted amount of time (eg ten minutes). Some possible sentences are: *It is five past eight. He works in Harlow. He takes the five o'clock train from Harlow. The Victoria train is in five minutes. It is quarter to eight. It is eight minutes past five. He is in the train. The train is in Harlow. It takes five minutes by train from Victoria to Harlow. He is ten.* etc...

Come/go If SS confuse these verbs, the following examples might help you explain:
Come: to/towards where the speaker is, was or definitely will be.
eg *He came to my house last night. He's coming towards me.*
Go: away from where the speaker is, was or definitely will be.
eg *Why don't you go home. Go away. He went to the cinema.*

NB *Will you come to Jane's party with me?* (I am definitely going and I would like you to accompany me). *Will you go to Jane's party with me?* (I have not decided whether I am going or not. Perhaps if you go, I will go.)

LANGUAGE DRILLS TAPESCRIPT

Drill 45

Look at the clocks. Say what the time is, like this:

P: 1 Can you tell me the time please?
R: *It's quarter past five.*

Now you try.
P: 2 What time is it please?
R: *It's half past six.*
P: 3 Have you got the right time please?
P: 4 Can you tell me the right time please?
R: *It's quarter to eight.*
P: 5 What time do you make it?

OFFICE ROUTINE

    R: *It's nine o'clock.*
    P: 6 What time does your watch say?
    R: *It's five to one.*
    P: 7 Do you know what time it is?
    R: *It's twenty to four.*

    R: *It's twenty past eight.*
    P: 8 Could you tell me the right time please?
    R: *It's ten past two.*

Aim: To practise saying the time; passive introduction to a variety of ways people ask for the time.

Drill 46 Look at the pictures and notes and answer these questions about Joy's daily routine, like this:

    P: Picture 2 What does Joy do at 9.30?
    R: *She starts work.*

Now you try.
    P: Picture 6 What does Joy do first?
    R: *She opens the post.*
    P: Picture 7 What does Joy do next?
    R: *She takes shorthand.*
    P: Picture 1 What does she do at eleven o'clock?
    R: *She makes coffee.*
    P: Picture 10 What does she do next?
    R: *She types letters.*
    P: Picture 8 What does she do at about one thirty?
    R: *She has lunch.*

    P: Picture 4 What does she do in the afternoon?
    R: *She sends telexes.*
    P: Picture 9 What does she do at four o'clock?
    R: *She makes tea.*
    P: Picture 3 What does she do after tea?
    R: *She does the filing.*
    P: Picture 5 What does she do at five thirty?
    R: *She goes home.*

Aim: Practice of present simple number recognition.

Drill 48 Pretend you are Joy. Look at the pictures in Exercise 46 and give short answers to these questions, like this:

    P: Do you start work at nine thirty?
    R: *Yes I do.*

    P: Do you do the filing in the morning?
    R: *No I don't.*

Now you try.
    P: Do you make coffee at four o'clock?
    R: *No I don't.*
    P: Do you take shorthand in the morning?
    R: *Yes I do.*
    P: Do you go home at five thirty?
    R: *Yes I do.*
    P: Do you type letters at four o'clock?
    R: *No I don't.*

    P: Do you have lunch at about one thirty?
    R: *Yes I do.*
    P: Do you open the post in the afternoon?
    R: *No I don't.*
    P: Do you make tea in the morning?
    R: *No I don't.*
    P: Do you send telexes at nine thirty?
    R: *No I don't.*

Aim: Comprehension; practice of short answers.

UNIT FOUR

Drill 49 Say these verbs in the third person singular of the present simple tense, like this:

P: Take
R: *He takes* /s/

Now you try. Be careful of the pronunciation of the final -*s*.

P: Do
R: *He does* /z/ NB pron /dʌz/
P: Catch
R: *He catches* /ɪz/
P: Travel
R: *He travels* /z/
P: Work
R: *He works* /s/
P: Telex
R: *He telexes* /ɪz/
P: Go
R: *He goes* /z/
P: Paint
R: *He paints* /s/
P: Drive
R: *He drives* /z/
P: Open
R: *He opens* /z/

P: Type
R: *He types* /s/
P: Wash
R: *He washes* /ɪz/
P: Photocopy
R: *He photocopies* /z/*
P: Start
R: *He starts* /s/
P: Send
R: *He sends* /z/
P: Say
R: *He says* /z/ NB pron /sez/
P: Rise
R: *He rises* /ɪz/
P: Leave
R: *He leaves* /z/

* Although the final sound is /ɪz/, the /ɪ/ is part of the verb stem.

Aim: Pronunciation practice of a final -s (SS can do this drill with their books closed).

Drill 50A Look at the exercise and answer these questions, like this:

P: Number 1 What time does the next train leave please?
R: *Six thirty-nine*

Now you try.

P: Number 2 What time does the next plane leave please?
R: *Eight forty-nine*
P: Number 3 What time does the next bus leave please?
R: *Thirteen oh six*
P: Number 4 What time does the next boat leave please?
R: *Twenty-three fifty-nine*
P: Number 5 What time does the next tube leave please?
R: *Six fifteen*
P: Number 6 What time does the next coach leave please?
R: *One oh six*

P: Number 7 What time does the next train leave please?
R: *Four twenty-five*
P: Number 8 What time does the next bus leave please?
R: *Twenty-one fifty-seven*
P: Number 9 What time does the next plane leave please?
R: *Fifteen forty-two*
P: Number 10 What time does the next boat leave please?
R: *Nineteen thirty-four*

Aim: Practice of saying times on the 24-hour clock.

OFFICE ROUTINE

Drill 50B

Ask questions about travelling, like this:

P: Train
R: *Excuse me. What time does the next train leave please?*

Now you try.
P: Bus
R: *Excuse me. What time does the next bus leave please?*
P: Boat
R: *Excuse me. What time does the next boat leave please?*

P: Coach
R: *Excuse me. What time does the next coach leave please?*
P: Plane
R: *Excuse me. What time does the next plane leave please?*

Aim: Practice of polite requests and means of transport (SS can do this drill with their books closed).

Drill 50C

Say the times in full, like this:

P: The train leaves at six thirty-nine.
R: *That's twenty-one minutes to seven.*

Now you try.
P: The bus leaves at eight forty-nine.
R: *That's eleven minutes to nine.*
P: The boat comes in at thirteen oh six.
R: *That's six minutes past one.*
P: The plane takes off at twenty-three fifty-nine.
R: *That's one minute to twelve.*
P: The train arrives at sixteen fifteen.
R: *That's quarter past four.*
P: The boat goes out at one oh eight.
R: *That's eight minutes past one.*

P: The bus is due at four twenty-five.
R: *That's twenty-five past four.*
P: The plane lands at twenty-one fifty-seven.
R: *That's three minutes to ten.*
P: The coach leaves at fifteen forty-two.
R: *That's eighteen minutes to four.*
P: The bus arrives at nineteen thirty-four.
R: *That's twenty-six minutes to eight.*

Aim: Recognition of times on the 24-hour clock; practice of saying the time (SS can do this drill with their books closed).

Drill 51

Ask about how long journeys take, like this:

P: Waterloo – London Bridge – train
R: *How long does the journey from Waterloo to London Bridge take by train?*

Now you try.
P: Waterloo – London Bridge – car
R: *How long does the journey from Waterloo to London Bridge take by car?*

P: Charing Cross – London Bridge – bus
R: *How long does the journey from Charing Cross to London Bridge take by bus?*

UNIT FOUR

P: Charing Cross – Waterloo – taxi
R: *How long does the journey from Charing Cross to Waterloo take by taxi?*
P: Charing Cross – London Bridge – tube
R: *How long does the journey from Charing Cross to London Bridge take by tube?*

P: Waterloo – London Bridge – bus
R: *How long does the journey from Waterloo to London Bridge take by bus?*

Aim: Fluency (SS can do this drill with their books closed).

Drill 52 Do Exercise 52 before you do this drill. Answer these questions, like this:

P: How does Sheila travel to work?
R: *She walks.*

Now you try.
P: How does Simon travel to work?
R: *He goes by train.*
P: How does Anne travel to work?
R: *She goes by bus.*

P: How does Luisa travel to work?
R: *She cycles.*
P: How does Fred travel to work?
R: *He drives.*

Aim: Comprehension; practice of the present simple and means of transport.

Drill 54A Look at the results of the survey and answer these questions, like this:

P: How many people always travel by bus?
R: *Four*

Now you try.
P: How many people occasionally travel by train?
R: *Four*
P: How many people never travel by tube?
R: *Fourteen*
P: How many people always cycle to work?
R: *One*

P: How many people occasionally walk to work?
R: *Seven*
P: How many people never drive to work?
R: *Thirteen*

Aim: Comprehension; number practice.

Drill 54B Ask questions about the result of the survey about how people travel, like this:

P: Always – bus
R: *How many people always travel by bus?*

P: Occasionally – walk
R: *How many people occasionally walk?*

46

Now you try.

P: Never – cycle
R: *How many people never cycle?*
P: Occasionally – tube
R: *How many people occasionally travel by tube?*

P: Always – train
R: *How many people always travel by train?*
P: Never – drive
R: *How many people never drive?*

Aim: Question practice in the present simple with transport vocabulary (SS can do this drill with their books closed).

WORKBOOK ANSWERS

Exercise 13 Times

0529 *Twenty-nine minutes past five.* 2059 *One minute to nine.* 0952 *Eight minutes to ten.* 0259 *One minute to three.* 1208 *Eight minutes past twelve.* 1820 *Twenty past six.* 1802 *Two minutes past six.* 0218 *Eighteen minutes past two.* 0812 *Twelve minutes past eight.* 0821 *Twenty-one minutes past eight.* 0128 *Twenty-eight minutes past one.* (The sentences can be in any order.)

This exercise practises converting times from the 24-hour clock. You can make up your own version of this exercise at any time for extra times/numbers practice.

Exercise 14 Transport puzzle

1 bus   2 bicycle   3 taxi   4 plane   5 car   6 coach
7 boat   8 train   9 tube

Exercise 15 A timetable

Liverpool Street	Seven Sisters	Harlow	Stortford
11.05	11.15	11.47	12.00
11.28	–	12.10	12.23
11.53	–	–	12.43
12.05	12.15	12.47	13.00
12.28	–	13.10	13.23
12.53	–	–	13.43

1 13.00 (One o'clock)   2 No   3 The 12.10 from Harlow (The 11.28 from Liverpool Street) This exercise is a reading comprehension from which SS have to fill in a railway timetable.

Exercise 16 Present simple and progressive tenses

1 works   2 is working   3 are redecorating   4 is typing
5 has   6 goes   7 paint   8 are painting

This exercise is to compare and contrast the two present tenses. You might introduce the time lines on TB pages 26

UNIT FOUR

and 36, if you have not done so already. Pre-teach: *decorate*, *redecorate* (you might point out that the prefix *re-* frequently means 'again' eg *rewrite*, *re-order*, *revise*), *decorator*, *to paint*, *ceiling*.

Exercise 17   A personal letter

> 2 Grenville Drive
> Bournemouth BM6 2GH
>
> 31st October 1992
>
> Dear Joy,
> Thank you very much for your letter. I'm sure your life isn't really boring.
> My life isn't very exciting at the moment. I'm in bed because I'm not very well.
> I'm looking forward to your visit next week and to the wedding.
>
> Love,
> Janet

This exercise is a reading comprehension, but it also provides practice in setting out a personal letter.

UNIT FIVE
ORDERING STATIONERY   5

> *Business content*:   An order; a business letter (reply to a request)
> *Structures*:   Count and mass nouns
>   Plurals
>   Adjectives
>   *Need*
>   *Have got*
> *Function*:   Expressing need
> *Lexis*:   Stationery, adjectives to describe
>   stationery, party food, numerical
>   expressions

TEACHING NOTES

Exercise 59   Comprehension

> Answers: *1 Twelve (12) 2 A couple (about 2) 3 Pencils and headed writing paper 4 We don't know but probably he controls stationery supplies.*

SS can probably do this exercise before the rest of the unit. Use this exercise to teach *a couple* (this literally means *two*, but in everday speech it may mean *two or three*, or even *a few*), *half a dozen* and *a dozen* (SS can work out what these mean from the dialogue). At the same time teach *a pair* (two of the same), *a few* (three, four or five), *several* (about seven) and *a lot of*. (See also WB Exercise 22)

NB   Although *a lot of* (or *lots of*) is informal, the formal *many* is not usually used as the object of a positive sentence. You might say *Many people did something*, but *There were a lot of people* (refer to a grammar book for precise rules).

Exercise 60   Plurals (LD)

> Answers: *See LDT*

Aim: To consolidate plural forms.

Consolidate the rules SS already know for making plurals and add to the list of irregular plurals (see SB page 42). The rules for the pronunciation of the final *-s* are the same as for the *-s* in the present simple third person singular (see TB page 38 and WB Exercise 18). The correct pronunciation is marked on the LDT. SS can do this exercise in class or for h/w.

Exercise 61   Unit nouns

> Answers: *a roll of sellotape; a bottle of ink; a box of paper clips; a sheet of paper; a glass of wine; a jar of coffee; a packet of cigarettes; a cup of tea*

UNIT FIVE

Aim: To introduce unit nouns.

NB Many other things can be talked about in this way eg *a box of matches, a cup of coffee, a bottle of milk, a bottle of wine, a packet of tea* etc.

The most common unit nouns are *piece* and *bit*, but weights and measures are also common unit nouns eg a *kilo* of potatoes, a *litre* of milk. Emphasise to SS how they are joined to the main noun with *of* and that unit nouns are countable, so it is the unit noun which becomes plural.

Teach *glass, cup, bottle, jar, packet* and *box* with real objects or pictures. Then introduce more than one of each and ask SS for the plurals. SS can then do this exercise (possibly with the help of a dictionary) working in pairs in class, or for h/w.

To teach 'have got' and count and mass nouns

The concept of count and mass (also called countable and uncountable) nouns is familiar in many other languages. Illustrate the concept by showing SS several things you can count eg *cup, pencil* etc and three things you cannot count, eg *tea* (in leaf form), *coffee* (granules or powder), *water* etc. Practise making sentences such as *What's this/that? It's tea/coffee/water* or *It's a cup/pencil*. Although you must stress the use of the indefinite article with the count nouns, be careful that you teach the sentences with a natural intonation pattern with the sentence stress on the noun. Hold up any of the objects and teach *I've got a pencil/some tea*. Hand objects round the class and ask SS what they have got. Teach the question *What have you got?* and ask them to move around the class asking what other SS have got and saying what they have got. Each time they have talked to another SS, they must swap objects with them. Ask everyone to talk to every other S in this way as quickly as possible (although you can stop the activity before this point if necessary). NB *Have got* is common spoken usage in England. The formal written form is *have* used as a main verb. In this book *have got* is used in spoken exercises and *have* in written work.

Exercise 62 Count and mass nouns

Answers:
Count: *catalogue, table, desk, bottle, filing cabinet, car, envelope* (pronounced /ɛnvɛləʊp/ or /ɔnvɛləʊp/) *paper clip, sheet*
Mass: *stationery, tea, paper, furniture, coffee, equipment, money, butter*
There are many words which could be added to both lists eg
Count: roll, packet, knife, shelf, typewriter
Mass: cheese, orange juice, sellotape, ink

Aim: To teach count and mass nouns.

ORDERING STATIONERY

SS can do this exercise in class in pairs or for h/w without preparation. When they have prepared their lists, discuss the oddities, like *money* which you can count, but which is a mass noun. Then ask SS to add two more words to each list, orally or for h/w. Introduce the implications of count and mass nouns (eg the use of *much/many* with questions and negatives etc) as they arise.

NB Some of these (and many other) mass nouns do have a 'count' meaning in certain circumstances eg *I'll have two teas please* (= two cups of tea); *That shop sells many different (kinds of) teas. I bought a (news)paper this morning. Could you take these papers (collection of documents) to Mrs Smith please?* At this stage it is enough for SS to learn one form. The additional uses can be pointed out as they occur.

Exercise 63 Planning a party (LD A & B)

Answers: *See LDT*

Aim: To practise *have got* and *need*.

You have already introduced *have got*, but you must also introduce *need* (this is the main verb, not the modal). Tell the class that you want to write a business letter and ask them for suggestions for all the things you *need*. They should give full answers: *You need*... In this way you can introduce or practise a lot of the vocabulary in this unit eg *typewriter, pen, pencil, rubber, paper, carbon, flimsy, envelope, stamp*. Then ask them what you need for a party, so that you can introduce the lexis for this exercise. You will also have to teach *Have we got any*...? at which stage you might also teach *No we haven't got any*... and *Yes we've got some*... Both these phrases could be used with the party examples as a preliminary to doing Exercise 63 from the book.

Exercise 64 Word quiz

Answers: *1 ruler   2 ballpoint   3 ream   4 drawing pins 5 rubber   6 typing paper   7 letter   8 sellotape   9 envelope   10 ink   11 file   12 paper clips   13 roll   14 pen 15 stationery   16 pencil*

Aim: Practice of stationery vocabulary.

SS can do this exercise in pairs in class or for h/w.

Exercise 65 Numbers

Answers: *See SB tapescript*

Aim: Listening comprehension (and number recognition).

See TB notes on Exercises 19 and 35. Here SS have to recognise the word which represents a number.

UNIT FIVE

To introduce adjectives

Coloured ballpoints or crayons are one of the best ways of introducing colours, with sentences such as:
I've got a blue ballpoint.   *I've got two blue ballpoints.*
This ballpoint is blue.   *These ballpoints are blue.*
It's blue.   *They're blue.*

Show that the adjective always stays the same (it does not agree with the noun) and show its possible positions in the sentence.

Let the SS talk about the colour of the ballpoints you hand round (or they have on their desks). You need the colours *black* and *blue* for Exercise 66, but you could take this opportunity to teach *green*, *red*, *brown* and *white* (which are needed for the shopping game on TB page 56) and any other colours you wish to introduce. If you teach the words *dark* and *light*, SS can also describe colours such as *dark blue*, *light green* etc.

Jumbled words (see TB notes on WB Exercise 7, page 23) Possible words to practise the position of adjectives are: *she – it – he – the – a – has – is – got –? –, –s – but – and – two – large – are – hard – black – small – not – pencil – envelope*. Sample sentences are: *He is small, but she is large. Has she got a large, black pencil?* (Point out the use of the comma when more than one adjective is used. NB We would not say, 'Has she got a *black, large* pencil?') *Is it small? The pencils are large and black.* (Note use of *and* with adjectives after the noun.) *The pencil is large, hard and black.*

Exercise 66   The stationery cupboard

Answers: A: *I need some black ballpoints and some narrow sellotape. I need some quarto typing paper and some A4 files. (I need some quarto typing paper, some A4 files and some short rulers.)* B: *I do not need any blue ballpoints or any wide sellotape. I do not need any A4 typing paper or any quarto files. (I do not need any A4 typing paper, any quarto files or any long rulers.)* C: *I need some small paper clips, but I do not need any large paper clips. I need some black ballpoints, but I do not need any blue ballpoints. I need some narrow sellotape, but I do not need any wide sellotape. I need some quarto typing paper, but I do not need any A4 typing paper. I need some A4 files, but I do not need any quarto files. I need some short rulers, but I do not need any long rulers.*

Aim: Writing practice using conjunctions.

This exercise can be done for h/w. Point out to SS the use of the words *and* (to join 2 or more equal things), *or* (to join things which are equal in a negative sentence) and *but* (to join things which are contrasted). Point out the use of the comma before '*but*'. Before SS can do the exercise you will have to introduce

ORDERING STATIONERY

the adjectives *hard, soft, wide* etc, although some classes might prefer to use the more technical terms as well or instead, eg *five H pencils, two B pencils, some thirty centimetre rulers, a fifteen centimetre ruler.*

NB In these compound adjectives (*thirty centimetre* etc), the second element remains in the singular (cf *a three-year-old boy, a four-day strike*). Although Britain has changed to the metric system, you may still meet inches (") and feet ('). *Quarto* and *foolscap* are gradually being replaced by their metric equivalents, but references to both sizes are still used in the UK (see SB page 99 for their relative sizes). A *ream* consists of 500 sheets. (See also WB Exercise 21)

Exercise 67 Helen's stationery order (LD A & B)

Answers: *See LDT*

Aim: Further practice of *need, have got* (in the negative) and adjectives.

All the language in this exercise has been introduced previously. You could introduce the form of the exercise as a dialogue (see TB page xxv).

Exercise 68 Mary's stationery order (LD A & B)

Answers: *See LDT*

Aim: Further practice of *have got* and *How many?*

This also practises structures which have been previously introduced. Like Exercise 67 it could be introduced as a dialogue (see TB page xxv).
Point out:
1 *How many* always takes a plural noun, *How many files...?*
2 Notice that 'mass' items (and some 'count' items) are asked for in fixed amounts using unit nouns eg *How many* rolls *of sellotape...? How many* boxes *of paper clips...* In general the question with 'mass' nouns is *How much?* but it does not occur in this unit.
3 The useful phrase, *Here you are.*

Exercise 69 Internal order form

Answers: *1 What is the order number? 2 How many boxes of small paper clips does Simon need? 3 Does Simon need wide sellotape or narrow sellotape? 4 How many rolls of sellotape does Simon need? 5 How many (hard) pencils does Simon need? 6 Does Simon need hard pencils or soft pencils? 7 How many rulers does Simon need? 8 Does Simon need long rulers or short rulers? 9 How many ballpoints does Simon need? 10 Does Simon need blue ballpoints or black ballpoints? 11 How many files does Simon need? 12 How many reams of typing paper does Simon need?* (Other questions may be possible)

UNIT FIVE

Aim: To introduce an internal order form and practise three question forms.

SS should be able to do this exercise (possibly for h/w) without preparation, although you might want first to revise or highlight the question forms. (See also WB Exercise 20)

Exercise 70   Roleplay and Exercise 71   Conversation

Sample dialogue:
Simon: *Hello, Charlie. How are you today?*
Charlie: *Fine thank you, Simon. Can I help you?*
S: *Yes, I need some stationery. Have you got any paper clips?*
C: *Yes, large or small?*
S: *I need three boxes of large paper clips and one box of small please.*
C: *Here are the large paper clips, but I'm afraid I haven't got any small ones. Anything else?*
S: *Yes. Five rolls of wide sellotape please.*
C: *Right.*
S: *And twelve (a dozen) hard pencils.*
C: *Yes. Here you are.*
S: *Two rulers.*
C: *Long or short?*
S: *Long please.*
C: *Here you are.*
S: *Have you got any blue ballpoints?*
C: *Yes. How many do you need?*
S: *Half a dozen (six) please. And fourteen A4 files.*
C: *I'm sorry. I haven't got any.*
S: *Have you got any typing paper?*
C: *A4 or quarto?*
S: *Quarto.*
C: *No. I'm sorry. Do you need anything else?*
S: *No. That's all thank you. Here's the official order.*
C: *Thanks.*

Aim: Creativity and fluency and dialogue building.

Exercise 70 gives SS the chance to improvise the conversation between Simon and Charlie, thereby practising much of the language introduced in this unit. 'Simon' should have his book open at the order form and 'Charlie' should only look at his list of stationery in stock. You should be available to help SS with problems, but intervene as little as possible. See notes on roleplay on TB page xxvi. Exercise 71 is a chance to write out a transcription of what the SS say in 70. They will have to write more accurately than they speak. The exercise can either be done in pairs in class, or written up for h/w.

Exercise 72   An order

Sample form: (see page 55)

ORDERING STATIONERY

```
BRIGHTER OFFICE SUPPLIES LIMITED

ORDER                                    B·O·S
                                         L I M I T E D
Order no: 6492
Date:     27 November 1992               Tel Harlow (0279) 26721
To:       BOS warehouse                  Fax (0279) 431109
          Mallary Street                 Telex 81259
          Croydon                        Cables/Telegrams BOS
                                         Harlow

Please supply and deliver:
Qty         Description                  Unit price
80 reams    typing paper (quarto)
200         files (A4)
72          rulers (30cm)
60 rolls    sellotape (2.5 cm)
50 boxes    paper clips (small)
60          ballpoints




Deliveries accepted only against our
official order                           Signed: C.Alexander
Please quote order no. & date            Purchasing officer

13 Mill Street, Harlow, Essex, CM20 2JR.
```

Aim: Listening comprehension; dictation.

SS should understand most of the tape, but they only need to show their understanding by completing the order form (or a copy of it). Everything is repeated fairly slowly, so SS should only need to listen once.

NB On the tape, Janet says *Goodbye*, and Charlie replies with the common short form *Bye/'bye*. We also frequently say *'morning, 'afternoon, 'evening* for *Good morning, good afternoon* and *good evening*.

Exercise 73   Standard business letters

Answers:
1 *Further to our telephone conversation this morning, I enclose our price list. We thank you for your enquiry and we look forward to doing business with you.*
2 *Further to our conversation yesterday afternoon, I enclose a job application form. We thank you for your enquiry and we look forward to hearing from you.*

UNIT FIVE

    3 *Further to our telephone conversation this morning, I enclose a cheque for £97. I/We apologise for the delay and I/we look forward to receiving your receipt.*

    4 *Further to our conversation this afternoon, I enclose our invoice. We look forward to receiving your payment.*

    5 *Further to your telex, I enclose our official order. I/We apologise for the delay and I/we look forward to receiving the goods.*

    6 *Further to our conversation at your office, I enclose a copy of the financial report. I look forward to hearing your opinion.*

Aim: To present some standard business letter terminology.

Make sure SS understand the meaning of all the phrases, and give them this transformation exercise to do for h/w. It is not necessary for SS to learn all the vocabulary in the six letters, but the standard phrases should be learnt by heart: *Further to ..., I + present simple ... I look forward to -ing ...* The writer uses *I* when writing on behalf of him/herself, and *we* when writing on behalf of the company. The exercises also tests whether SS can recognise the abbreviated forms of common words in the notes. Note-taking is a useful business/conference skill to acquire.

Exercise 74   Letter with order

Sample letter:

```
BRIGHTER OFFICE SUPPLIES LIMITED
```

```
                                        L I M I T E D
Attn: Mrs Janet Elvin
                                        13 Mill Street, Harlow,
BOS warehouse                           Essex CM20 2JR.
Mallary Street                          Tel Harlow (0279) 26721
Croydon                                 Fax (0279) 431109
                                        Telex 81259
                                        Cables/Telegrams BOS
25 November 1992                        Harlow

Dear Mrs Elvin

Further to our telephone conversation this
afternoon/morning, I enclose our official order.

I look forward to receiving the stationery/to hearing
from you.

Yours sincerely

Charlie Alexander

Mr Charlie Alexander
Purchasing Officer

Encl
```

ORDERING STATIONERY

Aim: To write a business letter unaided on the model of those in Exercise 73.

Additional activities

The shopping game This provides extra practice of many of the items introduced in this unit: Pre-teach: *What does x cost?* and *How much is that please?* (when asking for the total bill). Divide the class into four equal groups: A, B, C and D. Give each person a copy of one of the lists below (give a *Shopper A* card to everyone in group A, a *Stationer C* card to everyone in group C etc). If the class does not divide equally into four, the shopper groups should be bigger than the stationer groups.

SHOPPER – A

Go to the shops and buy:

30 cm ruler
1 pkt white envelopes
24 red ballpoints
rubber
1 pkt drawing pins
bottle blue ink
2 pkts small paper clips

Add up how much you spend.

SHOPPER – B

Go to the shops and buy:

2 × 15 cm rulers
7 pkts large paper clips
6 green ballpoints
2 bottles black ink
2 pkts drawing pins
rubber

Add up how much you spend.

STATIONER – C

You have in stock:

drawing pins @ 80p per pkt
ink (only blue) @ 90p per bottle
ballpoints (only green) @ 20p each
envelopes (only brown) @ 60p
 per pkt
15 cm rulers @ 30p each
large paper clips @ 50p per pkt

STATIONER – D

You have in stock:

rubbers @ 40p each
ink (only black) @ 90p a bottle
ballpoints (only red) @ 20p
envelopes (only white) @ 60p
 per pkt
30cm rulers @ 40p each
small paper clips @ 50p per pkt

The aim of the game is for each shopper to find a stationer and buy all the items on his/her shopping list. If that stationer does not have everything the shopper wants, the shopper must find another stationer who has. The shoppers must find out the cost of their items and note how much money they have spent. Stationers should keep a note of how much money they make.

Explain these rules and let SS discuss their lists in the groups for about a minute. They should be able to work out all the abbreviations. Only help if you are asked. However, you might briefly practise saying sums of money in English, eg *two pounds, twenty-five pee*. Then tell them to mix and go shopping. You can circulate among the SS and correct obvious errors, but do not intrude too much as the main aim of the activity is to give SS confidence and allow them to communicate with the language they know.

You can check that shoppers have completed the game correctly because at the end they should have spent £8.90p.

Fish A card game for 2 to 5 players, which practises numbers and *have got*. You need a pack of 52 cards (without jokers).

- The dealer deals 7 cards to each player.
- If any player (now or at any time in the game) has two cards of the same value (a pair) in his/her hand (eg two eights or two queens) that player puts them face down on the table in front of him/her.
- The player on the dealer's left (we will call her Mary) starts the game. Mary asks any other player for one of the cards in her hand, like this:
  Mary: *John, have you got an eight?*
  If John has got the number, he says: *Yes I have. Here you are*, and gives her the card. She puts the pair of cards on the table. Then she asks any other player for any card in her hand in the same way. Mary's turn continues until she asks a player for a card and the player does not have it.
  When a player does not have a card he/she is asked for, he/she says:
  No I haven't. Fish. Mary then picks up a card from the pack and her turn ends.
- The player on Mary's left has a turn in the same way and then it is the turn of the player on his/her left...etc.
  Remember: A player may only ask for a card if a card of the same value is in his/her hand (ie he/she is trying to make a pair).
- If a player puts his/her last two cards on the table as a pair, he/she may pick up 7 more cards from the pack and the game continues.

ORDERING STATIONERY

- The game ends when a player picks up the last card in the pack. Each player then counts the number of pairs on the table in front of him/her. The player with the most pairs is the winner.

Ace   King

Queen   Jack   Joker

LANGUAGE DRILLS TAPESCRIPT

Drill 60   Say the plural of these words, like this:

P: Pen   P: Box
R: *Pens* /z/   R: *Boxes* /ɪz/

Now you try. Be careful with the pronunciation.
P: Shelf   P: Lunch
R: *Shelves* /z/   R: *Lunches* /ɪz/
P: Customer   P: Cup of tea
R: *Customers* /z/   R: *Cups of tea* /s/
P: Sheet of paper   P: Letter
R: *Sheets of paper* /s/ R: *Letters* /z/
P: Secretary   P: Floor
R: *Secretaries* /z/   R: *Floors* /z/
P: Filing cabinet   P: Knife
R: *Filing cabinets* /s/ R: *Knives* /z/
P: Glass   P: Office
R: *Glasses* /ɪz/   R: *Offices* /ɪz/
P: Paper clip   P: Day
R: *Paper clips* /s/   R: *Days* /z/
P: Telex   P: Man
R: *Telexes* /ɪz/   R: *Men*

UNIT FIVE

P: Person
R: *People*
P: Company
R: *Companies* /z/

P: Woman
R: *Women* /wɪmɪn/

Aim: Plurals practice (SS can do this drill with their books closed). NB See note on plural of *person* on TB page 14.

Drill 63A

Ask questions about things for a party, like this:

P: Glasses
R: *Have we got any glasses?*

Now you try.
P: Bread
R: *Have we got any bread?*
P: Cheese
R: *Have we got any cheese?*
P: Plates
R: *Have we got any plates?*

P: Butter
R: *Have we got any butter?*
P: Knives
R: *Have we got any knives?*

Aim: Question practice with *have got/any* (SS can do this drill with their books closed).

Drill 63B

Look at Joy's list and answer Simon's questions, like this:

P: Have we got any glasses?
R: *Yes. We've got a lot of glasses.*

P: Have we got any bread?
R: *No. We need some bread.*

Now you try.
P: Have we got any cheese?
R: *No. We need some cheese.*
P: Have we got any plates?
R: *Yes. We've got a lot of plates.*
P: Have we got any butter?
R: *No. We need some butter.*
P: Have we got any knives?
R: *Yes. We've got a lot of knives.*

P: Have we got any orange juice?
R: *Yes. We've got a lot of orange juice.*
P: Have we got any wine?
R: *No. We need some wine.*

Aim: Practice of *have got* and *need*.

Drill 67A

Reply to these requests for stationery, like this:

P: I need some pencils please.
R: *Right. Hard or soft?*
You can also say –
R: *Right. Soft or hard?*

Now you try.
P: I need some paper clips please.
R: *Right. Large or small?*
P: I need some ballpoints please.
R: *Right. Black or blue?*

P: I need some sellotape please.
R: *Right. Wide or narrow?*
P: I need some typing paper please.
R: *Right. A4 or quarto?*

ORDERING STATIONERY

P: I need some files please.
R: *Right. A4 or quarto?*

P: I need some rulers please.
R: *Right. Long or short?*

Aim: Practice of adjectives (SS can do this drill with their books closed if they have learnt the adjectives).

Drill 67B

Reply to these requests for stationery, like this:

P: I need some pencils please.
R: *I'm sorry. I haven't got any pencils.*

P: I need some paper clips please.
R: *I'm sorry. I haven't got any paper clips.*

Now you try.
P: I need some ballpoints please.
R: *I'm sorry. I haven't got any ballpoints.*
P: I need some sellotape please.
R: *I'm sorry. I haven't got any sellotape.*
P: I need some typing paper please.
R: *I'm sorry. I haven't got any typing paper.*

P: I need some files please.
R: *I'm sorry. I haven't got any files.*
P: I need some rulers please.
R: *I'm sorry. I haven't got any rulers.*

Aim: Practice of *have not got/any* (SS can do this drill with their books closed).

Drill 68A

Answer these questions about stationery, like this:

P: Have you got any pencils?
R: *Yes. How many do you need?*

P: Have you got any paper clips?
R: *Yes. How many boxes do you need?*

Now you try.
P: Have you got any ballpoints?
R: *Yes. How many do you need?*
P: Have you got any sellotape?
R: *Yes. How many rolls do you need?*
P: Have you got any typing paper?
R: *Yes. How many reams do you need?*

P: Have you got any files?
R: *Yes. How many do you need?*
P: Have you got any rulers?
R: *Yes. How many do you need?*

Aim: Question practice with *How many*? (SS can do this drill with their books closed if they know which items of stationery are ordered using unit nouns).

Drill 68B

Ask for stationery, like this:

P: Pencils
R: *Have you got any pencils please?*

P: Paper clips
R: *Have you got any paper clips please?*

UNIT FIVE

Now you try.
P: Ballpoints
R: *Have you got any ballpoints please?*
P: Sellotape
R: *Have you got any sellotape please?*
P: Typing paper
R: *Have you got any typing paper please?*
P: Files
R: *Have you got any files please?*
P: Rulers
R: *Have you got any rulers please?*

Aim: Question practice (SS can do this drill with their books closed).

WORKBOOK ANSWERS

Exercise 18 Plurals pronunciation

/s/ *ballpoints, desks, graphs, paper clips*
/z/ *shelves, pens, rulers, pencils, days*
/ɪz/ *telexes, offices, boxes, glasses*

The pronunciation of the final plural -s is the same as that of the present simple third person singular (see TB page 38). This exercise is quite difficult as SS cannot hear the pronunciation. Ask them to try and work out the rules by looking back at the answers to Exercise 49.

Exercise 19 Word puzzle

Simon asks Charlie: *Have you got any paper clips?* Charlie replies: *There aren't any.*

Exercise 20 Questions

2 Where does Simon work?   3 How does Simon travel to work?   4 Why is Joy in a small office?   5 What is the order number? the order number?   6 When does Joy make coffee?

Exercise 21 Adjectives puzzle

1 hard   2 narrow   3 wide   4 blue   5 black   6 small   7 short   8 large   9 long   10 soft These are the adjectives used to describe stationery in this unit. SS could make up this kind of word puzzle for one another.

Exercise 22 Numbers crossword

Across *a-112   c-46   f-1998* Down: *a-12   b-24   d-608   e-19* This exercise practises numerical expressions. Pre-teach the word *score* meaning twenty.

CONSOLIDATION UNIT A
YOUR NEWS AND NEWS EXTRACTS

TEACHING NOTES

See note on TB page xii about the consolidation units. Pre-teach words connected with the news media, eg *newspaper, radio, news item, article, headline*.

Exercise 75   Headlines

Answers: *The order of the headlines is 6, 2, 8, 3, 4, 1, 7, 5*

Aim: To test SS' ability to match sounds to their written form.

SS do not have to understand the news items. Let SS read the headlines before you play the tape and then ask them to write the headlines in order. They should hand in this list for you to check their initial comprehension. After they have done Exercise 76, allow them to hand in a revised list if they wish to.

Exercise 76   Radio news

Answers: *1 The USA (North America) and Japan   2 7%   3 Tomorrow morning at 10 am   4 One pound (£1)   5 Three million   6 He is a salesman   7 3 am tonight   8 Scotland*

Aim: Listening comprehension.

The questions give clues to the meaning of the news items and the answers are very straightforward. Play the tape as many times as you think necessary. If SS are having a great deal of difficulty, teach the meaning of the headlines. Otherwise help SS use their deductive powers (see TB page xxi).

Exercise 77   Salesman of the year

Answers: *John/Ron;   Inskip/Woking;   52/53;   Marketing/Manufacturing;   travels by train/walks;   daughter/son;   going to London/prizes are coming tomorrow;   colour TV/stereo*

Aim: Linking spoken and written forms.

Pre-teach *daughter* and *son*, possibly with other family words, if you did not teach them in Unit 1. The written article helps SS understand the taped news item and they should be able to pick out the differences. Play the tape as many times as necessary.

Exercise 78   Car number spot

Answers: *See SB tapescript*

Aim: Number and letter dictation.

Only play this section of the tape once as the numbers are repeated in the programme.

CONSOLIDATION UNIT A

The record mentioned at the end of the radio programme is *Mr Monday* by Ken Wilson (pub. Longman 1971). It (and a similar record by the same person, *Goodbye Rainbow*) was specifically written for elementary SS. Each song practises one main structure.

Exercise 79 Summer time

Aim: To revise times and questions.

Notice that SS can make up times which are not written on the chart. Since SS do not have to answer their own questions, they will probably be more inventive about making up 'difficult' times.

Many countries besides Britain put the clocks forward one hour in spring and back one hour in autumn to 'save' daylight hours (particularly for farmers).

One way of doing this exercise is to eliminate the testing element and encourage group co-operation. Each S writes one question on a piece of paper. Everybody hands that piece of paper on to the S on their right. Everyone checks the question is correct and writes the answer. Each S now writes a second question and the papers are handed on to the right again. Follow this sequence for a maximum of 10 questions. Keep the questions circling within small groups of four or five SS, so that they feel responsible for the questions and answers in their own circle.

The exercise can also be done orally in pairs.

Exercise 80 The weather

Sample sentences: *It is hot and sunny in Athens today. It is warm and fine in Berlin today. Cairo: warm and fine; Copenhagen: cold and cloudy; Lisbon: hot and sunny; London: warm and foggy; Madrid: hot and sunny; Paris: warm and raining; Rome: hot and sunny; Stockholm: cold and snowing; Tokyo: cold and fine.*

Aim: Deciphering abbreviations to write about the weather.

Pre-teach *clouds, fine* etc. This exercise could also be done orally in pairs: S1: *What's the weather like in Amsterdam?* S2: *It's warm and cloudy.*

You could extend this practice into the classroom as a regular introduction to the class using the standard British format:

It's { nice weather / hot/cold / nice and sunny / wet/windy } today, isn't it? — { Mmm. Isn't it? / Yes it is, isn't it? }

CONSOLIDATION UNIT A

Exercise 81 Exchange rates

Aim: To revise nationalities in a business context.

See notes on Exercise 79 for an approach to this exercise. Exchange rates vary all the time. Ask SS to find out the current exchange rates (from a bank or from the newspaper) before they do this exercise. SS need only recognise the currencies so you do not need to pre-teach them.

You could briefly discuss with the class why it is important to be able to exchange money (it means that businessmen and companies trading internationally can pay or be paid in their own currency) and how the exchange rate continually changes according to economic or political factors. Ask them to look for any references to the exchange rate in newspapers in their own language.

Exercise 82 Britain

Answers: *1 The United Kingdom 2 Scotland, England, Wales and Northern Ireland 3 Approximately 56 million people 4 About 240,640 square kilometres 5 The Common Market 6 The EC countries and North America 7 Cars, machinery, textiles, chemicals 8 Banking, insurance and tourism*

Aim: Reading comprehension.

This passage may look complicated, but SS are only asked for short answers and the questions should help them understand the passage. Teach the words *visible*, *invisible* (in their normal context of able or not able to be seen), *imports* and *exports*. Briefly discuss with SS the difference between 'visible *goods*' and 'invisible *services*' which are ways of spending and earning money abroad.

Exercise 83 Abbreviations

Answers: *1 Ave 2 ° 3 Mr 4 £ 5 C 6 Oct 7 TV 8 Co 9 LTD 10 United States 11 dollar(s) 12 approximately 13 per cent 14 million 15 square 16 kilometre(s) 17 Great Britain 18 United Kingdom 19 afternoon (post meridiem) 20 European Community*

Aim: To introduce abbreviations and encourage SS to re-read all the news items closely.

The exercise is best done for h/w or in pairs in class.

Exercise 84 Focus on Italy

Sample article: *Italy consists of the mainland, Sardinia, Sicily, Elba and many other islands. It has frontiers with France, Switzerland, Austria and Yugoslavia. It has a population of approximately 56 million people (Its population is approximately the same as Britain's) and an area of about 324,000 square kilometres. Rome is the capital city. Italy's main exports are*

65

CONSOLIDATION UNIT A

machinery, cars, iron and steel and its main trading partners are West Germany, France and North America. Italy is a member of the EC.

Aim: Controlled writing practice and understanding notes.

SS should be able to write an article about Italy, using the format of the article about Britain and substituting the facts about Italy.

NB (a) *have got* is a spoken form and is replaced by *have* in written texts; (b) commas are needed in the lists of exports and trading partners. Allow SS to use a dictionary if they wish.

Exercise 85 A timetable

Sample sentences: *The Concourse leaves New York at quarter past three (in the afternoon) and lands at London at quarter to nine. The plane leaves London at five past three and arrives at Delhi at ten past ten. The plane takes off from Delhi at twenty past four (in the afternoon) and lands at London at twenty-five past eleven. The Concourse departs from Delhi at half past eleven (at night) and arrives at Sydney at twenty to seven (in the morning). The plane leaves Sydney at ten to eight (in the morning) and arrives at Delhi at five to three (in the afternoon).*

Aim: Revision of times and the present simple.

Verbs should be in the present simple because the sentences describe a timetable. Elicit from SS that *a* stands for *arrives/arrival* and *d* stands for *departs/departure*. This exercise could also be done orally in pairs by asking and answering questions such as: *What time does the 10 o'clock flight from London arrive at New York?*

Personnel competition

Answers: Back row, left to right: *personal assistant; managing director's personal secretary; sales assistant; receptionist;* Front row, left to right: *personnel manager; managing director; sales manager; sales representative*
Questions: 1 The sales representative 2 The sales assistant 3 The personnel manager and the sales manager

Aim: To revise prepositions and job vocabulary.

SS should be able to do this competition without any help. You can do it as a problem solving exercise if you follow the instructions for Exercise 132 (see TB page 104). The only difference is that you originally divide the class into five groups and read only one of the sentences from the SB to each group. Remember that you will have to draw a diagram of the people and SS should not look at the book.
NB The competition is out of date, so please do not send in any entries!

CONSOLIDATION UNIT A

Additional activities

Family vocabulary To revise and extend family vocabulary introduced in Exercise 77 (and possibly in Unit 1). Teach *wife, husband, father, mother, sister, brother, niece, nephew, uncle, aunt* (and possibly *grandmother, grandfather, granddaughter, grandson*) by building up a family tree like this:

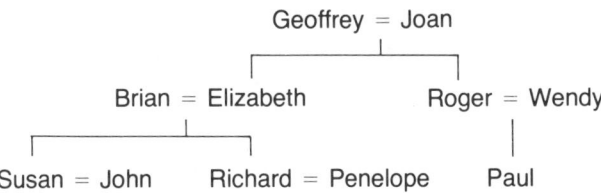

Elicit sentences such as *Geoffrey is Joan's husband. J is G's wife. Elizabeth is G + J's daughter. G is E and R's father.* etc.

1 SS test each other's knowledge of the names of family members by saying eg *My father's brother* or *My sister's son*. Another S answers *Your uncle* or *Your nephew*. This can be done in teams with points awarded for correct answers and points taken away for incorrect or slow answers.
2 A S describes his/her family (using first names only) and other SS draw the family tree. They can ask questions if they are not sure what to draw. Typical sentences will be *I've got two sisters. Their names are ... My mother's name is ... Is your uncle your father's brother or your mother's brother?*

There are no language drills for the Consolidation Units.

WORKBOOK ANSWERS – TEST A

Allow students a maximum of half an hour to do this test.

Part one Plurals

1 Their secretaries work in Harlow. 2 Are these your paper clips? 3 The books are on the shelves. 4 What do they do? 5 The stationery is in the drawers.

Mark this section out of 10. Give two marks for each sentence and subtract half a mark for each mistake up to a maximum of 2 marks per sentence.

Part two Prepositions

1 above/over 2 on 3 between 4 in 5 under

Give one mark for each correct answer.

CONSOLIDATION UNIT A

Part three Times

> 1 It is half past nine. 2 It is eighteen minutes past eleven.
> 3 It is quarter to eight. 4 It is twenty-one minutes to three.
> 5 It is twenty-six minutes past eight.

Give one mark for each correct answer. Subtract half a mark for each mistake up to a maximum of one mark per sentence.

Part four Question formation

> 1 Have you got any glasses? 2 Do you drive to work?
> 3 What do you do? 4 Are you married? 5 What are you doing?

Mark this section out of ten. Give two marks for each sentence and subtract half a mark for each mistake up to a maximum of two marks per sentence.

Part five Ordinal numbers

> 1 ninth 2 second 3 twelfth 4 eighth 5 twentieth

Give one mark for each correct answer.

Part six Pronouns

> 1–c 2–b 3–a 4–c 5–a

Give one mark for each correct answer.

The maximum number of marks for the test is 40. If you want to convert this total to a percentage, multiply the result by 4/10 (or 2/5).

See note on using the tests on TB page xiv.

UNIT SIX
JOY'S LEAVING PARTY

6

Structures:	*Would like* (*to* + infinitive)
	Articles: *a/the/one*
	Let's + infinitive
Functions:	Describing people; ordering a meal; invitations; suggestions
Pronunciation:	Word stress
Lexis:	Days of the week, adjectives to describe personal appearance, entertainment, a menu

TEACHING NOTES

This unit concentrates largely on social English. Although much of it is presented in a non-business context, some of the vocabulary and structures will be needed later in this book.

Exercise 86   Comprehension

Answers: *1 Luisa, the receptionist.   2 We do not know. He is giving Joy her present.   3 Simon smokes and Anne does not. 4 A present.*

SS can probably work out the answers to this exercise before they do the rest of the unit. There is some background party noise on the cassette which will make it slightly more difficult for the SS to hear the dialogue.

Teach from the tape: *Would you like a cigarette?* and introduce possible replies: *Yes please. I'd love one./Not at the moment thank you./No thank you. I don't smoke.* You can also teach the phrase: *Have you got a light?* and the replies: *Certainly. Here you are./I'm afraid not.*

Point out to SS that in English we feel obliged to give some explanation for refusing invitations or offers out of politeness. Also, we do not reply to an offer or invitation with exactly the same structure as is used to make it, eg we reply 'I'd *love* . . .' to 'Would you *like* . . .?'
NB   *Cigarette* can be stressed Ooo or ooO.

To describe people

Draw some basic caricatures on the board, eg: (see page 70)

Teach the adjectives: *1 long/straight hair   2 short/curly hair 3 tall/thin   4 short/fat   5 moustache   6 beard   7 glasses 8 pipe*

Practise these by saying to the SS: *I'm thinking of a person.* SS ask: *Is it the tall one? Is it the one with long hair?* etc.

69

UNIT SIX

Exercise 87   Joy's leaving party

Sample sentences: *A man with dark hair is talking to a woman with long, fair hair and a woman with short, dark, curly hair. A man with a pipe, a beard and glasses is talking to a man with fair, curly hair and glasses. A man with fair hair is sitting next to a woman with long, fair hair. etc*

Aim: To practise word order with adjectival phrases and vocabulary of personal description.

SS can use the tables of adjectival phrases at the end of the main sentence or inserted before the verb. They do not have to use words from each table in every sentence and all the sentences should describe people in the picture.

NB   *moustache* is normally stressed oO, however influence from the USA means that you can also sometimes hear it stressed Oo.

Point out to SS the order when there is more than one adjective to describe hair eg *short, dark, curly hair*.

Point out the difference between the indefinite article *a/an* (which refers to any one of a number of things) and the definite article *the* (which refers to a particular one or the only one). Incidentally, although the indefinite article cannot be used with mass nouns, the definite article can be used to refer to a particular mass noun eg *The money is on the table*.

This exercise can be done for h/w. Alternatively Exercises 87, 88 and 89 could be done by different groups in the class at different times (see notes on groupwork on TB page xix). (See also WB Exercise 24.)

Exercise 88   Guessing (LD)

Sample answers: *See LDT*

JOY'S LEAVING PARTY

Aim: To practise describing people in a game format.

SS can play in pairs or small groups of about four. Pre-teach *to smoke* and *to drink*. Before SS do the LD you should also teach *tie* and *to wear* (you could take this opportunity to teach other articles of clothing too). Note that in English we tend not to repeat main nouns. They are frequently replaced by *it* or *one* once the subject matter is established. (See WB Exercise 26)

NB Grammatical terms have been introduced throughout this book, but so far SS have not been expected to learn them or know what they refer to. Since *nouns, verbs, adjectives* and *articles* are specifically highlighted in this unit, you might like to spend a little time making sure that SS are clear what these terms refer to.

Pronunciation of *the*. Before a consonant sound (eg *man, glasses*) *the* is pronounced /ðə/, but before a vowel sound (eg *office, equipment*), it is pronounced /ðɪ/. NB *One* starts with the consonant sound /w/, so *the one* is pronounced /ðəwʌn/.

Exercise 89 Which man?

Answer: *The customer wants to talk to John.*

Aim: Listening comprehension.

By listening to the tape, SS can gradually eliminate the BOS staff the customer does not want to talk to. Play the tape as often as you think necessary for all the SS to know which man is being referred to.

Exercise 90 At the buffet table (LD A & B)

Answers: *See LDT*

Aim: To practise making and responding to offers.

The description of where things are in relation to one another on the buffet table is enough for SS to work out for themselves the necessary vocabulary for this exercise. You have already introduced *Would you like a cigarette?* and the short answers using the tape for Exercise 86. The remaining teaching point is the short answers *Yes I'd love one* (after a singular count noun) and *Yes I'd love some* (after a mass noun or a plural count noun). SS could write 8 sentences and short answers for h/w. (See also WB Exercise 23)

NB Sandwiches were supposedly named after the Earl of Sandwich in 1762. The story goes that he liked playing cards so much that he did not want to stop for meals. His meat was therefore brought to him between two slices of bread.

Exercise 91 Hidden word puzzle

Answers: 1 *Wednesday*   2 *Tuesday*   3 *Monday*
4 *Thursday*   5 *Saturday*   6 *Friday*   Hidden word: *Sunday*

UNIT SIX

Aim: To consolidate days of the week.

SS can work out the names of the days of the week from the puzzle as long as they know the meaning of *before* and *after* particularly as some of them were introduced in Unit 3. They can do the exercise for h/w or in pairs in class.

NB The days of the week are always written with capital letters even in their abbreviated forms. The pronunciation of the final *-ay* is either /ɪ/ or /eɪ/.

Your SS might be interested in the origins of the names for the days. *Sunday* is the day of the sun. *Monday* is the day of the moon. *Saturday* is named after the Roman god Saturn and the other days are named after the Norse gods Tiw, Woden, Thor and Freya.

To practise the days of the week T says, for example: *It is Saturday. What's tomorrow?* S: *Sunday*; T: *It is Thursday. What was yesterday?* S: *Wednesday.* etc... You might also like to teach *the day after tomorrow* and *the day before yesterday*.

You could also teach the times of day, eg *If it is Wednesday midday now*, then: Wed 5 pm = *this afternoon*; Wed 9 pm = *tonight*; Wednesday = *today*. You could introduce phrases such as the following in this way: *Tomorrow lunchtime, yesterday afternoon, this evening, tomorrow morning* etc. When you have practised this with the whole class, tell SS to pick another day and practise the phrases in pairs. (See also Unit 8 Exercise 125.)

Going out Exercise 92 (LD)

Answers: *See LDT*

Aim: To practise making and responding to invitations.

Teach the vocabulary in Simon's diary before SS practise this exercise in pairs. The structure is *Would you like* to do *something./Yes I'd love* to. The implication of this invitation is that Simon is offering to pay. SS could also write out the seven sentences for h/w.

Exercise 93 Suggestions (LD)

Answers: *See LDT*

Aim: To practise making and responding to suggestions.

The implication of *Let's do something* is that the people will share the cost. This is a suggestion not an invitation.

NB You will probably have to distinguish between *come* and *go* in this exercise if you have not already done so (see the note on TB page 42).

JOY'S LEAVING PARTY

Exercise 94 In a restaurant

Answers: Simon had: *soup, lamb cutlets, mashed potatoes, apple pie and coffee with cream.* Anne had: *Prawn cocktail, roast beef, chips, cheese and biscuits and black coffee.*

Aim: Listening comprehension.

Teach the items on the menu for recognition only. The SS will need to be able to pronounce them in the following exercise, but they can read them off the menu as they would in real life. Play the tape as many times as necessary. SS might find this exercise more difficult than previous ones as they have not met some of the structures. Guide them to an understanding of what Simon and Anne say, without looking at the tapescript. Intonation patterns might be of some help in guessing meaning. Note that the final *b* in *lamb* is not pronounced and that *gâteau* can either retain its French stress o O, or be stressed O o.

Exercise 95 Ordering a meal (LD A, B & C)

See the notes on dialogue presentation on TB page xxv. SS should practise ordering meals from one another with the 'customer' sitting down and the 'waiter' standing up. Once they have mastered the basic dialogue, encourage them to improvise, perhaps with another menu and with other partners.

Before SS do this exercise, revise the formation of a question with *would*:

You would like a cup of coffee.

You would like a cup of coffee. → *Would you like a cup of coffee?*

Would you like a cup of coffee? → *What would you like to drink?*

NB The contraction for *would like* in the affirmative is *'d like*.

SS might have noticed that there are different sorts of verbs which form questions in different ways. You could point out that most verbs are 'main verbs' eg smoke, walk, type etc, and different tenses are formed with the help of auxiliary verbs eg *is, do, would, have* (although *have* also has a main form – see note before Exercise 62 on TB page 5). This affects particularly the formation of questions, negatives and short forms. Point out other auxiliary and modal verbs as you come to them.

Exercise 96 Word stress: two-syllable words

Answers: *Jumper* (O o *stress on the first syllable*): *glasses, filing, Wednesday, office, question, answer* (Also: *Tuesday, Simon, coffee, orange, paper,* etc . . .) Supplies: (o O *stress on the second*

UNIT SIX

syllable): *machine, upstairs, canteen, moustache* (see note about *moustache* for Exercise 87, TB page 70)

Aim: To introduce word stress.

This exercise asks SS to recognise the stress in two-syllable words. Play the tape as many times as you think necessary for SS to recognise the stress. If they have difficulty, stop the tape after a word and say either *da-DAH* or *DAH-da* according to the stress. An alternative is to clap your hands or snap your fingers on the main stress. When SS have recognised the stress, ask them to repeat the words after the tape. Ask the class for suggestions for other two-syllable words in the first pattern.

Exercise 97 Word stress: three-syllable words

O o o cinema: *telephones   newcomer   envelopes   manager   ordering   furniture   typewriter   catalogue   Saturday*

o O o description: *equipment   September   promotion   department   enclosure   assistant*

Aim: To recognise word stress.

Again SS have to differentiate only between the two most common patterns. The less common pattern is o o O *entertain*.

Exercise 98 Word stress: different patterns

Answers: *director* o O o; *representative* o o O o o; *cabinet* O o o; *invitation* o o O o; *coffee* O o; *receptionist* o O o o; *personal* O o o; *application* o o O o; *orange* O o; *advertisement* o O o o; *personnel* o o O; *nationality* o o O o o

Aim: To recognise word stress.

This is a slightly more difficult exercise as SS have to hear the stress pattern for each word, they do not simply have a choice.

Exercise 99 Stress: phrases

Answers: *orange juice* O o o; *managing director* o o o o O o; *coffee pot* O o o; *fax machine* O o o; *personal secretary* o o o O o o; *personnel officer* o o O o o o; *per cent* o O; *word processor* O o o o; *sales representative* O o o o o o; *sales assistant* O o o o; *in-tray* O o; *limited company* o o o O o o.

Aim: To recognise word stress.

Point out that when two or more words make up a phrase, there is usually only one main stress. Notice also that here *secretary* is stressed O o o, and the final *tary* is pronounced /trɪ/. The word can also be stressed O o o o and pronounced /sekrətərɪ/. Similarly *stationery* can have three or four syllables.

Rather than doing Exercises 96 to 99 all at one time, you might prefer to do them over a number of lessons and make

74

JOY'S LEAVING PARTY

up further similar exercises if your SS need the extra practice. See also WB Exercises 40 and 66 and Additional activity: *Matching sentences* on TB page 156.

Exercise 100 Personal invitations

Sample reply:

```
                              33 Honister Avenue
                              Newcastle NE2 3PA

                              5th November
Dear David and Ann,

Thank you very much for your invitation
to dinner on Wednesday 11th November.
We'd love to come.


We look forward to seeing you both.

   Love,
            John & Susan
```

Aim: To continue the theme of invitations in written form.

SS have enough English to compose a simple invitation without looking at their books. Work with the class to write an invitation to dinner on the board. Then frame an acceptance with them. SS can compare the results with the samples in the SB. If SS want a less formal refusal than the one in the SB, replace the words underlined in the letter above with *We are very sorry we won't be able to come. We hope to see you both soon.* Exercise 100 can be done for h/w. (See also WB Exercise 25) Note the two possible spellings for the name *Anne/Ann*. Although dates are not fully introduced until Unit 8, teach *November* and *December* here.

Exercise 101 An invitation and a reply

SS should be able to do this exercise with little help from you, either in class or for h/w (although not necessarily both on the same day). You might like to hold a class party (if this is possible in your teaching situation) with SS writing formal invitations to one another or to another English class. If possible SS can bring in food and drink and greet one another and 'chat' in English. You could record snatches of conversation for error analysis either for your own information or to be listened to by the class or at a later date (see TB page xxvii).

UNIT SIX

LANGUAGE DRILLS TAPESCRIPT

Drill 88   Listen to these questions and ask for more specific information, like this:

  P: Is it the man with the moustache?
  R: *Which one? There are two men with moustaches.*

  Now you try.
  P: Is it the girl with dark hair?
  R: *Which one? There are two girls with dark hair.*
  P: Is it the man sitting down?
  R: *Which one? There are two men sitting down.*
  P: Is it the man standing near the door?
  R: *Which one? There are two men standing near the door.*
  P: Is it the girl talking to Fred?
  R: *Which one? There are two girls talking to Fred.*
  P: Is it the man wearing a tie?
  R: *Which one? There are two men wearing ties.*
  P: Is it the woman sitting at the table?
  R: *Which one? There are two women sitting at the table.*

  Aim: Practice of plurals (SS can do this drill with their books closed).

Drill 90A   Accept the things Simon is offering, like this:

  P: Would you like a cheese sandwich?
  R: *Yes please. I'd love one.*
  P: Would you like some crisps?
  R: *Yes please. I'd love some.*

  Now you try.
  P: Would you like a piece of cake?
  R: *Yes please. I'd love one.*
  P: Would you like a cigarette?
  R: *Yes please. I'd love one.*
  P: Would you like some cheese?
  R: *Yes please. I'd love some.*
  P: Would you like some sandwiches?
  R: *Yes please. I'd love some.*
  P: Would you like a glass of wine?
  R: *Yes please. I'd love one.*
  P: Would you like some orange juice?
  R: *Yes please. I'd love some.*

  Aim: Practice of accepting offers using *one/some* (SS can do this drill with their books closed).

Drill 90B   Offer things, as Simon does:

  P: A cheese sandwich
  R: *Would you like a cheese sandwich?*

  Now you try.

JOY'S LEAVING PARTY

P: Some cake
R: *Would you like some cake?*
P: A glass of wine
R: *Would you like a glass of wine?*
P: Something to eat
R: *Would you like something to eat?*

P: A cigarette
R: *Would you like a cigarette?*
P: A drink
R: *Would you like a drink?*

Aim: Practice of offering things (SS can do this drill with their books closed).

Drill 92

Invite Anne out, as Simon does:

P: Monday – go to the theatre
R: *Would you like to go to the theatre with me on Monday?*

Now you try.
P: Tuesday – have dinner
R: *Would you like to have dinner with me on Tuesday?*
P: Wednesday – see a film
R: *Would you like to see a film with me on Wednesday?*
P: Thursday – have lunch
R: *Would you like to have lunch with me on Thursday?*
P: Friday – go to a disco
R: *Would you like to go to a disco with me on Friday?*

P: Saturday – come to Jane's party
R: *Would you like to come to Jane's party with me on Saturday?*
P: Sunday – drive to the seaside
R: *Would you like to drive to the seaside with me on Sunday?*

Aim: Practice of invitations; fluency (SS can do this drill with their books closed).

Drill 93

Make suggestions about going out, as Mary does:

P: Monday – go to the theatre
R: *Let's go to the theatre together on Monday.*

Now you try.
P: Tuesday – have dinner
R: *Let's have dinner together on Tuesday.*
P: Wednesday – see a film
R: *Let's see a film together on Wednesday.*
P: Thursday – have lunch
R: *Let's have lunch together on Thursday.*
P: Friday – go to a disco
R: *Let's go to a disco together on Friday.*

P: Saturday – go to Jane's party
R: *Let's go to Jane's party together on Saturday.*
P: Sunday – drive to the seaside
R: *Let's drive to the seaside together on Sunday.*

Aim: Practice of suggestions; fluency (SS can do this drill with their books closed).

UNIT SIX

Drill 95A Look at the menu and listen to this dialogue. (Dialogue recorded in full.) Answer the waiter and order a meal. Order the first item in each section.

> P: What would you like to start with?
> R: *Soup please. And then I'd like steak and kidney pie with chips.*
> P: And for dessert?
> R: *I'd like fruit salad please.*

Drill 95B Answer the waiter again. This time order the second item in each section.

> P: What would you like to start with?
> R: *Pâté please. And then I'd like roast beef with roast potatoes.*
> P: And for dessert?
> R *I'd like black forest gâteau please.*

Drill 95C Answer the waiter again. This time order the last item in each section.

> P: What would you like to start with?
> R: *Prawn cocktail please. And then I'd like lamb cutlets with mashed potatoes.*
> P: And for dessert?
> R: *I'd like apple pie please.*

Aim: Practice in ordering a meal.

WORKBOOK ANSWERS

Exercise 23 Offers

> 1–d   2–e   3–c   4–b   5–a

Exercise 24 Description puzzle

> *1 glasses   2 short   3 curly   4 beard   5 moustache   6 fair   7 long   8 dark* This exercise practises words connected with personal appearance.

Exercise 25 An invitation

> *Mistakes:* Mowbray *Road* (not *road*); I *am* having (not *is*); a dinner party *on* 21st *November* (not *november*); Would *you* like *to* come? *Best wishes,* (not *Yours sincerely* – this is a friendly invitation).

Exercise 26 One

> *2 She is typing one.   3 He has got one/He has got an old one.   4 I am looking at one.   5 Would you like one?   6 She is making one.   7 That is one.   8 It is next to one.* This exercise makes explicit the use of *one* as a substitute for a person or object already mentioned.

UNIT SEVEN
THE IDEAL SECRETARY

7

> *Business content:* A survey; a memo; job advertisements; letters of recommendation
> *Structures:* Can + infinitive
> Was/were
> Prepositions (*revision*)
> *Function:* Giving opinions
> *Lexis:* Adjectives to describe personal qualities, *to give*

TEACHING NOTES

Exercise 102 Comprehension

Answers: *1 World at Work   2 Viewers   3 She is the winner of this year's 'Ideal Secretary' competition.   4 Yes   5 He thinks she can type and take shorthand, she's well-dressed and never late for work and she needs a lot of other qualities.   6 Michael Walton does not let her say.   7 No*

This exercise can be done as an introduction to the unit or after SS have studied *can* and some of the adjectives. Guide SS to an understanding of *ideal, presenter, studio, viewers* from the context, rather than explaining the words, by asking questions such as *'Is an ideal secretary a good secretary or a bad secretary?'* Mary has a slight Scottish accent. Before doing Exercise 107, you could review this interview to analyse why Michael Walton is such a bad interviewer. eg he does not let Mary speak, he answers his own questions. He should ask 'open' questions which allow Mary to give her own answer.

Exercise 103   A survey (LD A, B & C)

Answers: *See LDT*

Aim: To teach and practise the modal *Can*.

The explanation of the situation expresses the meaning of *can* (SS have already met the form as a polite request). The main teaching point is the pronunciation: *Can you* . . . ? /kæn/ *Yes I can* /kæn/ *No I can't* /kɑ:nt/ (= *cannot*).

When SS have carried out the survey, compile a list of the results on the board, eliciting full sentences in the form *Anne can* /kən/ *speak French*. Talk about the results before SS write the memo in Exercise 104: *Twelve people can speak French well* . . . etc. Teach the expression *not very well* and *not at all* (See also WB Exercise 27) If you talked about the difference between main and auxiliary verbs with the class in Unit 6, you can point out that *can* is a modal. Modals are very similar to

79

UNIT SEVEN

auxiliaries, but their meaning can change in different tenses and they are frequently 'defective' (they cannot be used in all tenses). Check with a grammar book for a fuller definition.

Exercise 104 A memo

Sample (the figures depend on your own class results.)

BRIGHTER OFFICE SUPPLIES LIMITED

MEMORANDUM

```
TO:       Sheila Baker
FROM:     Simon Young
DATE:     2 November 1992
Subject:  Translating advertising material
```

Here are the results of the survey:
Four people can speak French well, five people cannot speak French at all. Six people can type well, two people cannot type very well and four people cannot type at all. Ten people can use the photocopier and two people cannot use it at all.

Aim: To practise the format of a memo and *can*.

Point out the use of commas in a list of things, but not before *and*. This exercise can be written for h/w. Refer SS back to the format of a memo on SB page 24 if necessary.

Exercise 105 A news article (LD A, B & C)

Answers: *1 Where is Mary from? Where does Mary live? 2 What are her prizes? 3 Where does Mary work? 4 How old is Mary? 5 Who is Mary's boss? 6 How many languages can Mary speak?*

Aim: Reading comprehension and question practice.

SS should be able to understand the vocabulary from the context, particularly if they work in pairs. An alternative approach is to halve the class. Of one half, some pretend to be Fred and some pretend to be Mary. The other half of the class are journalists. They know Mary has won something but they do not know what or why. They prepare questions to ask Mary and her boss. 'Mary' and 'Fred' read the passage and prepare answers to questions they think the 'journalists' might ask. Collect the texts and arrange the SS in groups of four (a Fred, a Mary and two journalists). The journalists carry out the interview. For h/w the journalists write up the results of their interviews as an article (without looking at their text books) and 'Fred and Mary' write the questions in Exercise 105. This technique can be used as an approach to other reading passages.

THE IDEAL SECRETARY

The LD gives extended practice in question formation. Even if you do not normally use the LD you might do the drills in class if your SS are still having difficulties forming questions.

Exercise 106 Qualities

The decision about which qualities are suitable for bosses and secretaries is a purely personal one.

Aim: To express opinions.

It is not necessary for SS to learn all the adjectives, so the quickest solution is for them to look up their meanings in a dictionary. You will also need to practise the phrase with which SS can express opinions. One way of doing this exercise is to build up a *pyramid* effect: SS decide quickly in pairs a list of the qualities they think are important. Pairs then join together and try to decide on a common list between them (they might both have had the same list in the first place, or one pair will have to modify its list). Fours then join together into groups of eight, eights then join into groups of sixteen and finally the whole class comes together to agree a common list. During this process, SS use the adjectives again and again and they will have to start producing reasons (in English) to support their decisions. Supply extra words and phrases as necessary (or allow them to use their dictionaries). (See also WB Exercises 28 and 30)

Exercise 107 Radio (or television) programme

Aim: Fluency and creativity.

In WB Exercise 1 (or the answers on TB page 11) you will find the names of Jacques' assistant and secretary. You should put a time limit on the programme (eg 'five minutes on the air') and on the preparation time (eg 'you are on the air in exactly 20 minutes'). If SS work in groups of four or five they could be the presenter, an interviewer, Jacques and his assistant and secretary, all of whom can speak in the programme. If possible record the programmes on cassette or video and review them later, picking out one or two points for praise or correction from each programme (see notes on error analysis on TB page xxvii.)

Exercise 108 News article

Sample: (see page 82)

Aim: Written back-up to the previous exercise.

SS can write the article for h/w. They can base the format on the article about Mary Mackie. If SS use speech in their articles, point out the correct punctuation (comma and inverted commas).

UNIT SEVEN

> ### The Perfect Boss
>
> Jacques de la Plaine from Cairo is the winner of this year's 'Perfect Boss' competition. His prizes are a new car, a bottle of champagne and a meal for two in a famous London restaurant.
>
> Mr de la Plaine is a sales representative for Brighter Office Supplies Ltd. He lives in Cairo with his wife, but he is not Egyptian. He is French and his parents live in France. He is in England this month for a sales conference with his secretary, Chantal Dubois, and his assistant, Marie-Jo Braun. They both agree that he is the perfect boss. Chantal says, "He is very efficient, intelligent and hard-working and he can speak three languages: French, English and Arabic." Marie-Jo says, "He is an ambitious businessman but a considerate and helpful boss. He's also very attractive!"

Exercise 109 To give (LD)

Answers: *1 Please give him the book. 2 He always gives her presents. 3 Please give it to me. 4 They are giving a present to Joy. 5 They are giving Joy a present. 6 She is giving him a typewriter for Christmas. 7 She sometimes gives them to him. (She gives them to him sometimes.) 8 Can you give me the file please?*

Aim: To practise word order with direct and indirect objects.

SS should be able to do this exercise alone from the models given; it could be done as h/w, although it is probably more enjoyable if SS work in pairs in class. You could further check their grasp of the word order by doing the LD in class (you call out the prompts – and possibly make up more prompts) if you are not going to do it in the language laboratory.

Exercise 110 Differences (LD)

Answers: *See LDT for possible sentences.*

Aim: Revision of *There is/are*, prepositions and office furniture vocabulary.

Introduce the past tense of the verb *to be* (the explanation in the SB is probably presentation enough), although the past simple tense is not otherwise introduced until Unit 10. See TB notes for Exercises 21 and 22 on page 15 for other ways of exploiting this exercise.

Additional activity

Hunt the Thimble A game to practise vocabulary and prepositions. The instructions are: One person secretly hides the thimble. Other people in turn ask questions about where the thimble is, like this: *Is it near the desk? Is it under the chair?* The person who hides the thimble answers:
Hot (if the questioner is very near)
Warm (if the questioner is quite near)
Cold (if the questioner is a long way away)

The person who finds the thimble is the winner.
NB Do not play this game with more than 7 people. If your class is very big, play the game in small groups.
SS can 'hide' the thimble (it is a thing which protects your finger when you are sewing) in their imaginations in the picture of Simon and Anne's office (or in any other picture to practise other lexis).

Exercise 111 Experience

Answers:

name	work experience	typing	switchboard	shorthand	word processor	other notes
David	✗	✗	✓	✗	✗	at school gd. st. no exams
Carolyn	✗	✓	✓	✓	✓ some	at sec. college gd. speeds not lge co
Lorraine	✓	✓ a bit	✓	✗	✗	married and children older

Aim: Listening comprehension.

No preparation necessary. Play the tape as often as you think is necessary for SS to fill in the table. David has a slight northern accent and Carolyn has a slight west country (Somerset) accent. SS will have most difficulty with the final column 'other notes'. When they have finished talking about their notes, show them the abbreviated forms used in the sample answers.

Exercise 112 Job advertisements

Probable answers: *David Richards – filing clerk/person Friday. Carolyn Bennett – secretary. Lorraine Welder – receptionist.*

Aim: Reading comprehension and persuading in English.

Pre-teach *person Friday*. The expression comes from *Man Friday* in Defoe's book *Robinson Crusoe* – someone who does all the menial jobs. The expression was traditionally a *girl Friday*, but since it was made illegal in Britain to specify the sex of people required for jobs in advertisements it has changed to *person Friday*.

UNIT SEVEN

SS should be able to decipher enough to decide which person should have which job (and to give reasons). They can work in pairs or small groups and the class should be encouraged to reach a unanimous decision (which might entail a degree of persuasion in English). The jobs are advertised in the *classified* section of the paper. These advertisements are known as *classified ads* or *small ads*.

Exercise 113 Dictation

Answer:

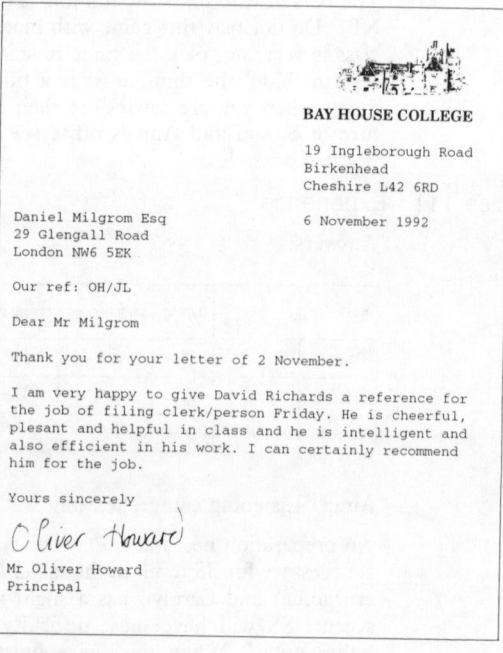

Aim: To practise the layout of a business letter, punctuation and capitalisation.

SS should now know the rules of capital letters and punctuation which apply to this letter (see Unit 11). Listening to the tape should help them understand the meaning of the letter, but they will need time to think about the punctuation. They could write the letter using the correct format for h/w.

British addresses

If SS are likely to have to make up British addresses in examinations, they should learn two or three by heart so that they are authentic. On the first line is the name of the company or house (Bay House College). Then comes the number of the building and the street name (19 Ingleborough Road). Instead of *Road* you might find *Street, Avenue, Close* or *Square*. Then comes the name of the town (Birkenhead) followed by the county (Cheshire) and the post code (L42 6RD). The first letter(s) of the post code is/are usually the initial letter(s) of the nearest city (here Liverpool). In London the first letters indicate the geographical district, so codes begin N (north), NE (north-east), NW, SW, SE, WC (West Central), W etc. Look at other addresses in this book and from other sources and notice any differences from this pattern. Modern style is to omit commas after the building number and at the end of each line of the address.

NB Esq *(Daniel Milgrom Esq)* is short for *esquire*. It is a somewhat old-fashioned term used after the name instead of the title *Mr* in addresses. SS should recognise it, not use it. The opening salutation is still *Dear Mr Milgrom*.

Exercise 114 Letter of recommendation

Sample letter:

```
LAWS SECRETARIAL COLLEGE
13 Cannonbury Lane  Inslip  Lancs PR4 2EL


Neil Warner Esq                      6 November 1992
Preston Goods
37 Highgate Road
Preston
Lancs PR4 41N

Our ref: BK/DG

Dear Mr Warner

Thank you for your letter of 2 November. I am happy to
give Carolyn Bennett  a reference for the job of
secretary.

She is very hard-working and efficient and her typing
and shorthand speeds are very good. I can certainly
recommend her for the job.

Yours sincerely

Brian Keith

Mr Brian Keith
Principal
```

Aim: To practise writing a letter of recommendation.

SS can write this letter for h/w based on the structure of the letter in Exercise 113. *Lancs* is short for *Lancashire*. 'PR' in the post code stands for *Preston*. Note the alternative position for the date.

UNIT SEVEN

NB SS cannot write a letter of recommendation for Lorraine Welder because it involves the use of the past tense which is not introduced until Unit 10.

LANGUAGE DRILLS TAPESCRIPT

Drill 103A Ask questions about what someone can do, like this:

P: Speak French
R: *Can you speak French?*

Now you try.
P: Type
R: *Can you type?*
P: Use a photocopier
R: *Can you use a photocopier?*
P: Drive
R: *Can you drive?*

P: Take shorthand
R: *Can you take shorthand?*
P: Use a telex machine
R: *Can you use a telex machine?*

Aim: Question practice with *can* (pronounced /kæn/) (SS can do this drill with their books closed).

Drill 103B Say what you can do, like this:

P: Speak French
R: *I can speak French.*

Now you try.
P: Type
R: *I can type.*
P: Use a photocopier
R: *I can use a photocopier.*
P: Drive
R: *I can drive.*

P: Take shorthand
R: *I can take shorthand.*
P: Use a telex machine
R: *I can use a telex machine.*

Aim: Practice of *can* (pronounced /kən/) (SS can do this drill with their books closed).

Drill 103C Say what you can't do, like this:

P: Speak French
R: *I can't speak French.*

Now you try.
P: Type
R: *I can't type.*
P: Use a photocopier
R: *I can't use a photocopier.*
P: Drive
R: *I can't drive.*

P: Take shorthand
R: *I can't take shorthand.*
P: Use a telex machine
R: *I can't use a telex machine.*

Aim: Practice of *can't* (pronounced /ka:nt/) (SS can do this drill with their books closed).

Drill 105A Turn these statements into questions, like this:

P: Mary's a secretary
R: *Is Mary a secretary?*

THE IDEAL SECRETARY

Now you try.
P: He's English.
R: *Is he English?*
P: You're married.
R: *Are you married?*
P: BOS is in Harlow.
R: *Is BOS in Harlow?*
P: They're sales representatives.
R: *Are they sales representatives?*
P: We're late.
R: *Are we late?*

Aim: Question practice with *to be* (SS can do this drill with their books closed).

Drill 105B Turn these statements into questions, like this:

P: Mary makes good coffee.
R: *Does Mary make good coffee?*

Now you try.
P: You like Harlow.
R: *Do you like Harlow?*
P: Fred drives to work.
R: *Does Fred drive to work?*
P: Jacques lives in Cairo.
R: *Does Jacques live in Cairo?*
P: They work for BOS.
R: *Do they work for BOS?*
P: You open the post every morning.
R: *Do you open the post every morning?*

Aim: Question practice with the present simple (SS can do this drill with their books closed).

Drill 105C Turn these statements into questions using the question word you hear, like this:

P: Mary is on the television programme. Why
R: *Why is Mary on the television programme?*
P: Mary comes from Epping. Where
R: *Where does Mary come from?*

Now you try.
P: Her prizes are a typewriter and a cassette recorder. What
R: *What are her prizes?*
P: She speaks two foreign languages. How many
R: *How many foreign languages does she speak?*
P: She's twenty-nine. How old
R: *How old is she?*
P: Mary's the winner of the Ideal Secretary Competition. Who
R: *Who's the winner of the Ideal Secretary Competition?*
P: Fred McLean is Mary's boss. Who
R: *Who's Mary's boss?*
P: Mary starts work at 9.30. What time
R: *What time does Mary start work?*

Aim: Question practice in the present using question words (SS can do this drill with their books closed).

UNIT SEVEN

Drill 109   Look at the word order with the verb 'to give'. Listen to this sentence. *They're giving Mary a prize.*
They're giving Mary a prize.
Change the sentence each time by substituting the new words you hear and changing the word order if necessary, like this: They're giving Mary a prize.

P: Her
R: *They're giving her a prize.*

Now you try.
P: A typewriter
R: *They're giving her a typewriter.*
P: Fred
R: *They're giving Fred a typewriter.*
P: To Fred
R: *They're giving a typewriter to Fred.*

P: It
R: *They're giving it to Fred.*
P: To Mary
R: *They're giving it to Mary.*
P: A prize
R: *They're giving a prize to Mary.*
P: Him
R: *They're giving him a prize.*

Aim: Practice of word order with direct and indirect objects (SS can do this drill with their books closed).

Drill 110   Talk about things that are different in Anne and Simon's office now, like this:

P: A photocopier on the table
R: *There was a photocopier on the table. Now there isn't.*
P: Six books on the top shelf.
R: *There were six books on the top shelf. Now there aren't.*

Now you try.
P: A calculator on Simon's desk
R: *There was a calculator on Simon's desk. Now there isn't.*
P: Three filing trays on Anne's desk
R: *There were three filing trays on Anne's desk. Now there aren't.*

P: A wastepaper bin under the table
R: *There was a wastepaper bin under the table. Now there isn't.*
P: Two telephones on Anne's desk
R: *There were two telephones on Anne's desk. Now there aren't.*

Aim: Practice of *was/were, is/are* (SS can do this drill with their books closed).

WORKBOOK ANSWERS

Exercise 27   Short answers

2 *Yes I am./No I'm not.*   3 *Yes I do./No I don't.*   4 *Yes I have./No I haven't.*   5 *Yes I am./No I'm not.*   6 *Yes I can./No I can't.*

THE IDEAL SECRETARY

Exercise 28   Hidden word puzzle

1 considerate   2 efficient   3 polite   4 hard-working   5 pleasant   6 ambitious   7 intelligent   8 well-dressed Hidden word: *reliable*   This exercise practises adjectives introduced in this unit.

Exercise 29   A description

Sample description: *In the office is a woman with short, dark hair and glasses. She is sitting at a desk reading a letter. A typewriter and a telephone are on the desk. A man with curly, fair hair is standing next to a photocopier. The photocopier is on a table and under the table is a wastepaper bin. On the wall on the left is a notice board and in the corner on the right is a filing cabinet. There are six shelves next to the filing cabinet. There are six books on the second shelf.* This exercise encourages creative writing using adjectives from this unit and Unit 6.

Exercise 30   Jumbled words

Sample sentences: *She is a very pleasant girl. She is always at work on time. She always works very hard. A good secretary is always pleasant. At work she is very pleasant. She is never on time. Girls always work hard. She is hard at work.* (Other sentences are possible.) This exercise allows SS to use language creatively within a controlled context (see note on WB Exercise 7, TB page 23).

Exercise 31   The alphabet

1 *(alternate letters)*   2 *O–U (One letter between A and C; two letters between C and F; three letters between F and J etc.)* 3 *X–C (Counting alternately backwards from the end of the alphabet and forwards from the beginning of the alphabet.)*   4 *O–U (The five vowels.)*   5 *H–J (Going consecutively through the alphabet omitting vowels.)*   6 *C–P (Counting alternate letters beginning at the beginning of the alphabet and half-way through.)* This exercise is to increase SS' awareness of the Roman alphabet.

Exercise 32   Can you do it?

The first number is straightforward: 9,999. The second number is a trick because *eleven hundred is one thousand one hundred*, so the answer is 12,111.

UNIT EIGHT
APPOINTMENTS

8

> *Business content*: Making appointments; business letters
> *Structures*: Present progressive with future reference
> *Must/have to/have got to*
> Imperatives (*revision*)
> *Functions*: Giving directions; expressing obligation
> *Lexis*: Dates, expressions of time, months

TEACHING NOTES

Exercise 115   Comprehension

Answers: *1 At 1.30 (half past one)*   *2 He is having lunch with Richard Bean.*   *3 Thursday afternoon*   *4 (Because) it is her birthday.*

SS should recognise the form of the present progressive from Unit 3. Teach that the answer to a *Why* question begins with *Because*. Use this exercise to elicit that here the present progressive is being used about the future and that it is referring to definite appointments.

If your SS are false beginners, they may think of the future in English as being expressed by *will*. Reassure them that there are several ways of expressing the notion of futurity according to the precise meaning you want to express and that *will* is frequently used to express other notions (eg the invitation: *Will you come to my party?*) The present progressive is always used to refer to definite future appointments (just as we use the present simple to talk about timetables). The *will* future is introduced in Unit 11 to express a decision taken at that moment. (See also note on introducing dates on the next page).

Exercise 116   Appointments (LD)

Answers: *See LDT*

Aim: To practise the present progressive with future reference.

Check that SS understand *attend a sales conference*, *board meeting* (a meeting of the directors who can also be called the *board* or the *board of directors*) and *warehouse*, before they do the exercise in pairs. You might talk briefly about the expressions of time (*at the weekend* etc) but these are dealt with more fully in Exercise 125. (See also WB Exercise 35)

APPOINTMENTS

Exercise 117 Arranging an appointment (LD)

Sample dialogue: (Anne's part only).
A: *Certainly, Mrs Balzarini. When would you like to come?*
A: *I'm afraid she's attending a sales conference in Brighton all day on Thursday.*
A: *I'm sorry. She's busy all day on Tuesday. What about lunchtime today or on Wednesday?*
A: *Are you doing anything on Friday?*
A: *Oh. Mrs Baker's free in the afternoon, but she's busy in the morning.*

Aim: To practise the present progressive with future reference and dialogue building.

SS have to take into account what Marisa says both before and after each statement of Anne's (which is why they must prepare the exercise before they do the LD). They can do this exercise for h/w or in pairs in class.

Exercise 118 Things to remember (LD A, B & C)

Answers: *See LDT*

Aim: To present and practise ways of expressing obligation.

This exercise introduces three ways of expressing obligation, but only two question forms. *What does she have to do?* is also possible, but *What has she to do?* is not very common. Introduce the forms one at a time and allow SS to practise each separately, referring to Helen's list. SS can also write five sentences using each form for additional h/w.
NB Notice that this is the unstressed form of *must* /məst/, expressing mild obligation. It is not the emphatic /mʌst/, which expresses some form of compulsion.

Exercise 119 Personal lists

Aim: Creative practice in expressing obligation.

SS can choose which structure(s) they use in this exercise. Each list will presumably be different, so allow SS to talk to more than one partner.
NB Ask SS not to make sentences in the negative as the negative forms of *must* and *have to* have different meanings. *Must* is a modal verb.

To introduce dates

Teach the list of months and/or ask SS to learn them for h/w. Point out that they are always written with capital letters, even in their abbreviated forms. SS might also need to look again at the list of ordinal numbers in the language notes for Unit 3. Elicit the difference between the spoken and written forms using Exercise 115.

UNIT EIGHT

Practise the spoken forms *the first of May* and *May the first* one form at a time round the class asking SS about their birthdays and famous dates (eg New Year's Day, Christmas Day, Christmas Eve, American Independence Day etc). This is also a chance to note which dates are important in the UK and US compared to SS' countries.

Exercise 120 Dates (LD A, B & C)

Answers: *See LDT*

Aim: To practise dates (and revise ordinal numbers).

Teach the US and UK forms of the dates and let SS work out this exercise together in pairs. They can write out the dates in full for h/w.

NB 12/12/79 is the same in the US and the UK and 15/10/90 is an impossible date in the US. You could further test SS' understanding of the two systems by asking them to write more dates which are the same and dates which are impossible in the UK and US systems. On future occasions for revision, eight SS could each make up and call out a date in the form 7/12/96. Everyone in the class writes down these numbers (as a number dictation) and writes out the dates in full (US and UK style) for h/w. It does not matter which system SS use as long as they are consistent. It is sensible to write dates in full to avoid misunderstanding.

LD 120C practises the prepositions used with dates and times. If you do not usually use the LD, you might like to call out the prompts yourself for class practice. (See also WB Exercise 36)

Pronunciation The sound /θ/ occurs with many of the ordinal numbers (six*th*, eigh*th* etc) and also mon*th*, *Th*ursday. Contrast /θ/ with /ð/ (as in *this*, *that* etc) or with /t/ or /s/ according to which your SS find most difficult. (See note on minimal pairs on TB page xxiv.)

Listening For listening practice, call out *What day is it?* (to which they reply *Monday*) or *What date is it?* (they reply *the 17th of March* or whatever the date really is). The correct reply shows they have differentiated between the two questions.

Exercise 121 A calendar (LD)

Answers: *See LDT*

Aim: Further practice of dates.

NB *The office is being decorated* is a passive form, but it follows the pattern of the drill, so you need not refer to it at this stage. The passive is introduced in Unit 13. Note that when only two dates are next to each other you use the preposition *on* rather than *from...to* (eg Mary's weekend in Paris).

APPOINTMENTS

Exercise 122   A map of Harlow

Answers: *A – supermarket*   *B – newsagent's*   *C – post office*
D – bank   *E – BOS*   *F – cinema*

Aim: Listening comprehension.

Pre-teach the names of the shops, but SS can deduce the meaning of *T-junction*, *crossroads* and *roundabout* from the road signs. Check that SS know that the British drive on the left in England.

SS should remember expressions like *Turn right* from Unit 3, but you might want to check directions (perhaps by doing Exercise 123) before listening to the tape. Play the tape as many times as necessary for SS to identify the places on the map.

Exercise 123   Asking the way (LD) and Exercise 124 Where am I?
(LD)

Sample answers: *See LDT.*

Aim: Practising asking for and giving directions.

This oral practice can be done before or after Exercise 122. You could divide your SS into three groups which take it in turns to have the tape recorder to do the listening comprehension in 122 while the other two groups do these exercises in pairs (see TB page xix). Exercise 124 could also be done by asking SS to write 5 sets of instructions for h/w and giving them to someone else in class to follow the next day.

Exercise 125   Expressions of time

Answers: *1–c   2–h   3–l   4–j   5–b   6–e   7–i
8–g   9–k   10–f   11–a   12–d*

Aim: Learning expressions of time by deducing their meaning.

SS should be able to work out by themselves both the answers and what words must mean, particularly if you introduced some of the terms in Unit 6 (see TB page 72). Let SS do this exercise alone, but later consolidate their learning by practising the expressions in class.

Exercise 126   A business letter

Answer: (see page 94)

NB   The underlined words are the ones missing from the original.

Aim: Reading comprehension.

SS will find it more rewarding to do this exercise in pairs or small groups. They can each write out the complete letter for h/w. This technique can be used for other letters (or short reading passages). Make enough copies of the letter for one

UNIT EIGHT

```
        BRIGHTER OFFICE SUPPLIES LIMITED
                                              [BOS logo]
        Mrs Joyce McAndrew
        45 Norman Avenue                      L I M I T E D
        Canterbury
        Kent CT1 39X                          13 Mill Street, Harlow,
                                              Essex CM20 2JR.
        Our ref: SB/AB                        Tel Harlow (0279) 26721
                                              Fax (0279) 431109
                                              Telex 81259
        10 November 1992                      Cables/Telegrams BOS
                                              Harlow

        Dear Ms McAndrew

        Thank you for your application for the post of sales
        representative.

        Please come to my office for an interview on 23
        November at 11am. My office is number 103.

        To get to BOS by car from Harlow town centre, drive up
        Central Avenue and go straight ahead at the roundabout
        into Fifth Avenue. Take the first turning on the left.
        BOS is the tall, white building on the left.

        I look forward to meeting you.

        Yours sincerely

        Sheila Baker

        Mrs Sheila Baker
        Sales manager
```

between four SS and cut them up line for line or every two lines. With longer passages you can cut them into paragraphs, so that SS can appreciate the development of the passage through the paragraphs. If SS do not immediately notice all the bits missed out of the letter, let them do Exercise 127 first.

Exercise 127 Comprehension

Answers: *1 Ms Joyce McAndrew   2 Sheila Baker   3 Anne Bell (see our ref SB/**AB**)   4 In Canterbury (45 Norman Avenue, Canterbury, Kent CT1 39X)   5 We do not know (Ms can mean Miss or Mrs)   6 Yes. She writes Mrs before her name.   7 On 23 November   8 Sales representative 9 By car   10 White*

Aim: To check reading comprehension.

Exercise 128 Letter writing

Sample letter: (see page 95)

Aim: Practice of letter writing and giving written directions.

SS can base this letter on that written to Joyce McAndrew. They should refer to the map on SB page 65 for the directions.

Additional activities

Appointments   For further practice of the present progres-

APPOINTMENTS

```
┌─────────────────────────────────────────────────────┐
│  BRIGHTER OFFICE SUPPLIES LIMITED                   │
│                                      BOS            │
│  Mrs Rachel Snell                                   │
│  93 Lee Road                         L I M I T E D  │
│  London SE3 4XB                                     │
│                                      13 Mill Street, Harlow,
│                                      Essex CM20 2JR.
│  10 November 1992                    Tel Harlow (0279) 26721
│                                      Fax (0279) 431109
│                                      Telex 81259
│  Our ref: SY/JB                      Cables/Telegrams BOS
│                                      Harlow
│
│  Dear Ms Snell
│
│  Thank you for your application for the post of sales
│  representative.
│
│  Please come to my office for an interview on 23
│  November at 11.45. My office is number 103.
│
│  To get to BOS from the station, go straight ahead and
│  take the second exit at the roundabout. Take the first
│  road on the right. BOS is the tall white building on
│  the left.
│
│  I look forward to meeting you.
│
│  Yours sincerely
│
│  Sheila Baker
│
│  Mrs Sheila Baker
│  Sales manager
└─────────────────────────────────────────────────────┘
```

sive for future appointments in a freer context, divide the class into three groups (A, B and C) and ask them to make blank diaries for Monday to Friday, dividing each day into *morning* and *afternoon*. Secretly tell each group to mark an x against different days, like this:

Group A marks:

Mon	am	x
	pm	
Tue	am	x
	pm	x
Wed	am	
	pm	
Thu	am	
	pm	
Fri	am	
	pm	x

Group B marks:

Mon	am	
	pm	
Tue	am	x
	pm	
Wed	am	
	pm	x
Thu	am	
	pm	
Fri	am	x
	pm	x

Group C marks:

Mon	am	
	pm	x
Tue	am	x
	pm	
Wed	am	
	pm	
Thu	am	x
	pm	x
Fri	am	
	pm	

Tell the whole group to mark a definite appointment against each cross. Each person can write anything s/he likes as long as it takes the whole morning or afternoon. Then ask SS to get into groups of three with an A, a B and a C in each group. SS

UNIT EIGHT

must negotiate a time when they can all meet. They cannot change any of their appointments, they must speak in English and they must not show each other their diaries. The only time they are all free is Wednesday morning (but let them discover this by trying to make their arrangements).

LANGUAGE DRILLS TAPESCRIPT

Drill 116   Look at Sheila Baker's diary. Today is Monday. Answer Sheila's questions about things she's doing, like this:

P: Am I doing anything this morning?
R: *You're seeing Mr Smith at 10 o'clock and Mr Parker at 11.*
P: And what about lunch?
R: *You're not doing anything at lunchtime.*

Now you try.
P: What am I doing this afternoon?
R: *You're going to a board meeting.*
P: Am I doing anything tomorrow morning?
R: *You're seeing Mr Matthews at 10.30.*
P: And at lunchtime?
R: *You're having lunch with Lorenzo Magnani.*
P: What am I doing in the afternoon?
R: *You're showing Lorenzo Magnani round the department.*

P: Am I doing anything on Wednesday morning?
R: *You're interviewing new sales staff.*
P: What about lunch?
R: *You're not doing anything at lunchtime.*
P: And in the afternoon?
R: *You're visiting the new warehouse.*
P: And on Thursday?
R: *You're attending a sales conference in Brighton all day.*

Aim: Practice of present progressive with future reference.

Drill 117   Do Exercise 117 before you do this drill. Look at Sheila's diary and say Anne's part in this conversation with Marisa Balzarini. There is more than one correct answer. Just say what you think Anne says: (see dialogue in SB and sample answers on TB page 91).

Aim: Fluency and creativity.
NB   Since the SS' responses have to fit in with what Anne says before and afterwards, the dialogues must be prepared beforehand, although SS should not just read what they have prepared.

Drill 118A   Talk about the things Helen's got to do, like this:

P: Send a telex to New York
R: *She's got to send a telex to New York.*

APPOINTMENTS

Now you try.
P: Phone Mr Parker
R: *She's got to phone Mr Parker.*
P: Write to Mr Jones
R: *She's got to write to Mr Jones.*
P: Order the stationery
R: *She's got to order the stationery.*

P: Type a letter to Miss Negus
R: *She's got to type a letter to Miss Negus.*
P: Photocopy the report
R: *She's got to photocopy the report.*

Aim: Practice of expressing obligation with *have got to* (SS can do this drill with their books closed).

Drill 118B Talk about the things Helen's got to do, like this:

P: Send a telex to Paris
R: *She must send a telex to Paris.*

Now you try.
P: Do the filing
R: *She must do the filing.*
P: Make an appointment to see Chris Foord.
R: *She must make an appointment to see Chris Foord.*
P: Give the order to Simon
R: *She must give the order to Simon.*

P: Type the report
R: *She must type the report.*
P: Arrange an appointment with Mr Smith
R: *She must arrange an appointment with Mr Smith.*

Aim: Practice of expressing obligation with *must* (SS can do this drill with their books closed).

Drill 118C Talk about the things Helen has to do, like this:

P: Send a telex to Cairo
R: *She has to send a telex to Cairo.*

Now you try.
P: Type the memo
R: *She has to type the memo.*
P: Ring Mr Donaldson
R: *She has to ring Mr Donaldson.*
P: Take a message to Luisa
R: *She has to take a message to Luisa.*

P: Give the report to Fred
R: *She has to give the report to Fred.*
P: Answer the letter from Mrs Cox
R: *She has to answer the letter from Mrs Cox.*

Aim: Practice of expressing obligation with *have to* (SS can do this drill with their books closed).

Drill 120A Say these dates, like this:

P: The first of May
R: *May the first*

UNIT EIGHT

Now you try.
P: The fifth of September
R: *September the fifth*
P: The second of August
R: *August the second*
P: The twelfth of December
R: *December the twelfth*

P: The third of June
R: *June the third*
P: The seventh of April
R: *April the seventh*
P: The fifteenth of October
R: *October the fifteenth*

Aim: Practice of saying dates (SS can do this drill with their books closed).

Drill 120B

Say these dates, like this:

P: January the fifth, nineteen forty-two
R: *The fifth of January, nineteen forty-two*

Now you try.
P: May the ninth, nineteen eighty-four
R: *The ninth of May, nineteen eighty-four*
P: February the eighth, nineteen sixty-five
R: *The eighth of February, nineteen sixty-five*
P: December the twelfth, nineteen seventy-nine
R: *The twelfth of December, nineteen seventy-nine*
P: March the sixth, nineteen eighty-two
R: *The sixth of March, nineteen eighty-two*

P: July the fourth, nineteen eighty-one
R: *The fourth of July, nineteen eighty-one*
P: October the fifteenth, nineteen ninety
R: *The fifteenth of October, nineteen ninety*

Aim: Practice of saying dates (SS can do this drill with their books closed).

Drill 120C

Say the correct preposition with these dates and times, like this:

P: September
R: *In September*
P: September the fifth
R: *On September the fifth*

Now you try.
P: Six fifteen
R: *At six fifteen*
P: Monday six o'clock
R: *On Monday at six o'clock*
P: The weekend
R: *At the weekend*

P: The afternoon
R: *In the afternoon*
P: October 1969
R: *In October 1969*
P: Lunchtime
R: *At lunchtime*

Aim: Practice of the prepositions used with dates and expressions of time (SS can do this drill with their books closed).

APPOINTMENTS

Drill 121 Look at the BOS calendar and answer these questions, like this:

P: When's the sales conference?
R: *It's on the twelfth of November.*
P: When's the stocktaking?
R: *It's from the seventeenth to the nineteenth of November.*

Now you try.
P: When's Sheila's trip to Italy?
R: *It's from the first to the eighth of December.*
P: When's Mary's weekend in Paris?
R: *It's on the twelfth and thirteenth of December.*
P: When's the Christmas party?
R: *It's on the twentieth of December.*
P: When's the Christmas holiday?
R: *It's from the twenty-fourth to the twenty-sixth of December.*
P: When's the bank holiday?
R: *It's on the first of January.*

P: When's the office being decorated?
R: *It's from the twelfth to the twenty-second of January.*
P: When's the Director's conference?
R: *It's on the twenty-eighth of January.*
P: When's the union's general meeting?
R: *It's on the eighth of February.*
P: When's the office outing?
R: *It's on the nineteenth of February.*

Aim: Further practice of saying dates.

Drill 123 Ask your way to places politely, like this:

P: The newsagent's
R: *Excuse me. Can you tell me the way to the newsagent's please?*

Now you try.
P: The bank
R: *Excuse me. Can you tell me the way to the bank please?*
P: Brighter Office Supplies.
R: *Excuse me. Can you tell me the way to Brighter Office Supplies please?*
P: The post office
R: *Excuse me. Can you tell me the way to the post office please?*

P: The cinema
R: *Excuse me. Can you tell me the way to the cinema please?*
P: The supermarket
R: *Excuse me. Can you tell me the way to the supermarket please?*

Aim: Practice of asking the way (SS can do this drill with their books closed).

UNIT EIGHT

Drill 124 Do Exercise 122 before you do this drill. Listen to these directions and follow them on the map. Say which building they direct you to. Start from the station.

P: Go straight ahead. At the roundabout take the second exit. Then take the first road on the right. Which building is on the left?
R: *BOS – Figure E*
P: Start from the station again. Go straight ahead. At the roundabout turn right. Which building is on the left?
R: *The cinema – Figure F*
P: This time start from the cinema and walk back down the road. At the roundabout, turn right and then take the first road on the left. At the T-junction turn left and go round the corner. Which building is on your left?
R: *The post office – Figure C*
P: Which building is on your right?
R: *The bank – Figure D*
P: Start from the station again. At the roundabout, take the first exit. Take the first turning on the right and then turn right again. Which building is on the right?
R: *The supermarket – Figure A*
P: Come out of the supermarket and turn right. Take the next road on the right. Which building is on the right?
R: *The newsagent's – Figure B*

Aim: Comprehension; following directions on a map.

WORKBOOK ANSWERS

Exercise 33 Days and months

The missing month is *April*. The missing day is *Friday*.

Exercise 34 Vocabulary

pencil	*boss*	*telex*	Tuesday	*typewriter*	*January*
rubber	*secretary*	*memo*	Saturday	*calculator*	*May*
ruler	*assistant*	*letter*	*Friday*	*photocopier*	*August*

Ask SS to think of titles for each category eg stationery, jobs, correspondence/written communication, days, office equipment/machines, months.

Exercise 35 Appointments

Sample sentences: *On Monday Lorenzo Magnani is having lunch with Fred McLean. In the afternoon he is going to a board meeting. On Tuesday he is meeting Sheila Baker for lunch and he is visiting the sales department in the afternoon. On Wednesday morning he is meeting (going to see) Howard Spencer. He is not doing anything (he is free) at lunchtime. On Monday afternoon he is visiting the (a) new warehouse and in the evening he is going to the theatre with Marisa Balzarini.* (Other variations on these sentences are possible.) This exercise practises the present progressive for future appointments.

Exercise 36 Prepositions

1 *in* January   2 *on* January 23   3 *of* 9 March   4 *on* Friday   5 *at* 6 o'clock   6 *at* the weekend   7 *in* the afternoon   8 (*no preposition*)   9 *at* lunchtime   10 *in* 1999   This exercise practises the prepositions used with expressions of time.

UNIT NINE
JOB SATISFACTION   9

Business content: Pie chart; report; petty cash; time and motion study
Structures: Verbs and expressions of liking + *ing*
Should/why don't...
Present simple tense (*revision*)
Function: Suggestions
Lexis: Fractions, jobs, report and petty cash vocabulary, numbers (*revision*)

TEACHING NOTES

Exercise 129   Comprehension

Answers: *1 One (a) month   2 She thinks it is boring. 3 She is not feeling very well.   4 Mary (because she is going home).*

SS will probably understand the dialogue well enough to answer the questions even before the main structures are presented.

NB   When verbs describe states rather than actions they are not usually used in the progressive tenses (eg *She thinks it is boring*). Note however that we say both *She feels ill* and *She is feeling ill*.

Exercise 130   Problems and suggestions (LD A & B)

Answers: *See LDT.*

Suggestions for Simon: *Why don't you send a fax? You should fax him/her. You should telephone him/her. You should send an express letter.*

Aim: To teach and practise suggestions.

Introduce Mary's problem *I've got a cold* by playing her role and inviting suggestions from the SS about what to do (go to bed, keep warm, call the doctor etc.) Check that SS know the necessary vocabulary before you teach one (or both) of the structures. Then introduce the full dialogue (see TB page xxv).
NB   This is the unstressed *should* /ʃəd/, not *should* /ʃʊd/ to express obligation.

SS can further practise the dialogue by substituting Helen's problem and the suggestions from the book, however further suggestions for her, and suggestions for Simon, should be discussed and practised with the whole class working together as they are partly business problems. (Helen could take out a loan, or a mortgage on a house, she could sell something, she could ask for a rise or an advance on her wages/salary etc.)

JOB SATISFACTION

Exercise 131   Likes and dislikes (LD)

Answers: *See LDT* (sentences are in a different order)

Aim: Written practice of verbs and expressions + *ing*.

This is a written transformation exercise using verbs and expressions which take the *ing* form of the verb (see SB page 25 for the spelling rules). They are all to do with liking and disliking and they are all 'stative' (they describe states rather than actions and are not usually used in the progressive tenses).

Ask SS to look up each expression in the dictionary and then arrange sentences 2 to 7 in order of strength (from mild irritation to absolute hate). The distinction between some of the expressions is a fine one, but one possible order is that in the LD. The exercise can be done orally and/or for h/w, either before or after Exercises 132 and 133.

Exercise 132   Problem Solving

Answers:

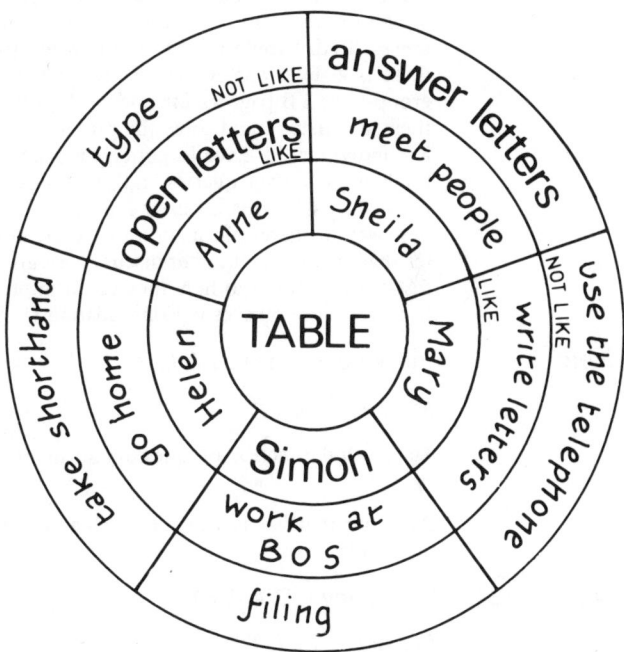

Note that you only get all the information by reading the Questions too.
Remind SS that *like* takes *ing*.
NB   In many cases, *like doing* and *like to do* are interchangeable, but since this is not always the case, only introduce the one

103

ized themselves and how they could improve on this another
UNIT NINE

form at the moment. *Like doing* always means *enjoy doing*, but *like to do* can mean that you do something for some other reason than enjoyment, so you can say *'I like to shop at the best shops'* even though you do not like (enjoy) shopping; and you can say *'I like to go to the dentist for a check up every year'* even if you hate going to the dentist.

Although this exercise can be done for h/w as a reading comprehension, a more satisfactory exploitation is to do it as a problem-solving information-gap exercise with the whole class (see TB page xx) which gives a lot of oral practice of *like/don't like + ing*:

SS must not open their books. Draw the diagram from the SB on the board and write up the two questions. Read the general introduction to the class and tell them they will each be given some of the information. They will have to share their facts with other people in order to solve the problem. Divide the class into three equal groups, A, B and C. Quickly and secretly tell sentences 1 and 2 from the SB to group A; tell sentences 3 and 4 to group B; and tell sentences 5 and 6 to group C. Go back to each group to check that they can repeat their sentences. Redistribute the SS into new groups of 5 or 6 so that there is at least one A, one B and one C in each of the new groups (see TB page xx for how to do this). SS can now share their information and solve the problem. Do not interfere unless individual SS have forgotten their information, but do be available to answer queries and make sure the SS keep speaking in English. This is partly a managerial problem about the best way to share information and some groups will cope better than others. You might discuss with groups how they organised themselves and how they could improve on this another time. (See also puzzles in Consolidation Units A and B).

Exercise 133   Check questions (LD A & B)

   Answers: *See LDT*

   Aim: Oral practice of question form of *like/doesn't like + ing*.

   Point out that *like* is a regular verb and forms the question in the regular way.

Exercise 134   Job survey (LD A & B)

   Answers: *See LDT*

   Aim: Further practice of verbs + *ing* and question tags.

   SS can do this exercise in pairs. Listen to the LDT for the (falling) intonation of the question tag. (See also WB Exercise 38)

JOB SATISFACTION

Additional activity

To introduce or give further practice in this question tag form, ask the SS to stand in a circle. Go up to a S and check his/her name, like this: *You're Helmut, aren't you?* (or *Your name's Helmut, isn't it?*) Take his place in the circle and fold your arms. Helmut must then approach any other S and check his/her name in the same way. Helmut then takes that S's place in the circle and folds his arms. This continues until everyone is in a new place in the circle with folded arms (SS cannot approach anyone whose arms are folded already). The last S approaches you (unfold your arms to indicate this) and the game ends.

With a multi-national class you could practise nationalities in the same way with sentences such as: *You're Italian, aren't you?* (See note on Exercise 11 on TB page 5).

Exercise 135 Job advice (LD)

Aim: To practise *like* + *ing* and *should*.

Either pre-teach some of the jobs or ask SS to try to work out what they are from the clues which lead to them. They can check their conclusions in a dictionary. Only play the game for about 5 minutes in class, but SS could write sentences for h/w following various paths and commenting on what a person doing each job likes, eg *Jennifer is a journalist. She likes writing, but she does not like selling things or working in a factory. She does not like working in an office, but she likes meeting people.* (See also WB Exercise 39)

NB If you did not play the game from Unit 1 (TB page 7) to practise jobs, you could play it now with a greater range of jobs. Alternatively you could play the name game which involves jobs (see alternative version of game 3 on TB page 1). Remind SS to use the indefinite article before jobs.

Exercise 136 Petty cash

Answers:

OCTOBER	travel	postage	stationery	sundries	
First week	£8.20	£3.92	£1.58	£13.96	
Second week	£4.80	£2.40	£2.34	£7.60	
Third week	£6.40	£4.68	£3.20	£12.64	TOTAL
Fourth week	£5.60	£4.00	£2.88	£16.04	EXPENDITURE
TOTAL	£25.00	£15.00	£10.00	£50.00	£100.00

Aim: Number dictation in a business context.

Remind SS how sums of money are spoken and written. Play the tape only once while SS write down the numbers (numbers

UNIT NINE

are repeated on the tape). SS can then fill in the totals. If they have the correct totals, they probably heard the figures correctly. (See also WB Exercise 37)

NB Note the repeated rising intonation when reading a list aloud except for the fall on the last item in the list.

Exercise 137 Pie chart

Answers:

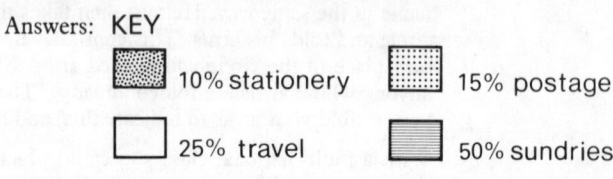

SS work in pairs to check their answers to Exercise 136 and fill in the key to the pie chart. Discuss this way of presenting information visually through a pie chart and how to judge the size of the segments (eg 50% = ½ the circle; 25% = ¼; 10% is ⅖ of the remaining segment).

Exercise 138 Time and motion study

Answers: *1 Anne spends 8 hours at work. 2 She spends 2½ hours typing; ½ hour filing; ½ hour taking shorthand; 1½ hours on the phone; ½ hour making tea and coffee; 1 hour at lunch; 1½ hours doing everything else. 3 Typing – 31¼%; filing – 6¼%; taking shorthand – 6¼%; phoning – 18¾%; making tea and coffee – 6¼%; at lunch – 12½%; miscellaneous – 18¾%*

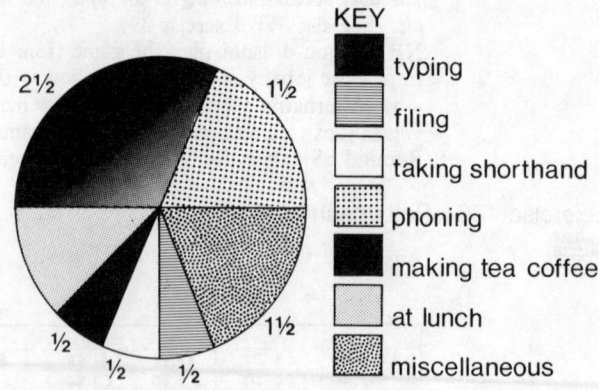

Aim: Exploitation of a reading comprehension text in a business context.

If necessary, explain to SS that a time and motion study is done to see how employees spend their time, with a view to finding more productive ways of working.

SS can do this exercise in pairs. They should not need any help working out the different times, although you should

JOB SATISFACTION

check they are correct before they go on to work out the percentages (with the help of the formula)

Additional activity

Project SS could either make accurate records of or estimate how they spend an average 24 hours or week (eg sleeping, eating, working, playing sport, other forms of recreation etc). They could present the information in the form of a pie chart (or block chart, see SB page 32).

Exercise 139 Percentages (LD)

Answers: *See LDT*

Aim: Fluency; saying fractions; revision of present simple tense.

Teach SS how to say fractions: Most fractions have an ordinal number at the bottom, eg *a third* ($1/3$), *a sixth* ($1/6$), *a ninety-ninth* ($1/99$) etc. The exceptions are: *a quarter* ($1/4$) and *a half* ($1/2$). (See language notes on SB page 76)

If any number other than *one* is at the top of the fraction, the bottom number must be in the plural eg *five-sixths, three-quarters*. If you say a whole number followed by a fraction you must insert the word *and*: *six and nine-tenths*.

NB If the number at the top of the fraction is bigger than the number at the bottom, you can turn the fraction into a whole number plus a fraction eg $7/6 = 1 1/6$; $9/4 = 2 1/4$. If the number at the top of the fraction is the same as the number at the bottom, the answer is 1 eg $2/2 = 1$; $87/87 = 1$. If the number at the top can be divided by the same number as the number at the bottom, the fraction can be reduced: $8/10 = 4/5$ (8 and 10 can both be divided by 2); $3/9 = 1/3$ and $5/100 = 1/20$.

SS can say further fractions for their partners to write down for extra practice. (See also WB Exercise 42)

This exercise also involves the use of the present simple tense and now is a good time to revise the use of this tense for habitual actions if SS are making mistakes.

Exercise 140 Hidden word puzzle

Answers: 1 *recommendations* 2 *report* 3 *findings* 4 *petty cash* 5 *personal* 6 *expenditure* 7 *savings* 8 *figures* 9 *carbon paper* 10 *rent* 11 *rates*
Hidden word: *conclusions*

Aim: To present the format of a report and practise deducing the meaning of words from context.

For extra numbers practice, introduce the report by having half the class cover the figures for 1981 and the other half cover the figures for 1980. SS from different halves of the class

UNIT NINE

can then ask each other for the figures they have not got, like this:
S1: *What was the figure for rent and rates in 1991 last year?*
S2: *Thirty-four thousand, one hundred pounds.*

SS can also work out which figures have risen and by how much, ie light and heat by £6,000; telephone £7,900; telexes and cables £500; postage £10,000; stationery £1,800; photocopying £900; petty cash £1,400.

No other preparation is necessary to do the exercise. SS need only understand the general meaning of the report, although you could ask general comprehension questions (or ask them to ask each other). Exercise 141 further exploits the *recommendations* section.

Point out the order in which information is presented so that SS will be able to write their own reports using the same format in the future.

Exercise 141   A memo (LD)

Sample:

BRIGHTER OFFICE SUPPLIES LIMITED

MEMORANDUM

TO: All staff
FROM: Peter Hall,
           Accounts department
DATE: 19 November 1992
Subject: Saving money

My recent report on expenditure shows that we are spending a lot of money. Here are some ways we can save money:
Please use the phone after 1pm when it is cheaper.
Please do not make personal phone calls at work.
Please switch off lights when you go out of the office.
Please use carbon paper not the photocopier.
Please order stationery from the warehouse, do not buy it on petty cash.
Please send post to the postroom. Do not buy stamps on petty cash.
Please re-use envelopes.

Thank you.

Aim: To revise the format of a memo and the imperative; to introduce the function of polite suggestion.

If you did not introduce the negative imperative in Unit 3, teach it now. For practice you could play *The Boss Says* (see TB page 28) with the difference that SS only obey your commands (positive and negative) if you say *please*. Practise the

JOB SATISFACTION

Exercise 142 A survey and a report

Aim: Revision of *like doing* and *would like to do* in a business context.

This exercise is a short project involving a survey (see Exercises 54 and 103), presenting the figures in some other form eg a block graph and writing a properly laid out report.

Compare and contrast *like doing* with *Would you like to do*? if necessary. (See also WB Exercise 41)

Comparing and contrasting

WB Exercise 41 is the first in a series of exercises over the next few units which differentiate between structures and phrases which are very similar and which SS might be confusing. Even if the SS are not using the WB regularly, you might like to do these exercises (WB Exercise 44, SB Exercise 177, WB Exercise 54) and devote a particular time in each lesson to them (eg first thing in the lesson – to encourage SS to be on time). For extra practice in class when the words sound the same (eg their, they're, there), you could prepare a short dictation or sentence containing the problem words. SS have to write down either the whole sentence, or just the problem word in each sentence.

LANGUAGE DRILLS TAPESCRIPT

Drill 130A Helen hasn't got any money. Give her some suggestions, like this:
P: Borrow some
R: *Why don't you borrow some?*

Now you try.
P: See your bank manager
R: *Why don't you see your bank manager?*
P: Ask for a pay rise
R: *Why don't you ask for a pay rise?*
P: Get a new job
R: *Why don't you get a new job?*
P: Sell something
R: *Why don't you sell something?*

Aim: To practise making suggestions (SS can do this drill with their books closed).

Drill 130B Mary's not feeling very well. Give her some suggestions, like this:

P: Go home
R: *You should go home.*

Now you try.
P: Lie down
R: *You should lie down.*

UNIT NINE

P: Take an aspirin
R: *You should take an aspirin.*
P: Keep warm
R: *You should keep warm.*
P: Have a hot drink
R: *You should have a hot drink.*
P: See a doctor
R: *You should see a doctor.*

Aim: To practise making suggestions (SS can do this drill with their books closed).

Drill 131 Helen doesn't like being a secretary. Listen to what she says about her job and make sentences, like this:

P: I write a lot of letters and I don't like it.
R: *I don't like writing letters.*

Now you try.
P: I write memos all the time and I'm tired of it.
R: *I'm tired of writing memos.*
P: I open the mail every morning and I'm bored with it.
R: *I'm bored with opening the mail.*
P: I answer the telephone all day long and I'm fed up with it.
R: *I'm fed up with answering the telephone.*
P: I use the photocopier a lot, but I don't like it.
R: *I don't like using the photocopier.*

P: I type all day long and I hate it.
R: *I hate typing.*
P: I take shorthand every day and I can't stand it.
R: *I can't stand taking shorthand.*
P: But I go home on Fridays and I love it.
R: *I love going home on Fridays.*

Aim: Practice of verbs and expressions which take *ing* (SS can do this drill with their books closed).
NB These sentences in the drill are in a different order from the sentences in the SB (see TB page 103).

Drill 133A Ask questions about what people like, like this:

P: Open letters
R: *Who likes opening letters?*

Now you try.
P: Meet people
R: *Who likes meeting people?*
P: Write letters
R: *Who likes writing letters?*
P: Work at BOS
R: *Who likes working at BOS?*
P: Go home
R: *Who likes going home?*

Aim: Question practice with *like + ing* (SS can do this drill with their books closed).

Drill 133B Ask questions about what people don't like, like this:

P: Take shorthand
R: *Who doesn't like taking shorthand?*

JOB SATISFACTION

Now you try.
P: Type
R: *Who doesn't like typing?*
P: Answer letters
R: *Who doesn't like answering letters?*
P: Use the telephone
R: *Who doesn't like using the telephone?*
P: Do the filing
R: *Who doesn't like doing the filing?*

Aim: Negative question practice with *like + ing* (SS can do this drill with their books closed).

Drill 134A

Give short answers to agree with these questions, like this:

P: Anne likes filing, doesn't she?
R: *Yes she does.*
P: Helen doesn't like typing, does she?
R: *No she doesn't.*

Now you try.
P: Helen hates taking shorthand, doesn't she?
R: *Yes she does.*
P: Mary loves working for BOS, doesn't she?
R: *Yes she does.*
P: Mary doesn't like filing, does she?
R: *No she doesn't.*
P: Anne loves being a secretary, doesn't she?
R: *Yes she does.*

Aim: Comprehension and practice of short answers.

Drill 134B

Make questions from these statements to confirm your opinion by adding a question tag, like this:

P: Anne likes filing.
R: *Anne likes filing, doesn't she?*
P: Helen doesn't like typing.
R: *Helen doesn't like typing, does she?*

Now you try. Listen carefully to the intonation of the question tag and try to copy it.
P: Helen hates taking shorthand.
R: *Helen hates taking shorthand, doesn't she?*
P: Mary loves working for BOS.
R: *Mary loves working for BOS, doesn't she?*
P: Mary doesn't like filing.
R: *Mary doesn't like filing, does she?*
P: Anne loves being a secretary.
R: *Anne loves being a secretary, doesn't she?*

Aim: Practice of question tags in the present simple (SS can do this drill with their books closed).

Drill 135

Ask questions about what someone likes, like this:

P: Meet people
R: *Do you like meeting people?*

UNIT NINE

Now you try.
P: Work in an office
R: *Do you like working in an office?*
P: Sell things
R: *Do you like selling things?*
P: Write
R: *Do you like writing?*
P: Help people
R: *Do you like helping people?*
P: Take shorthand
R: *Do you like taking shorthand?*

Aim: Question practice with *like* + *ing* (SS can do this drill with their books closed)

Drill 139

Do Exercise 138 before you do this drill. Answer these questions, like this:

P: How much time does Anne spend typing?
R: *She types for thirty-one and a half per cent of the time.*

Now you try.
P: How much time does Anne spend at lunch?
R: *She's at lunch for twelve and a half per cent of the time.*
P: How much time does she spend doing the filing?
R: *She does the filing for six and a quarter per cent of the time.*
P: How much time does she spend taking shorthand?
R: *She takes shorthand for six and a quarter per cent of the time.*
P: How much time does she spend making tea and coffee?
R: *She makes tea and coffee for six and a quarter per cent of the time.*
P: How much time does she spend on the phone?
R: *She's on the phone for eighteen and three-quarters per cent of the time.*
P: How much time does she spend doing everything else?
R: *She does everything else for eighteen and three-quarters per cent of the time.*

Aim: Comprehension and fluency; practice of fractions.

Drill 141

Suggest ways the staff at BOS can save money, like this:

P: They should use the phone after one pm.
R: *Please use the phone after one pm.*
P: They shouldn't leave the lights on.
R: *Please don't leave the lights on.*

Now you try.
P: They shouldn't make personal phone calls at work.
R: *Please don't make personal phone calls at work.*
P: They should re-use envelopes.
R: *Please re-use envelopes.*
P: They should order stationery from the warehouse.
R: *Please order stationery from the warehouse.*
P: They shouldn't buy stamps on petty cash.
R: *Please don't buy stamps on petty cash.*

JOB SATISFACTION

Aim: Practice of polite suggestions using imperatives (SS can do this drill with their books closed).

WORKBOOK ANSWERS

Exercise 37 Figures

115% a (one) hundred and fifteen per cent. £574 five hundred and seventy-four pounds (sterling). $420 four hundred and twenty dollars. 180° a (one) hundred and eighty degrees. 92p ninety-two pence. £5,237 five thousand, two hundred and thirty-seven pounds. This exercise revises the written form of numbers.

Exercise 38 Question tags

3 You're a doctor, aren't you? 4 She doesn't work at BOS, does she? 5 Her job's very exciting, isn't it? 6 They've got to leave soon, haven't they? 7 Simon's sitting next to Helen, isn't he? 8 Mary's got a cold, hasn't she? 9 He's not very efficient, is he? 10 They can take shorthand, can't they? This exercise practises the formation of question tags with a variety of modal and auxiliary verbs.

Exercise 39 Jobs

*1 doctor   2 journalist   3 farmer   4 accountant
5 craftsman   6 vet   7 musician   8 writer   9 nurse
10 salesman* This exercise practises job vocabulary.

Exercise 40 Word stress

O o   o O   O o o   O o   O o o   O o   O o o
circle per cent writer report percentage suggestion secretary/
O ooo   o o Ooo   O o o   o Ooo   o O o   O o o o
secretary★ secretarial journalist activity depressing interested/
O o o   O o o   o o O   O o o   o O o   o O o
interested★ shopkeeper petty cash expenditure accountant computer

See also SB Exercises 96–99 and WB Exercise 66. NB★ See TB page 74.

Exercise 41 Would like to do/like doing

*1 typing   2 to go   3 would   4 do   5 would   6 does
7 would   8 going* (See note on TB page 109).

Exercise 42 Fractions

*2 a half (three sixths)   3 one and a quarter   4 one (three thirds)   5 a third   6 two ninths   7 ten and a quarter
8 three and four fifths*

UNIT TEN
JOB APPLICATIONS

10

Business content:	Curriculum vitae; job interviews; letters of application
Structures:	Past simple tense Question words: *Who saw...? Who did...see?*
Functions:	Describing past actions; discussing biographical information
Pronunciation:	Final *-d*
Lexis:	Regular and irregular verbs

TEACHING NOTES

Exercise 143   Comprehension

Answers: *1 In 1988   2 We do not know.   3 No. He sold telephone equipment.   4 The telephone company   5 Yes he did*

You might prefer to teach the past simple tense before you do this exercise. Teach from the tape *actually*, as a means of correcting someone (it does not mean *now*), and *anything else*.

To introduce the past simple tense

Establish a sequence of actions on the board using regular verbs, eg:

1 *Simon is opening the post.*   2 *He is typing a letter.*   3 *He is phoning a customer.*   4 *He is posting a letter.*

Practise these sentences in the present progressive. Then tell the SS what Simon did yesterday: *He opened the post yesterday.* Elicit from the SS the regular past tense of the other verbs. Give plenty of practice round the class. Show SS how the reg-

JOB APPLICATIONS

ular past tense is formed from the infinitive (see SB page 84) and point out that the past simple is the same in all persons.

Practise the tense with a substitution drill such as:

T: *Simon opened the post at 8 o'clock*   S1: *Simon opened the post at 8 o'clock.*
T: *I*   S2: *I opened the post at 8 o'clock.*
T: *a letter*   S3: *I opened a letter at 8 o'clock.*
T: *typed*   S4: *I typed a letter at 8 o'clock.*
T: *two*   S5: *I typed two letters at 8 o'clock.*
T: *yesterday*   S6: *I typed two letters yesterday.*

Exercise 144   The past simple (LD)

Answers: *See LDT*

Aim: To practise the form and pronunciation of the past simple.

Ask SS to write the past tense of the verbs in this exercise. Let them try to work out the spelling from their knowledge of other spelling rules in English (plurals, present participles etc). When they have done this (possibly for h/w) let them listen to the three different ways the final -*d* is pronounced and see if they can recognise the sounds from the tape.

NB Teach SS that the final -*d* is pronounced /ɪd/ after the sounds /d/ and /t/. It is not necessary to teach the /d/ and /t/ rules to SS: it is pronounced /t/ after all other voiceless sounds ie: /p/ /f/ /θ/ /k/ /s/ /ʃ/ /tʃ/; it is pronounced /d/ after all other voiced sounds ie: /b/ /v/ /ð/ /g/ /z/ /ʒ/ /dʒ/ /l/ /n/ /m/ /ŋ/ /w/ /r/ and all vowel sounds (although this can be modified by doubling consonant sounds).

Point out that most of the common verbs are irregular (they already know *was/were*) and they should learn them as they meet them. For a start they could learn the list on SB page 84 (see also LD 155). Later you could ask them to learn the list on SB page 139, a few at a time.

Pronunciation If SS have difficulty distinguishing /d/ and /t/ you could do some work on minimal pairs containing these sounds (see TB page xxiv) eg *din−tin; pat−pad; drunk−trunk; water−warder* etc.

Exercise 145   Some time ago (LD A & B)

Answers: *See LDT*

Aim: Written practice of the past simple.

Teach the concept of *ago*:
T: *It's 12 o'clock on Wednesday.*
   I did it at 9 o'clock   S1: *3 hours ago*
   I did it on Monday   S2: *2 days ago*
   I did it last Wednesday   S3: *a week ago*

UNIT TEN

SS can write these sentences in the past tense for h/w. All the verbs are regular.

The LD also practises questions with the past simple. SS could write questions in the same way for h/w. Just as the present simple negative and question are formed with *do*, so they are formed in the past simple with *did* (the past tense of *do*):
He typed a letter.

He typed a letter. (with handwritten "Did" before and "?" after)	→	*Did he type a letter?*
He typed a letter. (with handwritten "did not")	→	*He did not (didn't) type a letter.*
Did he type a letter? (with handwritten "what" above "a letter")	→	*What did he type?*

Exercise 146 Late for work (LD)

Answers: *See LDT*

Aim: Story building in the past simple.

This exercise introduces a number of irregular verbs which SS should learn for h/w. If you pre-teach the vocabulary *church bell*, *knock*, *go off*, *put on* and *wake up* the SS can work out the story and the past tenses either in class or for h/w. When SS retell the story without looking at the notes, make sure they use the conjunctions *then*, *but*, *and*, *so*.
NB You can point out that *go off*, *put on* and *wake up* are called 'phrasal verbs' and that the prepositions give the verb a different meaning (*go off* has a different meaning from *go*). Since usage and word order only becomes problematic when the object is a pronoun, SS need not be bothered by this at present.

Exercise 147 Anne's day (LD A & B)

Answers: *See LDT*

Aim: Further practice of the past simple.

This exercise involves putting the whole of Exercises 46/47 into the past tense. (SS will not necessarily have a record of the time of each action, so you may need to check this, possibly by listening to Exercise 46 again). Refer SS to the list of irregular verbs on SB page 84 before they do the exercise in pairs. They can write a short passage in the past tense (like Exercise 47) for h/w.

Exercise 148 Who? (LD A & B)

Answers: *See LDT*

Aim: Question practice.

Explaining the difference between these two questions depends on the SS understanding the difference between the subject and the object of the verb. The subject is the person who 'does' the action and the object is the person or thing it is 'done to'. In the sentence *John saw Mary*, John is the subject and Mary is the object. If you want to ask about the subject of the verb you make the question like this:

/ ~~John~~ *Who* saw Mary. (?) Who saw Mary?

If you want to ask about the object:

√ John ~~saw~~ *Who did see* ~~Mary~~. (?) Who did John see?

NB Some Grammar books maintain that the correct form is *Whom did John see?* but this form is very rarely heard nowadays. SS can do the exercise in class or for h/w.

The LD also practises recognition of sentence stress. If SS are not using the LDs regularly, you might like to do these drills in class.

Exercise 149 A curriculum vitae

Answers:

CURRICULUM VITAE

(Please write in block capitals)

Surname: **WELDER**
First name(s): **LORRAINE**
D.o.b.: **18th APRIL 1963**
Marital status: **MARRIED**
Children: **TWO**

Address: **13 QUEEN'S CRESCENT**
LONDON SW1T 5JJ
Tel no: **081- 673 - 9201**

Education and further studies

Dates	Schools/colleges (names and addresses)	Qualifications
1974-9	YORK GRAMMAR SCHOOL, YORK	5 GCE O LEVELS
1979-80	PRESTON PARK 6TH FORM COLLEGE, PRESTON, LANCS.	
1980-1	LONGFORD SECRETARIAL COLLEGE, BRIGHTON	SECRETARIAL DIPLOMA

Experience

Dates	Place of work (with address)	job	pay
1981-2	CHAMBERS TRUCKS, 33 JEVINGTON ROAD, BRIGHTON, SUSSEX BR2 50B	SECRETARY TO THE MANAGER	£40 pw £2080 pa
1982-5	BUFFALO BOOKS, 29 BAKER ST, LONDON W1F 4AB	RECEPTIONIST	£5,600 - £8,200

Names and addresses of three referees

MS E SPINK, LONGFORD SECRETARIAL COLLEGE, BRIGHTON, SUSSEX BR9 HRD

MR J CHAMBERS, CHAMBERS TRUCKS, 33 JEVINGTON ROAD, BRIGHTON, SUSSEX BR9 50B

MRS MAYER, BUFFALO BOOKS, 29 BAKER STREET, LONDON N1F 4AB

UNIT TEN

Aim: Listening comprehension in a business format.

Curriculum vitae is a Latin phrase to describe the outline of your education and career. In the USA it is called a *résumé*.

SS (or you) can prepare copies of this CV form if you do not want them to write in their books. Ask SS what they think *Dob* (date of birth) *marital status* and *tel no* mean. Play the tape as many times as necessary for the SS to fill in the CV. Some of the addresses they need are at the bottom of the form. Stop them after they have written their first word to see if they have noticed the instruction to 'write in block capitals'. The salaries are rather low by today's standards, but they are representative of salaries for the years mentioned.

Exercise 150 An interview (LD)

Aim: Creative use of language and dialogue building.

SS can use the information in Lorraine's CV to complete this dialogue. The exercise can be done for h/w, but it is better done in pairs in class. SS then listen to SB cassette.
NB Please do not use the Drill Cassette for this exercise as dates do not match those in SB. (See also WB Exercises 46 and 47)

Exercise 151 Questions

Answers: *What is the salary? How long are the holidays? When can/do I start the job? Where is my office? Who is my boss? What time do I start work?* (Other questions may be possible.)

Aim: Question practice.

Check that the SS know that a *salary* is money expressed as a sum *pa* (*per annum*) but usually paid monthly (*wages* are usually paid weekly). They should be able to work out the questions quickly in pairs or for h/w. The questions might be useful in the roleplay in the next exercise.

Exercise 152 Roleplay

Aim: Fluency and creativity.

SS prepare their own CVs; younger SS might have to invent details. Each S decides which job s/he would like to apply for (either from the advertisements in SB Unit 7 or taking advertisements from the British press). In pairs, the 'interviewer' is given a copy of the interviewee's CV and the job advertisement and carries out an interview acting as a personnel manager or a senior member of the firm. You could also have SS in groups of three or four, where each interviewee is interviewed by a panel. When the first interview is complete, discuss with the SS how they felt about the interviews. Could they do it better? Do they need any more language? Supply extra words or phrases if necessary, but encourage SS to experiment with

JOB APPLICATIONS

Exercise 153 Letter of application

Answers: *1 saw 2 like 3 apply 4 enclose 5 see 6 worked 7 had 8 use 9 can 10 gave 11 left 12 growing 13 would 14 go 15 look 16 hearing*

Aim: Verb recognition in a business context.

Do not pre-teach any of the verbs. SS should be able to work out which goes where by recognising a combination of meaning and grammatical form. The exercise can be done in pairs in class or for h/w. When SS have done the exercise, elicit the meaning of *to apply for*. Link it with the noun *an application*.

Exercise 154 Writing a letter

Aim: Creative writing in a controlled business context.

For revision SS could also write a letter of reference for Lorraine Welder based on the letter and facts in Unit 7.

Exercise 155 Hidden word puzzle (LD)

Answers: *1 applied 2 hear 3 see 4 put on 5 go off 6 waited 7 left 8 knocked 9 sold 10 wake up*
Hidden words: *past tense*

The LD practises the past tense of the irregular verbs in this unit (see list on SB page 84).

Additional activity

Past tense verb game For further practice of irregular past tenses.

Sit in groups of 5 to 7 people. Each S secretly writes down any eight of the irregular verbs on SB page 84 on a piece of paper in the past tense. Each S gives his/her piece of paper to the S on his/her left so that each S now has a new set of verbs. S1 says one of the verbs on his/her paper and crosses it off. Any other S who has the same verb can also cross it off. The SS say one verb each in turn, crossing off the verbs that are said, until someone crosses off his/her last verb. That person then shouts 'Finished' and is the winner.
NB If a S makes a mistake with one of the past tenses, no-one can cross that verb off.

If you play the game at a later date, you can add to the list of irregular verbs any verbs that the SS know.

Verb Bingo by Nina Hajnal (Longman) also practises past tense forms.

UNIT TEN

LANGUAGE DRILLS TAPESCRIPT

Drill 144 Say the past tense of these regular verbs, like this:

P: Look
R: *Looked* /t/

Now you try. The verbs are all regular. Be careful about the pronunciation of the final '*d*'.

P: Move
R: *Moved* /d/
P: Wait
R: *Waited* /ɪd/
P: Visit
R: *Visited* /ɪd/
P: Work
R: *Worked* /t/
P: Order
R: *Ordered* /d/
P: Stop
R: *Stopped* /t/
P: Walk
R: *Walked* /t/
P: Wash
R: *Washed* /t/
P: Photocopy
R: *Photocopied* /d/*

P: End
R: *Ended* /ɪd/
P: Type
R: *Typed* /t/
P: File
R: *Filed* /d/
P: Open
R: *Opened* /d/
P: Start
R: *Started* /ɪd/
P: Stay
R: *Stayed* /d/

* Although the final sound is (ɪd), the /ɪ/ is part of the verb stem.

Aim: Practice of regular past tenses and pronunciation of final -*d*.

Drill 145A Turn these sentences into questions using the given question word, like this:

P: I wanted the stationery last Friday. When
R: *When did you want the stationery?*

Now you try.
P: Peter worked for BOS in 1979. When
R: *When did Peter work for BOS?*
P: He stopped work in January. Why
R: *Why did he stop work in January?*
P: I answered the telex at ten o'clock. What time
R: *What time did you answer the telex?*
P: They travelled to Scotland last Monday. When
R: *When did they travel to Scotland?*

P: Simon opened the mail at ten o'clock. Who
R: *Who opened the mail at ten o'clock?*
P: Mr Passas visited BOS in October. Who
R: *Who visited BOS in October?*
P: Simon posted the letter on Tuesday. What
R: *What did Simon post on Tuesday?*

JOB APPLICATIONS

Aim: Question practice in the simple past (SS can do this drill with their books closed).
NB   The date in SB (Question 2) is different.

Drill 145B   Talk about how long ago people did things, like this:

P: I want the stationery. A week
R: *I wanted the stationery a week ago.*

Now you try. Remember the sentences are in the past tense.

P: Peter works for BOS. Two years
R: *Peter worked for BOS two years ago.*
P: I'm answering the telex. Five minutes
R: *I answered the telex five minutes ago.*
P: Simon's opening the mail. An hour
R: *Simon opened the mail an hour ago.*

P: Mr Passas is visiting BOS. Three months
R: *Mr Passas visited BOS three months ago.*
P: Simon is posting the letter. Two days
R: *Simon posted the letter two days ago.*

Aim: Practice of past simple with *ago* (SS can do this drill with their books closed).

Drill 146   Do Exercise 146 before you do this drill. Look at the pictures and tell the story, like this:

P: Picture 1
R: *One morning Fred McLean's alarm clock didn't go off.*

Now you try.
P: Picture 2
R: *He woke up at eleven o'clock.*
P: Picture 3
R: *He put on his clothes and ran out of the house.*
P: Picture 4
R: *He went to the bus stop and waited for a bus, but the bus didn't come.*
P: Picture 5
R: *He saw a taxi, but there was someone in it.*

P: Picture 6
R: *So he ran to work.*
P: Picture 7
R: *He knocked on the door, but no-one was there.*
P: Picture 8
R: *Then he heard the church bell. It was Sunday.*

Aim: Story telling practice.

UNIT TEN

Drill 147A

Look at the pictures showing Joy's routine in Exercise 46. Anne does the same things as Joy did. Answer these questions about what Anne did last Wednesday with short answers, like this:

P: Picture 2 Did Anne start work at nine thirty?
R: *Yes she did.*

P: Picture 6 Did she do the filing first?
R: *No she didn't.*

Now you try.
P: Picture 2 Did Anne start work at eight thirty?
R: *No she didn't.*
P: Picture 6 Did she open the post first?
R: *Yes she did.*
P: Picture 7 Did Anne take shorthand next?
R: *Yes she did.*
P: Picture 1 Did she make coffee at ten o'clock?
R: *No she didn't.*
P: Picture 10 Did she have lunch next?
R: *No she didn't.*

P: Picture 8 Did she have lunch at about one thirty?
R: *Yes she did.*
P: Picture 4 Did she send telexes in the morning?
R: *No she didn't.*
P: Picture 9 Did she make tea at four o'clock?
R: *Yes she did.*
P: Picture 3 Did she do the filing before tea?
R: *No she didn't.*
P: Picture 5 Did she go home at five thirty?
R: *Yes she did.*

Aim: Comprehension; practice of short answers in the simple past.
NB The examples are not repeated in this drill.

Drill 147B

Look at the pictures showing Joy's routine in Exercise 46. Anne does the same things as Joy did. Answer these questions about what Anne did last Wednesday, like this:

P: Picture 2 What did Anne do at nine thirty?
R: *She started work.*

Now you try.
P: Picture 6 What did Anne do first?
R: *She opened the post.*
P: Picture 7 What did Anne do next?
R: *She took shorthand.*
P: Picture 1 What did she do at eleven o'clock?
R: *She made coffee.*
P: Picture 10 What did she do next?
R: *She typed letters.*
P: Picture 8 What did she do at about one thirty?
R: *She had lunch.*

P: Picture 4 What did she do in the afternoon?
R: *She sent telexes.*
P: Picture 9 What did she do at four o'clock?
R: *She made tea.*
P: Picture 3 What did she do after tea?
R: *She did the filing.*
P: Picture 5 What did she do at five thirty?
R: *She went home.*

Aim: Practice of simple past.

JOB APPLICATIONS

Drill 148A Make questions from these sentences using the question word *'who'*. Ask the question about the person who is named with a stressed intonation, like this:

P: *John* saw Mary.
R: *Who saw Mary?*
P: John saw *Mary*.
R: *Who did John see?*

Now you try.
P: *Sheila* phoned Fred at ten o'clock.
R: *Who phoned Fred at ten o'clock?*
P: *Simon* went to the bank on Wednesday.
R: *Who went to the bank on Wednesday?*
P: Simon asked *Joy*.
R: *Who did Simon ask?*

P: *Joy* asked Simon.
R: *Who asked Simon?*
P: *The accountant* wrote the report.
R: *Who wrote the report?*
P: They liked *Helen*.
R: *Who did they like?*

Aim: Recognition of sentence stress; practice of questions with *who* (SS can do this drill with their books closed).

Drill 148B Answer these questions using the sentences in Exercise 148. Stress one word in the sentence according to the question you're asked, like this:

P: Who saw Mary?
R: John *saw Mary*.
P: Who did John see?
R: *John* saw Mary.

Now you try.
P: Who phoned Fred at ten o'clock?
R: Sheila *phoned Fred at ten o'clock*.
P: Who went to the bank on Wednesday?
R: Simon *went to the bank on Wednesday*.
P: Who did Simon ask?
R: *Simon asked* Joy.

P: Who asked Simon?
R: Joy *asked Simon*.
P: Who wrote the report?
R: The accountant *wrote the report*.
P: Who did they like?
R: *They liked* Helen.

Aim: Practice of sentence stress.

Drill 150 Unfortunately we have been unable to rerecord the Drill cassettes in updating this course. Please do not use Drill 150 as the dates do not reflect those in SB.

UNIT TEN

Drill 155 Say the past tense of these irregular verbs, like this:
P: Do
R: *Did*

Now you try.
P: Go
R: *Went*
P: Have
R: *Had*
P: Read /ri:d/
R: *Read* /red/
P: Make
R: *Made*
P: See
R: *Saw*
P: Wake
R: *Woke*
P: Run
R: *Ran*
P: Leave
R: *Left*
P: Give
R: *Gave*

P: Hear
R: *Heard* /hɜ:rd/
P: Come
R: *Came*
P: Put
R: *Put*
P: Send
R: *Sent*
P: Sell
R: *Sold*
P: Take
R: *Took*

Aim: Practice of some common irregular past tenses in this unit.

WORKBOOK ANSWERS

Exercise 43   Odd-man-out

2 *German* (It does not end -*ish*)   3 *has* (It is not part of the verb *to be*)   4 *typed* (The final *d* is pronounced /t/ and not /d/)   5 *catalogue* (It is the only count noun)   6 *read* (It is the only irregular verb)   7 *ago* (It is not used with the present tense)   8 *twenty-three* (The ordinal number is not made by adding *-th*)   9 *May* (The name of the month is complete)   10 *Sun* (It is part of the weekend. It is not a weekday) You may find reasons for other words being the odd-man-out which are as acceptable as the suggestions above. This exercise is to alert SS to look for patterns within the language which might aid their memories.

Exercise 44   They're/their/there

1 *their*   2 *They're*   3 *there*   4 *They're – there*   5 *There*   6 *their* A further exercise in the series to differentiate between structures and phrases SS might confuse (see TB page 109).

Exercise 45   Categories puzzle

1 *calculator*   2 *furniture*   3 *chair*   4 *photocopier*   5 *pencil*   6 *ruler*   7 *stationery*   8 *equipment*   9 *desk* See WB Exercise 34 which is also to do with categories of words. You

JOB APPLICATIONS

might discuss with SS any other 'category' words they can think of (eg machinery, jobs, clothing, etc), and words which fit into those categories as a way of practising and/or enlarging their vocabulary.

Exercise 46   Curriculum vitae

1 Anne Lesley Bell   2 1 October 1960   3 No. She is single. 4 She lives at 42 Montreal Drive, Stubbington, Hants. 5 Fareham Comprehensive School in Fareham, Hants. (NB Hants is the abbreviation for Hampshire) *6 5 GCE O levels and one GCE A level (in English)   7 Star Secretarial College, Queens Road, London SW1 ORD.   8 Yes. A secretarial diploma.   9 Typing: 40 words per minute. Shorthand: 120 words per minute.   10 She worked at/for the Commercial Bank in Fareham, Hants.*

Exercise 47   Experience

Sample paragraph about Anne's life and experience (variations are possible):

Anne Lesley Bell is single and she lives in Montreal Drive in Stubbington, Hants. Her date of birth is 1st October 1960. (or *She is...years old.* NB Her age will vary according to the year in which you are using this book). *She went to Fareham Comprehensive School from 1972 to 1979 and she got five GCE O levels and one GCE A level. The A level was in English. From 1979 to 1980 she went to (the) Star Secretarial College in London and she got a secretarial diploma. Her secretarial speeds were 40 wpm for typing and 120 wpm for shorthand. From 1980 until 1987, Anne worked at the Commercial Bank in Fareham as a clerical assistant: From 1987 until she joined BOS, she worked at the same bank as a department secretary.*

CONSOLIDATION UNIT B
YOUR NEWS AND NEWS EXTRACTS

TEACHING NOTES

In this unit the listening exercises are done after the exercises on the written articles so that SS have had some exposure to the new vocabulary before they hear it.

See notes on consolidation units on TB page xii.

Exercise 156   The USA

Sample questions (other questions are possible): *1 What is the capital of the USA?   2 How many states are there in the USA?   3 When did Leif Ericsson discover America?   4 Who rediscovered America in 1492?   5 Which colony did Sir Walter Raleigh start?/What was the (name of the) first British Colony in America?   6 When did the American Revolution start?   7 When is Independence Day?   8 Who was the first president of the US?*

Aim: Reading comprehension and question practice.

Despite some new vocabulary in this article, SS should be able to write questions for the answers on their own. The exercise can be done in class in pairs, under test conditions or for h/w. Allow SS to use their dictionaries (preferably English-English) if necessary.

Exercise 157   Hidden word puzzle

Answers: *1 wages   2 factory   3 rise   4 strike   5 conditions   6 increasing   7 management*
Hidden word: *working*

Aim: To deduce the meaning of words from context.

No preparation necessary. The answer to number 6 (increasing) is in a different tense to the verb in the article.

Exercise 158   Raise/rise; found/find

Answers: *1 founded   2 found   3 raised   4 rises   5 raise   6 find   7 found   8 rose*

Aim: To differentiate between similar transitive and intransitive verbs. You could introduce these verbs and give some examples before the SS do the exercise: *We* found *companies and new colonies, but we* find *things that were lost. Prices and wages* rise, *but we* raise *prices and wages.*
NB   *To raise* is a transitive verb (it has to have an object); *to rise* is an intransitive verb (it cannot have an object).

Exercise 159   Financial Times Index

Suggested description of the FT Index (other descriptions are possible): *The index went down slightly at lunchtime on Tuesday to 476 and then rose sharply by 2 points to 478. On Wednesday the*

CONSOLIDATION UNIT B

index rose to 479. On Thursday the index dropped sharply at lunch-time to 476, but then went up by 1.5 points to 477.5. On Friday the index fell slightly again. It closed at 476.5.

Aim: Writing practice on a business topic.

SS could prepare this exercise orally in pairs after you have set the pattern: S1: *What happened on Monday?* S2: *The index closed at 476.5.*
* said: *four seven six point five.*

The *Financial Times* is a British newspaper which publishes the London Stock Exchange share prices in its index.

Exercise 160 A graph

Answer:

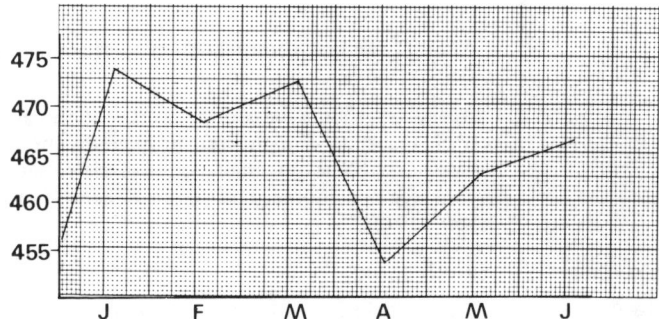

Aim: Aural recognition of numbers and the ability to express these in visual form.

SS can prepare a blank graph in their books before they do this exercise. They can take down the figures in note form as a number dictation from the tape and fill in the graph afterwards.

Exercise 161 Radio news

Answers: *1 True 2 False. The oil producing countries (OPEC) are discussing oil prices and this affects the industrial countries. 3 True 4 False. The workers at Jones Brothers Engineering Works are on strike. 5 True 6 True 7 False. It fell slightly in February. 8 True*

Aim: Listening comprehension.

Pre-teach the words *bomb, scare* and *go off* (meaning 'explode' – cf Fred's alarm clock *went off* in Unit 10). See if SS remember *on strike* from Exercise 157. The Minimum Lending Rate (MLR) used to be called the bank rate. It is 'the advertised minimum rate at which the Bank of England will discount

CONSOLIDATION UNIT B

approved bills of exchange'. In practical terms it is the rate on which all interest rates are based, so the man in the street pays interest on loans (ie borrows money) at slightly more than the MLR, and receives interest on savings in banks etc at slightly less than the MLR.

The exercise can be done with the SS working together or independently. SS should be able to work out the correct answers without any more pre-teaching. The questions help the SS understand the aural text. You may have to move backwards and forwards on the cassette, so it is a good idea to make a note of the counter numbers on the cassette player.

Exercise 162 News comprehension

Answers: *1-b 2-c 3-b 4-d* (this is a matter of opinion; some people may think the answer is 'c'); *5-c 6-d 7-d 8-a* (there was only a bomb *scare*).

Aim: Listening comprehension (perhaps leading to discussion).

Again, SS should be able to work out the answers on their own. Question 4 might lead to some disagreement, in which case allow SS to put their points of view, encourage them to convince one another and accept either (c) or (d) as the correct answer.

Exercise 163 Bomb scare

Aim: Creative writing from an aural stimulus.

Ask SS why the story was interrupted (there was a fault on the radio). Each version of the story will be different. A possible explanation (since this was a bomb scare and not an explosion) was that someone thought the sandwich-box was a bomb and called the police. Discuss possible scenarios before SS write this exercise. SS are free to write whatever they want, but sentences describing a story in the past should be in the past simple tense.

SS are free to write whatever they want, but sentences describing a story in the past should be in the past simple tense.

Exercise 164 Traffic news

Answers: *1-B   2-E   3 Egyptian Street   4 Motorists should turn left at the roundabout in Italian Grove and use Holland Road and German Avenue.*

Aim: Listening comprehension and deducing words from context.

Let SS listen to this section of the tape as often as necessary. Only offer help if SS ask for it. The exercise revises some countries and nationalities in the names of the streets, so now would be a good time to extend this revision if necessary. (See also 'prize puzzle' on the next page.)

CONSOLIDATION UNIT B

Exercise 165 Newspaper project

This is an optional class project, but one which is usually very popular. Go through the suggestions in the SB, preferably while looking through some real (preferably British or American) newspapers, eliciting the meaning of the words from the SS.

Decide which of these things you all want to include and make sure everyone has something to do (people can work together on projects). Allow SS to make as many decisions as possible, but allocate jobs and responsibilities if they take too much time. Encourage SS to work out of class time, but have a strict deadline (eg a week) by which time all 'copy' must be handed in, neatly presented for 'publication'. Either assemble the material on the wall or make up a newspaper by sticking the material to large pieces of paper. If you are going to photocopy the result make sure everyone writes in black ink.

Additional activity

You could prepare a newspaper quiz (see Exercise 239 and TB page 182).

Prize puzzle Answer: *The Italian company* (The Japanese company produces cars and trades with Britain.) The German company produces machinery and trades with Brazil. The Italian company produces chemicals and trades with France.)

Aim: Further revision of countries, nationalities and the present simple.

The exercise uses vocabulary introduced in the consolidation units. Check that SS know the meaning of the words. The exercise can either be done as a reading comprehension or you could do it as a problem-solving information-gap exercise (see TB page 104). NB The competition is out of date. Please do not send in any entries!

There are no language drills for the Consolidation Units.

WORKBOOK ANSWERS – TEST B

Allow students a maximum of half an hour to do this test.

Part one Structure formation

1 You should go ~~to~~ home. 2 He (did) not drive to work yesterday. 3 Let's ~~to~~ go ~~to~~ the theatre. 4 Did you (do) the filing? 5 It took twelve and (a) half per cent of the time.

Mark this section out of 5. Give one mark for each correct answer.

CONSOLIDATION UNIT B

Part two Dates

1 The thirteenth of November (or November the thirteenth), nineteen eighty-two. 2 The twenty-third of February (or February the twenty-third), nineteen sixty-four. 3 The thirty-first of July (or July the thirty-first), eighteen eighteen. 4 The twenty-second of December (or December the twenty-second), nineteen ninety-five. 5 The thirtieth of May (or May the thirtieth), nineteen seventy-three. Give two marks for each correct answer. Subtract half a mark for each word which is wrong, up to a maximum of two marks for each sentence.

Part three Short answers

1 Yes I do. 2 No I can't/cannot. 3 No I'm not/am not. 4 Yes he is. 5 No they aren't/they're not/they are not. Give one mark for each correct answer.

Part four Question formation

1 Who does not like typing? 2 Would you like a sandwich? 3 Can Mary type? 4 Who gave it to Fred? 5 When is she meeting him for lunch?

Mark this section out of 10. Give two marks for each correct answer but subtract half a mark for each mistake up to a maximum of 2 marks per sentence.

Part five Prepositions (with expressions of time)

1 on 2 in 3 at 4 in 5 in

Give one mark for each correct answer.

Part six Tenses

1–b 2–b 3–c 4–b 5–c

Give one mark for each correct answer.

This test is marked out of forty. You can convert the totals to a percentage by multiplying the totals by 4/10 (or 2/5).

UNIT ELEVEN
A MEETING

11

Business content:	Job experience; letters of enquiry; interviews
Structures:	Present perfect tense
	Adverbs used with the present perfect
	Could/would you...?
	Will future
	Possessive pronouns
	Capital letters and punctuation
	Question words: *Whose? Who's?*
Function:	Polite requests

TEACHING NOTES

Exercise 166 Comprehension

Answers: *1 The accountant's report/Peter's report   2 About saving money   3 He has seen the bank manager about borrowing some more money.   4 Peter*

SS can do this exercise as an introduction to the unit, but you might prefer to wait until you have presented the present perfect tense.

To introduce polite requests and 'will'

Elicit the *Can you?* form for polite requests and ask SS to suggest several sentences they could use for polite requests eg *Can you open/close the door please?... clean the board... stand up... sit down* etc. Teach the *Could you/Would you* forms which are more polite than *Can you* and practise the same sentences (and perhaps make up others).
NB *Will you do something?* can also be used as a polite request, but it is better not to confuse SS with this at present as *will* is introduced as having a different function in this unit.

Ask SS to ask you to do things, to which you reply using the *will* future before you do the action, eg *Certainly. I'll stand up at once.* (Remember to stand up or the words lose their meaning.) Point out that *at once* means *immediately* (now) and that *I'll* is short for *I will*. NB Some grammars still say that the first person of *will* is *shall*, but the distinction is blurred in everyday speech.

Ask SS to do things, to which they respond with sentences using *will* before they do the actions. They might also enjoy refusing to do actions using *No I won't* even though (or perhaps because) this would be considered very rude in England. NB *Will* is an auxiliary verb.

131

UNIT ELEVEN

Pronunciation You could contrast the pronunciation of *won't* /wəʊny/ with *want* /wɒnt/ as a minimal pair (see TB page xxiv). Other minimal pairs contrasting the same sounds are *own-on*, *coat-cot*.

Exercise 167   Polite requests (LD A, B & C)

Answers: *See LDT*

Aim: To practise polite requests and the *will* future.

SS can do this exercise orally in pairs and they can also write some of the sentences for h/w.

To introduce the present perfect tense

Illustrate on the board four things to do in an office using regular verbs, eg:

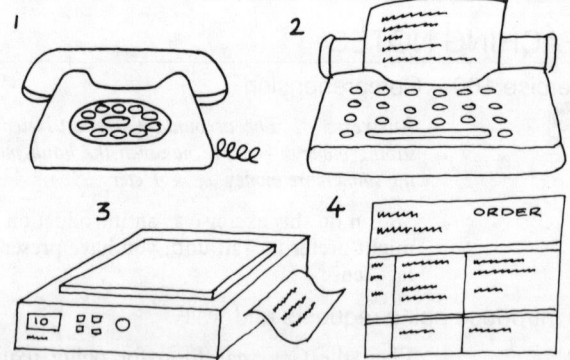

1 Phone Mr Middle   2 Type the letter   3 Photocopy the memo   4 Order the stationery

Practise this vocabulary by getting the SS to ask you politely to do these things: *Could you phone Mr Middle please?*

As the SS ask you to do things, mime the actions so that it is clear they have all been done satisfactorily and that they are now actions in the past. Then get the SS to ask you to do them again, to which you reply: *I've phoned Mr Middle.* Ask the SS to mime the four actions and then elicit from them the form of the regular present perfect tense (it is the same as the regular past tense). When the SS have practised the four verbs, write the sentences on the board in the present perfect and highlight the grammatical form. Ask them to say the sentences beginning: *Simon...* to make sure they recognise the verb *have* which becomes *has* in the third person singular. Emphasise that the action is in the past, but that it is relevant to the present (there is no reason for you to do the action again *now*; it has already been done). The action itself is more important than the time it took place (in contrast to the simple

A MEETING

past tense when the time the action took place is important). Introduce the two adverbs *just* and *already* and practise saying them in the sentences.

If your SS are false beginners, they may have met other uses of the present perfect before. The present perfect is one that many foreigners find difficult, so the use introduced in this book is the easiest to comprehend to start with.

Exercise 168   Action taken (LD A & B)

Answers: *See LDT*

Aim: To practise the present perfect tense.

Pre-teach the irregular past participles *sent, written, given* and *done* (SS could also start learning the irregular past participles from the list on SB page 139). Some of the sentences could be written for h/w.

Exercise 169   Things to do (LD)

Answers: *See LDT*

Aim: To practise the present perfect negative.

Elicit from the SS how to make the question and negative form of the present perfect before they do this exercise:

I have phoned Mr Smith.

I have/phoned Mr Smith. (not ... yet) → *I have not (haven't) phoned Mr Smith yet.*

He has phoned Mr Smith.

✓*He (has) phoned Mr Smith* (yet?) → *Has he phoned Mr Smith yet?*

Have here is an auxiliary verb and the short answer is *Yes he has/No he hasn't*. (Contrast its use as a main verb meaning *has got*, see TB page 50).

I'm afraid means *I'm sorry*. The function Helen is expressing is apology.

SS can write some questions and negative sentences from Helen's list for h/w after they have done the exercise orally in class.

Exercise 170   A meeting (LD)

Answers: *See LDT*

Aim: To revise the past simple and contrast it with the present perfect.

Practise these sentences in the past simple to familiarise SS with the vocabulary. Make sure SS understand *a branch* (a

UNIT ELEVEN

division of a company, eg *BOS Ltd has branches in various towns throughout Britain*), *a pension scheme* (the employees and the company save regularly to provide the workers with a regular sum of money, *a pension*, when they retire), *employees* (this can be stressed ooO or oOo) *a record number* (the greatest number ever) and *a charity* (a society which helps people in need). Stress again that Fred uses the past simple because he is interested in *when* these things happened, but the people who express interest using the present perfect are more interested in *what* happened and the effect on the company now.

SS can write the sentences in the past simple and present perfect for h/w.

Exercise 171 Questions (LD)

Answers: *See LDT*

Aim: Fluency and further practice of the present perfect.

This exercise is quite demanding in that it practises two structures at the same time, but the prompt has already been practised in the previous exercise. (See also WB Exercise 50)

Exercise 172 Word puzzle

Answers: *1 already   2 yet   3 just   4 since   5 never   6 ever   7 before*

Aim: To draw SS' attention to adverbs which are frequently used with the present perfect.

SS can find examples of all these adverbs in the language notes on SB page 96. It is not important to learn them all at present.

Exercise 173 Work experience

Answers:

take shorthand	✓	work a switchboard	✓
take the minutes at a meeting	✗	type reports	✗
use a photocopier	✓	order stationery	✓
send a telex	✗	keep a petty cash book	✗

Aim: Listening comprehension.

SS have only to understand enough of the tape to complete the table although they will probably understand most of the conversation. Play the tape as often as you think necessary.

Exercise 174 Talking about experience (LD A & B)

Answers: *See LDT*

Aim: To practise the question form and short answers of the present perfect.

A MEETING

After doing the exercise orally, SS could write the eight questions for h/w.

Exercise 175 Roleplay

Aim: Fluency and creative use of the present perfect.

See the notes on roleplay on TB page xxvi.

Give SS time to think of the experience the jobs require before you start the roleplay. Encourage SS to talk about their past experience and how that makes them suitable for the job, rather than talking about their plans for the future.

Although these examples seem unlikely (and this might add some amusement to the exercise), they are not impossible. A British company has exported wholewheat spaghetti to Italy and another company has sold sand to Abu Dhabi (the grains of sand were a special shape for filtering water).

Possessive pronouns

SS can learn the list of possessive pronouns from SB page 96 for h/w. To practise them in class, send three SS out of the room and collect one item belonging to each SS remaining in the class. Put all the objects on your desk and call the three SS back in. They have to decide who the objects belong to and try to give them back, saying *Is this/Are these yours?* If they are wrong, the S replies: *It's not mine/ours. I think it's his/hers/theirs.*

Exercise 176 Whose? (LD)

Answers: *See LDT*

Aim: To practise possessive pronouns.

Pre-teach *stapler* and *rubber bands*. SS can do the exercise orally in pairs and write the sentences for h/w. (See also WB Exercise 49)

Exercise 177 Who's/whose?

Answers: *1 Who's (who is)   2 Whose   3 Who's (who is)   4 Who's (who has)   5 Whose   6 Who's (who has)*

Aim: To differentiate between two similar and confusing forms.

This exercise continues the series of exercises which differentiate between similar words and structures SS might confuse (see TB page 109).

Exercise 178 Punctuation

Answers: (see page 136)

Aim: Listening comprehension; practice of prepositions; to teach the names of punctuation marks.

UNIT ELEVEN

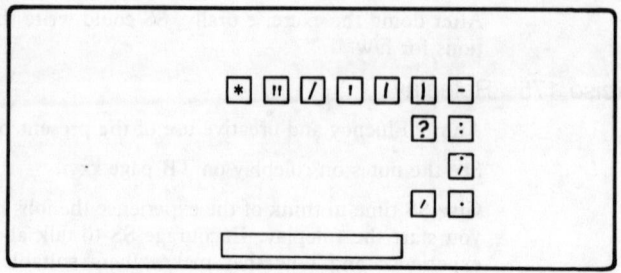

Although SS' attention has been drawn to punctuation throughout the book and they have been expected to use it correctly, the names are introduced here for ease of reference.

Pre-teach the word *key*. Play the tape as many times as necessary for SS to determine the positions of the marks on the keyboard. There is a note on the use of punctuation marks on SB page 97. (See also WB Exercise 51)

Exercise 179 Capital letters

Answers: *John – Atlantic Ocean – I – Mr Spencer – Italian – Monday – BOS Ltd – Milgrom & Co – Egypt – Mount Everest – River Thames – Paris – December – English*

Aim: To highlight the rules of capitalisation.

Just as with punctuation, SS have been expected to use capital letters correctly. They should do this exercise without preparation to see whether they really know which words are capitalised and which are not. Discuss the rules with them afterwards. There is a note on the use of capital letters on SB page 97.

Exercise 180 Dictation

Answer: (see page 137)

Aim: A guided dictation in a business context.

SS need only write down the words from the tape. They can write out the letter with the correct format, address etc afterwards (possibly for h/w). Some of the vocabulary is provided in the form of notes. (See also WB Exercise 52)

Exercise 181 Letters of enquiry

Answers:
1 *I have heard about your typewriters from the Commercial Attaché at the British Embassy. I would be grateful if you would send me more information about them.*

UNIT ELEVEN

BAY HOUSE COLLEGE

19 Ingleborough Road
Birkenhead
Cheshire L42 6RD

Brighter Office Supplies Ltd   25 November 1992
13 Mill Street
Harlow
Essex CM20 2JR

Our ref: OH/JL

Dear Sirs

I have seen your advertisement for office equipment in
the Evening Star.

I would be grateful if you would send me a full
catalogue and price list.

I look forward to hearing from you.

Yours faithfully

Oliver Howard

Mr Oliver Howard
Principal

2 *I have talked to your representative about your equipment. I would be grateful if you would send me your brochure showing your range of desks.*

3 *I have seen your publicity material about your range of stationery. I would be grateful if you would send your representative to visit us.*

Aim: To teach some of the conventional phrases of business letters.

This is a written exercise which can be done for h/w. SS need only write the body of the letter unless they particularly need practice in laying out letters with the correct format. SS do not have to learn all the vocabulary in this exercise but they should learn the standard terminology (and possibly use it to write to companies in Britain to ask for brochures etc).

LANGUAGE DRILLS TAPESCRIPT

Drill 167A   Ask Helen to do things, like this:

P: Phone Mr Smith
R: *Could you phone Mr Smith please?*

UNIT ELEVEN

Now you try.
P: Send the telex to New York
R: *Could you send the telex to New York please?*
P: Write to Paul Sawyers
R: *Could you write to Paul Sawyers please?*
P: Photocopy the report
R: *Could you photocopy the report please?*
P: Type the letters
R: *Could you type the letters please?*

Aim: Practice of polite requests (SS can do this drill with their books closed).

Drill 167B

Ask Helen to do things, like this:

P: Phone Mr Smith
R: *Would you phone Mr Smith please?*

Now you try.
P: Give the memo to Sheila
R: *Would you give the memo to Sheila please?*
P: Ask Miss Matthews to come in
R: *Would you ask Miss Matthews to come in please?*
P: Make some coffee
R: *Would you make some coffee please?*

Aim: Practice of polite requests (SS Can do this drill with their books closed).

Drill 167C

Answer as Helen does when Mr Spencer asks her to do things, like this:

P: Could you phone Mr Smith please?
R: *Certainly. I'll phone him at once.*

Now you try.
P: Would you send the telex to New York please?
R: *Certainly. I'll send it at once.*
P: Could you write to Paul Sawyers please?
R: *Certainly. I'll write to him at once.*
P: Would you photocopy the report please?
R: *Certainly. I'll photocopy it at once.*
P: Could you type the letters please?
R: *Certainly. I'll type them at once.*
P: Would you give this memo to Sheila please?
R: *Certainly. I'll give it to her at once.*
P: Could you do the filing please?
R: *Certainly. I'll do it at once.*
P: Would you ask Miss Matthews to come in please?
R: *Certainly. I'll ask her to come in at once.*

Aim: Practice of *will* future and pronouns (SS can do this drill with their books closed).

A MEETING

Drill 168A Reply as Mary does when Fred asks her to do things, like this:

P: Could you phone Mr Smith please?
R: *I've already phoned him.*

Now you try.
P: Would you send this telex to New York please?
R: *I've already sent it.*
P: Could you write to Paul Sawyers please?
R: *I've already written to him.*

P: Would you photocopy the report please?
R: *I've already photocopied it.*
P: Could you type the letters please?
R: *I've already typed them.*

Aim: Practice of present perfect with *already* (SS can do this drill with their books closed).

Drill 168B Reply as Mary does when Fred asks her to do things, like this:

P: Could you phone Mr Smith please?
R: *I've just phoned him.*

Now you try.
P: Would you give the memo to Sheila please?
R: *I've just given it to her.*
P: Could you do the filing please?
R: *I've just done it.*

P: Would you make some coffee please?
R: *I've just made it.*
P: Could you ask Miss Matthews to wait please?
R: *I've just asked her.*

Aim: Practice of present perfect with *just* (SS can do this drill with their books closed).

Drill 169 Helen hasn't done any of the things on her list. Make sentences like this:

P: Phone Mr Smith
R: *I'm afraid I haven't phoned Mr Smith yet.*

Now you try.
P: Send the telex to New York
R: *I'm afraid I haven't sent the telex to New York yet.*
P: Write to Paul Sawyers
R: *I'm afraid I haven't written to Paul Sawyers yet.*
P: Photocopy the report
R: *I'm afraid I haven't photocopied the report yet.*
P: Type the letters
R: *I'm afraid I haven't typed the letters yet.*

P: Give the memo to Sheila
R: *I'm afraid I haven't given the memo to Sheila yet.*
P: Do the filing
R: *I'm afraid I haven't done the filing yet.*
P: Make the coffee
R: *I'm afraid I haven't made the coffee yet.*

Aim: Practice of negative sentences in the present perfect with *yet* in the context of an apology (SS can do this drill with their books closed).

UNIT ELEVEN

Drill 170 Comment on these statements, like this:

P: Last May we opened a branch in Liverpool.
R: *Oh, so we've opened a branch in Liverpool.*

Now you try.

P: Two years ago we started a pension scheme for the employees.
R: *Oh, so we've started a pension scheme for the employees.*
P: We sold a record number of desks in 1978.
R: *Oh, so we've sold a record number of desks.*
P: We hired fifty more employees in January.
R: *Oh, so we've hired fifty more employees.*

P: In 1979 we raised our prices by seven per cent.
R: *Oh, so we've raised our prices by seven per cent.*
P: We gave three thousand pounds to charity last year.
R: *Oh, so we've given three thousand pounds to charity.*
P: We increased sales by ten per cent in 1980.
R: *Oh, so we've increased sales by ten per cent.*

Aim: Practice of present perfect (SS can do this drill with their books closed).
NB The dates are different in the updated SB.

Drill 171 Question Fred about the things he said in his speech, like this:

P: We opened a branch in Liverpool.
R: *You say we've opened a branch in Liverpool. Could you tell us when exactly?*

Now you try.

P: We started a pension scheme for the employees.
R: *You say we've started a pension scheme for the employees. Could you tell us when exactly?*
P: We sold a record number of desks.
R: *You say we've sold a record number of desks. Could you tell us when exactly?*
P: We hired fifty more employees.
R: *You say we've hired fifty more employees. Could you tell us when exactly?*

P: We raised our prices by seven per cent.
R: *You say we've raised our prices by seven per cent. Could you tell us when exactly?*
P: We gave three thousand pounds to charity.
R: *You say we've given three thousand pounds to charity. Could you tell us when exactly?*

Aim: Fluency practice with the present perfect (SS can do this drill with their books closed).

Drill 174A Howard asked Anne about her secretarial experience when she applied for a job with BOS. Ask questions like this:

A MEETING

P: Take shorthand
R: *Have you taken shorthand before?*

Now you try.
P: Take the minutes at a meeting
R: *Have you taken the minutes at a meeting before?*
P: Use a photocopier
R: *Have you used a photocopier before?*
P: Send a telex
R: *Have you sent a telex before?*
P: Work a switchboard
R: *Have you worked a switchboard before?*
P: Type reports
R: *Have you typed reports before?*
P: Order stationery
R: *Have you ordered stationery before?*
P: Keep a petty cash book
R: *Have you kept a petty cash book before?*

Aim: Practtice of short answers with the present perfect.
do this drill with their books closed).

Drill 174B Do Exercise 173 before you do this drill. Look at the work experience card you have filled in. Answer Howard's questions with short answers, as Anne does:

P: Have you taken shorthand before?
R: *Yes I have.*

Now you try.
P: Have you used a photocopier before?
R: *Yes I have.*
P: Have you sent a telex before?
R: *No I haven't.*
P: Have you worked a switchboard before?
R: *Yes I have.*
P: Have you taken the minutes at a meeting before?
R: *No I haven't.*
P: Have you typed reports before?
R: *No I haven't.*
P: Have you ordered stationery before?
R: *Yes I have.*
P: Have you kept a petty cash book before?
R: *No I haven't.*

Aim: Practice of short answers with the present perfect.

Drill 176 Change these sentences using possessive pronouns, like this:

P: It's my ruler.
R: *It's mine.*

Now you try.
P: It's their stapler.
R: *It's theirs.*
P: They're her rubber bands.
R: *They're hers.*
P: They're his drawing pins.
R: *They're his.*
P: That's your pencil.
R: *It's yours.*
P: Those are our envelopes.
R: *They're ours.*

Aim: Practice of possessive pronouns (SS can do this drill with their books closed).

UNIT ELEVEN

WORKBOOK ANSWERS

Exercise 48 Contractions

didn't – did not; we'll – we will; hasn't – has not; I'm – I am; it's – it is/it has; can't – cannot (NB one word); *won't – will not; I'd – I would* (*I'd* can also stand for *I had*, but the past perfect has not yet been introduced) *they're – they are; we've – we have; who's – who is/who has.*

This exercise practises deciphering the contracted forms of verbs. Although this book encourages the use of contractions in speech, it is important SS know what they stand for.

Exercise 49 Pronouns

3 It is broken. 4 This is their office. 5 This is mine. 6 That is ours. 7 Have you seen her memo? 8 They were over there. 9 It is hers. 10 We are going to the conference.

Exercise 50 Remembering

1 became 2 has moved 3 has received 4 has opened 5 have organised 6 went 7 joined 8 have launched 9 has left 10 won

In this exercise SS have to differentiate between the past simple tense (when the time something happened is important) and the present perfect tense (when the time is not known or not important).

Exercise 51 Word trail

The *apostrophe* is not in the word trail.

Exercise 52 Punctuation

This exercise practises the use of punctuation marks and capital letters within the format of a letter. If SS do this exercise, you might like to discuss with them whether they think it is a business letter or a personal letter. It is a business letter because it conveys information which is important within the business context. However, although it follows a business format, the tone is informal, since Sheila and Lorenzo, are obviously friendly, and he does not use the conventional business opening and closing salutation. It is quite important sometimes that SS (particularly younger SS) are reminded that business letters are between real people and are not just a series of exercises.

Mrs Sheila Baker
Sales manager
Brighter Office Supplies Ltd
13 Mill Street
Harlow
Essex CM20 2JR

via Foscolo 4   21016 Milan Italy

27 November 1992

Our ref: LM/FA

Dear Sheila

Thank you for your letter of 18 November. I am very pleased that you are coming to Milan to visit BOS Italia.

Can you tell me the date and time you are arriving? I will meet you at the airport. How long are you staying? Would you like me to book you a hotel room? Please write and give me all the details.

I look forward to seeing you again.

Best wishes

Lorenzo Magnani

Mr Lorenzo Magnani
Sales representative

UNIT TWELVE
BOS IS THE BEST

12

Business content:	Advertising circulars; reprographics; a survey
Structures:	Comparatives and superlatives Short answers (*So can I/I can't*)
Functions:	Comparing objects, processes and situations
Lexis:	Adjectives, abbreviations

TEACHING NOTES

Exercise 182 Comprehension

Answers: *1 No he did not. 2 Yes he does. 3 Office equipment 4 Brighter Office Supplies 5 Both Simon and the man.*

SS will almost certainly be able to do this exercise as an introduction to the unit.

To introduce comparatives and superlatives

Draw shapes like this on the board:

A
B
C
D

Elicit the adjectives *long* and *short*. Point out the relationship between A and B and teach the sentence: *B is longer than A.* Ask SS to compare the other rods in the same way, and then see if they can make sentences such as: *A is shorter than B.* You can also teach the superlatives at the same time: *A is the shortest* and *D is the longest.* Then draw three rings on the board:

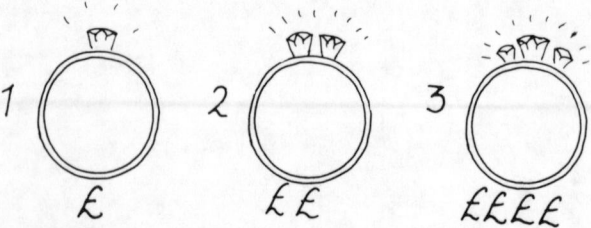

Teach the adjective *expensive*. Teach that with long words (adjectives of three syllables or more) the comparative and superlative are formed with *more* and *the most*.

144

Exericse 183 Comparative and superlative (LD A & B)

Answers: *1 cheaper – the cheapest   2 more efficient – the most efficient   3 heavier – the heaviest   4 wider – the widest   5 easier – the easiest   6 quieter – the quietest   7 dirtier – the dirtiest   8 thinner – the thinnest   9 bigger – the biggest   10. darker – the darkest   11 taller – the tallest   12 cleaner – the cleanest   13 more intelligent – the most intelligent   14 more attractive – the most attractive   15 longer – the longest   16 noisier – the noisiest. See also LDT.*

Aim: To practise the spelling of the comparative and superlative of adjectives.

SS can do this exercise in class or for h/w. Let them try to work out the spelling for themselves, and then discuss the spelling in class after they have done the exercise.

Exercise 184 Comparisons (LD A & B)

Answers: *See LDT*

Aim: Using comparatives and superlatives in an office context.

Pre-teach *length* and *width*.

If possible bring in real sheets of paper of the correct sizes so SS know what they are actually discussing. SS could write sentences comparing the different sizes of paper for h/w.

Exercise 185 Word puzzle

Answers: Simon's typewriter: *expensive, small, light, electric, clean, quiet, easy to use, new*; Anne's typewriter: *cheap, big, heavy, manual, dirty, noisy, difficult to use, old.*

Aim: Deducing vocabulary from knowledge of word structure.

Even without knowing what the words mean, SS should be able to find them in this word square from the clues and their knowledge of English word formation. Afterwards you can teach the meaning of the words (or SS can look them up in a dictionary).

Exercise 186 Comparing two things (LD)

Answers: *See LDT*

Aim: Further practice of the comparative of adjectives.

The adjectives that cannot be compared are *electric* and *manual*.

UNIT TWELVE

Exercise 187   Comparing three things (LD)

       Answers: *See LDT*

       Aim: Further practice of the superlative of adjectives.

Exercise 188   Reprographics

       Sample comparisons (other comparisons may be possible and they can be expressed in a number of ways):   *Using a spirit duplicator is dirtier than using a photocopier. Using a spirit duplicator takes more time/longer than using a photocopier. Using a spirit duplicator costs less than using a photocopier.* (And the reverse:) *Using a photocopier takes less time, is cleaner and costs more money than using a spirit duplicator.*

       Aim: Creativity of language in a business setting.

       NB   Notice the word stress of duplicator (Oooo).

       The exercise is best done in pairs or small groups although you should set up the exercise carefully with the whole class first. SS could write a few sentences of comparison for h/w. (See also WB Exercise 53) If you have a photocopier and spirit duplicator in the school it would be a good idea to show both systems to SS. You could initiate a similar discussion asking SS to compare different methods of communication e.g. telephone, fax, post and telex.

Exercise 189   Listening Comprehension

       Answers:

	6 months	35	£10,000	3 weeks
	1 year	40	£12,000	1 month
	3 months	20–30	£15,000	2 months

       Richard is the youngest.

       Aim: Listening comprehension.

       Pre-teach *training, holidays, per annum/pa* (or *per year; annum* is Latin for year) and *per week/pw*. (You can also say '£2,000 *a* year' or '*a* week', but the *per* form is used in this book.) Play the tape as often as necessary.

       NB   The superlative of *old* when used about people in a family is *the eldest*. Look in a good dictionary for a full explanation of the difference between *oldest* and *eldest*.

Exercise 190   Comparing jobs

       Sample sentences: *Richard works more hours per week than*

Penelope or Susan. Susan works fewer hours per week than Richard or Penelope. Susan had a shorter training than Richard or Penelope. Richard had a longer training than Penelope or Susan. etc.

Aim: Written practice of comparatives.

Make sure SS know that the comparative of *a little* or *some* is *less* (used with mass nouns) and the comparative of *a few* or *some* is *fewer* (used with count nouns). SS can write the sentences in class or for h/w.

Exercise 191 Superlative sentences

Sample sentences: *Susan earns the most. Penelope earns the least. Susan has the longest holidays. Penelope has the shortest holidays.* etc.

Aim: Written practice of superlatives.

Pre-teach *the least* and *the fewest* before SS do this exercise in class or for h/w.

Exercise 192 A survey

Aim: Question practice and creative practice of superlatives (and possibly comparatives).

Give SS the opportunity of writing true or imaginary things about themselves, (schoolpupils will have to make up at least some of the information). Then let them move around the class asking each other questions (which you should check with them before they start): *How old are you? How long was your training? How many hours per week do you work? What is your salary?*

They should keep a note of the highest and lowest figures they hear and who these figures refer to. When SS have had the chance to speak to about six people, stop the activity and collect the information on the board, making sure that SS are making sentences using comparatives and superlatives. See notes on whole-class activities on **TB page xx**.

Further practice/revision of comparatives and superlatives: For further practice (possibly at a later date) you could turn back to various charts and questionnaires in this book to make sentences such as: *It takes longer to travel by bus from Charing Cross to Waterloo than (it does) to travel by train.* (Exercise 50); *More people travel by bus than by tube.* (Exercise 54/55); *It's hotter in Amsterdam than (it is) in Copenhagen.* (Exercise 81); *The man with glasses and a pipe is taller than the woman with short dark hair.* (Exercise 87); *More people can type than (can) speak French.* (Exercise 103); *The sales department spent more on postage in the first week than they did in the second week.* (Exercise 136); *Anne spends more time typing than she spends filing.* (Exercise 138); *BOS spent more in 1992 on postage than they did in 1991.* (Report,

UNIT TWELVE

SB page 74); *The FT index was higher/lower on Wednesday than (it was) on Tuesday.* (Exercise 162/163).

Exercise 193 The Guinness Book of Records

Sample questions (other questions are possible): *1 How much did a Jawa (a Nepalese ¼ dam) weigh? 2 What was the heaviest coin? 3 How long did Violet Gibson Burns type? 4 Who holds the record for typing on a manual typewriter? 5 Who is the fastest typist? 6 Who earned the highest recorded salary in the world? 7 What are the fastest recorded shorthand speeds? 8 Who is the holder of the shorthand speed record? 9 Who probably have (has) the longest working week? 10 How long is the shortest working week?*

Aim: Reading comprehension and question practice.

The Guinness Book of Records is a well-known book in Britain. It contains records of all kinds. This extract is slightly modified.

When SS have done the exercise (in class or for h/w), ask them to make up two more questions on the passage, each of which is to be answered by another S.

Exercise 194 Abbreviations

Answers: *2 kg/kgs 3 min/mins 4 g/gs 5 pa 6 wpm*

Aim: Deciphering abbreviations.

SS have encountered other abbreviations (eg in Consolidation Unit A) which they could also talk about.

Exercise 195 Comparing situations (LD A & B)

Answers: *See LDT*

Aim: To practise short responses with a variety of modal and auxiliary verbs.

You can do this exercise orally in class before SS do it for h/w. (See also WB Exercise 55)
NB Note the use of a past time with the present perfect in number 5: *I've typed a lot of letters this week.* Times such as *this morning, this week, this year* etc may be used with the present perfect as long as the period referred to is still continuing. At 11 am you can say, 'I've done something this morning', but at 2 pm you would have to say, 'I did it this morning'.

Exercise 196 Advertising circulars

Three sample letters: *I am writing to tell you about our newest/most recent/latest car. It is probably the fastest/most exciting/most reliable you can buy. It is also more economical/cheaper than any other model. It makes your short journeys more enjoyable/brighter and your long journeys shorter. I enclose a brochure for you to look at. I look forward to hearing from you when you have read it. For a test drive or further information, please ring John Jones on 01-459 4114 or 01-459 4686.*

We are writing to tell you about our most recent/newest/latest soap powder. It is probably the best you can buy. It is also cheaper/more efficient/cleaner than any other brand. It makes your coloured washing brighter and your white washing whiter. We enclose a sample for you to try. We look forward to hearing from you when you have used it. For the name of your nearest supplier, please write to Mary Smith at Smith & Co, 57 Westgate Road, London SW1B 7XY.

We are writing to tell you about our latest/newest/most recent cooker. It is probably the most reliable/best you can buy. It is also more economical/cheaper/cleaner/more efficient than any other make. It makes your cakes and tarts lighter and your fried food crispier . . . etc.

Pre-teach *model, brand* and *make* eg: *Ford is a make of car. Ford produce many models eg Fiesta, Sierra, Escort etc. You usually have brands of packaged goods eg soap powder, sugar, butter etc.*

Aim: Guided reading and writing practice in a business context.

Point out to SS the link between the word *circular* and the words *circle* and *circulate*.

Ask SS to do this exercise without your help, but if necessary allow them to look up words in the dictionary. SS can work together in class to produce the first letter, but they can write the other two for h/w. (They might also enjoy trying to write the most ridiculous letter from the table).

LANGUAGE DRILLS TAPESCRIPT

Drill 183A Say the comparative of these adjectives in short sentences, like this:

P: This computer is very small.
R: *Mine's smaller.*

P: His calculator is very expensive.
R: *Mine's more expensive.*

Now you try.
P: My typewriter's very heavy.
R: *Mine's heavier.*
P: Her secretary's very efficient.
R: *Mine's more efficient.*
P: His desk is very wide.
R: *Mine's wider.*
P: The photocopier is very noisy.
R: *Mine's noisier.*

P: My boss is very attractive.
R: *Mine's more attractive.*
P: My assistant is very intelligent.
R: *Mine's more intelligent.*

UNIT TWELVE

Aim: Practice of regular comparatives in short sentences (SS can do this drill with their books closed).

Drill 183B Say the superlative of these adjectives in short sentences, like this:

P: These computers are very small.
R: *Mine's the smallest.*

P: Their calculators are very expensive.
R: *Mine's the most expensive.*

Now you try.
P: Our departments are very efficient.
R: *Mine's the most efficient.*
P: Our working day is very long.
R: *Mine's the longest.*
P: These machines are very dirty.
R: *Mine's the dirtiest.*

P: Their offices are very big.
R: *Mine's the biggest.*
P: Our products are very cheap.
R: *Mine's the cheapest.*
P: His secretary's very attractive.
R: *Mine's the most attractive.*

Aim: Practice of regular superlatives in short sentences (SS can do this drill with their books closed).

Drill 184A Look at the pieces of paper drawn to scale. Answer the questions about them like this:

P: Is A4 longer than quarto?
R: *Yes it is.*

P: Is foolscap wider than quarto?
R: *No it isn't.*

Now you try.
P: Is quarto wider than A5?
R: *No it isn't.*
P: Is foolscap narrower than A5?
R: *Yes it is.*

P: Is A5 longer than A4?
R: *No it isn't.*
P: Is quarto shorter than A4?
R: *Yes it is.*

Aim: Comprehension.

Drill 184B Compare the sheets of paper in your book, like this:

P: Foolscap and A4
R: *Foolscap is longer and narrower than A4.*
You can also say: *Foolscap is narrower and longer than A4.*
P: A5 and A4
R: *A5 is shorter than A4.*

Now you try.
P: Foolscap and quarto
R: *Foolscap is longer than quarto.*
P: Quarto and A5
R: *Quarto is longer and narrower than A5.*

P: A5 and foolscap
R: *A5 is shorter and wider than foolscap.*
P: A4 and quarto
R: *A4 is longer and wider than quarto*

Aim: Comprehension; practice of comparatives in a business context.

BOS IS THE BEST

Drill 186 Compare two typewriters, like this:

P: My typewriter's big.
R: *You're right. It's bigger than mine.*

P: My typewriter's difficult to use.
R: *You're right. It's more difficult to use than mine.*

Now you try.
P: My typewriter's light.
R: *You're right. It's lighter than mine.*
P: My typewriter's expensive.
R: *You're right. It's more expensive than mine.*

P: My typewriter's clean.
R: *You're right. It's cleaner than mine.*
P: My typewriter's quiet.
R: *You're right. It's quieter than mine.*

Aim: Practice of regular comparatives (SS can do this drill with their books closed).

Drill 187 Ask questions about three typewriters, like this:

P: Old
R: *Whose typewriter is the oldest?*

Now you try.
P: Heavy
R: *Whose typewriter is the heaviest?*
P: Easy to use
R: *Whose typewriter is the easiest to use?*
P: Expensive
R: *Whose typewriter is the most expensive?*
P: Noisy
R: *Whose typewriter is the noisiest?*

P: Cheap
R: *Whose typewriter is the cheapest?*
P: Difficult to use
R: *Whose typewriter is the most difficult to use?*
P: Clean
R: *Whose typewriter is the cleanest?*

Aim: Practice of regular superlatives (SS can do this drill with their books closed).

Drill 195A Mary's situation is the same as Anne's. Comment on Anne's statements as Mary does:

P: I can type very well.
R: *So can I.*

P: I've got a lot of work to do.
R: *So have I.*

Now you try.
P: I'm very efficient.
R: *So am I.*
P: I earn a good salary.
R: *So do I.*
P: I've typed a lot of letters this week.
R: *So have I.*
P: I photocopied six reports yesterday.
R: *So did I.*

P: I was top of my class at school.
R: *So was I.*
P: I went to a good secretarial college.
R: *So did I.*
P: I'm going out for lunch.
R: *So am I.*
P: I can drive.
R: *So can I.*

Aim: Practice of short answers with a variety of auxiliary and modal verbs (SS can do this drill with their books closed).

UNIT TWELVE

Drill 195B Helen's situation is different from Anne's. Comment on Anne's statements as Helen does:

P: I can type very well.
R: *I can't.*

P: I've got a lot of work to do.
R: *I haven't*

Now you try.
P: I'm very efficient.
R: *I'm not.*
P: I earn a good salary.
R: *I don't.*
P: I've typed a lot of letters this week.
R: *I haven't.*
P: I photocopied six reports yesterday.
R: *I didn't.*

P: I was top of my class at school.
R: *I wasn't.*
P: I went to a good secretarial college.
R: *I didn't.*
P: I'm going out for lunch.
R: *I'm not.*
P: I can drive.
R: *I can't.*

Aim: Practice of short responses with a variety of auxiliary and modal verbs (SS can do this drill with their books closed).

WORKBOOK ANSWERS

Exercise 53   Comparisons

Sample sentences: *Typewriter A is newer, cleaner and lighter than typewriter B. The girl in office A is younger and has shorter hair than the woman in office B. There is a light in office B, but there is not one in office A. The woman in office B smokes, but the girl in office A does not. There is a duplicating machine in office B, but a photocopier in office A.*

This is a creative writing exercise in which SS can practise vocabulary from previous units as well as comparisons.

Exercise 54   It's/its

2 *its*   3 *It's (it is)*   4 *It's (it has)*   5 *It's (it has)*   6 *Its*
This exercise continues in the series differentiating between similar structures and phrases (see also TB page 109).

Exercise 55   Comparing situations

3 *So is Mary. Helen's not. Helen isn't.*   4 *So does Mary. Helen doesn't.*   5 *So has Mary. Helen hasn't.*   6 *So did Mary. Helen didn't.*   7 *So was Mary. Helen wasn't.*   8 *So did Mary. Helen didn't.*   9 *So is Mary. Helen isn't.*   10 *So can Mary. Helen can't.*

UNIT THIRTEEN
COMPLAINTS

13

Business content:	Post room procedures; telexes; a letter of complaint
Structures:	The passive Short answers (*Nor do I/I do*)
Functions:	Comparing situations; discussing procedures; complaining
Lexis:	Numbers (*revision*), world exports

TEACHING NOTES

Exercise 197 Comprehension

Answers: *1 Yes. They are very popular. 2 Nothing. It is free. 3 The furniture he ordered was damaged. A chair seat was torn, a typewriter was dented and a desk handle was broken. 4 This is partly a matter of opinion, but probably the chair.*

SS will probably be able to do this exercise before you have taught the passive. The only word they might not know is *free*.

Exercise 198 What's wrong? (LD)

Answers: *See LDT*

Aim: To introduce and practise the passive.

In this exercise past participles are used as adjectives and can be taught as such. Teach the four verbs *tear, crack, dent* and *break* as a group. SS can deduce the meanings of the other verbs. The exercise can be done orally, but then SS can write six sentences for h/w.

Exercise 199 A speech (LD)

Answers: *See LDT*

Aim: Written practice of sentences in the passive.

The form of the passive was introduced in the previous exercise, but you could highlight it before SS do this exercise. Point out that we use the passive when what was done is more important than who did it or when we do not know who did it. (This could easily be the case with all the examples from Fred's speech.) SS are already familiar with the vocabulary in this exercise. It can be prepared orally in class and written for h/w. Note that you can say '£3,000 *was* given to charity' (thinking of the sum of money) or '£3,000 *were* given' (referring to the plural word *pounds*).

Exercise 200 Numbers revision (LD)

Answers: *See LDT* Also: *9,056 – nine thousand and fifty-*

UNIT THIRTEEN

six; 9,065 – nine thousand and sixty-five; 9,650 – nine thousand, six hundred and fifty; 9,560 – nine thousand, five hundred and sixty; 6,590 – six thousand, five hundred and ninety; 6,905 – six thousand, nine hundred and five; 6,509 – six thousand, five hundred and nine; 6,059 – six thousand and fifty-nine; 6,095 – six thousand and ninety-five; 5,609 – five thousand, six hundred and nine; 5,690 – five thousand, six hundred and ninety; 5,906 – five thousand, nine hundred and six; 5,960 – five thousand, nine hundred and sixty; 5,069 – five thousand and sixty-nine; 5,096 – five thousand and ninety-six; 7,211 – seven thousand, two hundred and eleven; 7,112 – seven thousand, one hundred and twelve; 1,271 – one (a) thousand, two hundred and seventy-one; 1,721 – one (a) thousand, seven hundred and twenty-one; 1,712 – one (a) thousand, seven hundred and twelve; 1,127 – one (a) thousand, one hundred and twenty-seven; 1,172 – one (a) thousand, one hundred and seventy-two; 8,003 – eight thousand and three; 3,080 – three thousand and eighty; 3,800 – three thousand, eight hundred.

Aim: Revision of numbers.

SS can do this in class or for h/w. You can give any four (or more) figure numbers for practice of this kind at any time.

Point out to SS the use of commas in numbers. With long numbers commas are inserted after every three figures starting from the right eg 6,000,000; 56,435,567,876. This is particularly important as in some countries a comma can denote a decimal place. For numbers beginning with *one*, you can say either *one* or *a*. In everyday speech we usually use 'a' eg *I've been here for a week. He gave me a hundred pounds.* 'One' is used when numbers are said in isolation or when 'one' is stressed in contrast to another number: *Oh you've been here for two weeks, have you? – No. One week.*

NB Although in Britain we say 'two hundred *and* twenty-five' it is perfectly correct in the US to say 'two hundred twenty-five'.

Exercise 201 Calculations (LD)

Answers: *See LDT and SB tapescript*

Aim: Revision of numbers and introduction of simple calculations.

Teach the four basic calculations and let the SS practise in pairs (they can make up calculations for one another – possibly as they are done in the LD) before they do this listening exercise and certainly before they do the LD. For 6 + 4 you can also say *six and four*; for 2 × 4 you can say *two multiplied by four*.

NB Pronunciation of *minus* is /'maɪnəs/; *plus* is /plʌs/.

COMPLAINTS

Exercise 202 Flowchart

Answers: *1 delivered   2 sorted   3 business   4 personal
5 opened   6 distributed   7 collected   8 sorted
9 internal post   10/11 First class letters/second class letters
12 parcels   13 weighed if necessary   14 wrapped
15 labelled   16 weighed   17 franked*
Simon put his memo in an envelope by mistake and it was sent with the outgoing post. He wanted it sent by internal post.

Aim: Listening comprehension.

SS should be able to follow the description and use the notes to fill in the diagram from the tape without help. Ask SS to deduce the meanings of the verbs from their context after doing the activity. They will probably need to hear the tape more than once.
Note that on the tape, Simon uses the short form *"Morning, George'* for *'Good morning, George'*.
NB   If the agent (the person who does an action) is mentioned in the passive, we use the preposition *by*, eg *The post was delivered by the postman.*

George does not mention overseas post. Ask the SS to describe the system using foreign mail.

For revision of adjectives ask SS to describe what they think George looks like. They should be able to form an impression of him and what they think he is wearing from his voice (even if different SS have different pictures).

Exercise 203 Post room procedures (LD)

Answers: *See LDT* Also: *1 delivered 2 postman 3 post room
4 sorted   5 business   6 distributed   7 collected   8 sorted
9 parcels   10 letters   11 post   12 postbox   13 internal post*

Aim: Consolidation of vocabulary in Exercise 202.

No preparation necessary. Possible h/w exercise. (See also WB Exercise 57)

Exercise 204 Advertisements (LD)

Answers: *See LDT*

Aim: Further practice of the passive.

SS are given all the information they need to do this exercise. After they have done the sentences orally, they can write them for h/w.
NB   You might want to highlight the questions with *make*: *Made by* Of-Op Ltd: Of-Op Ltd are the producers. *Made of* silk: silk is a raw material. It is the only material in the blouse. *Made with* coconut: coconut is one of several ingredients. For a fuller explanation, refer to a good grammar book (See TB page xv).

UNIT THIRTEEN

Exercise 205 World exports (LD)

Answers: *See LDT*

Aim: Further practice of the passive relating language study to SS' general knowledge.

SS can get an idea of the meaning of most of the vocabulary from the pictures under the map.

Discuss (or ask SS to find out for h/w) which products are most closely associated with which countries. When they have done the exercise orally, they could write sentences about the exports for h/w.
NB You might also ask SS whether these are visible or invisible exports (they are all visible, see TB page 65 Exercise 84). The exercise can also be used to revise countries and nationalities eg *It's Brazilian coffee, Sri Lankan tea* (pronounced /sri:/ or /ʃri:/); *New Zealand butter*, etc. Note that Sri Lanka used to be called Ceylon. (We still sometimes talk of 'Ceylon tea'.)

Exercise 206 Project

Aim: To encourage SS to work out of school hours and to relate language and business to the everyday world; to practise language from Exercises 204 and 205 in a creative context.

If SS are interested in the project, different SS could look at different types of goods eg food, clothing, electrical equipment, cars etc. The research is to be done in the SS' own time and discussed briefly in class before they write a report on their findings. The report should be properly set out (see SB page 74) and say where the research was done. If possible find out (or ask SS to find out) your country's main imports and trading partners from official figures and see whether these facts confirm the SS' research.

Exercise 207 Comparing situations (LD A & B)

Answers: *See LDT*

Aim: Practice of short responses to negative sentences.

(See also Exercise 195 and WB Exercises 55 and 58) The exercise can be prepared orally in class and/or written for h/w.

Additional activity

Matching sentences For extra practice of short responses, write several of the sentences from Exercises 195, 207, WB 55 and WB 58 (or similar positive and negative sentences) on pieces of paper and write a possible short answer for each on another piece of paper. Make sure that the sentences are in pairs which have interchangeable answers:

COMPLAINTS

I can't swim. *Nor can I.*
I can't type. *He can.*

Write enough sentences and short answers so that you have one piece of paper for everyone in the class, plus about four more. Mix up the pieces of paper and hand out one to each person in the class. SS have to find a partner so that their two sentences make a statement and a response. They should *say* their sentences, not show their paper to other SS. When SS find a partner they bring their papers to you for checking; you then give them each another paper. Their sentences can now be mixed into the pool of spares to be handed out to the next SS who find partners. Do not play the game for more than about 5 minutes.

NB This game can be used to practise many other structures or language items eg you could have words with different stress patterns on the pieces of paper. (Four or five words for each stress pattern; SS have to find a partner whose word has the same stress pattern. See Exercises 96 to 99.)

Exercise 208 Telexes

Answers: *1 PLEASE SEND 20 FILING CABINETS TYPE SD52; 2 CONFIRM AGENT ARRIVING GATWICK SATURDAY 22 AUGUST; 3 PLEASE CONFIRM DESPATCH ORDER 520; 4 REGRET ORDER 665 DELAYED CUSTOMS; 5 SMITH ARRIVING WATERLOO 1530 PLEASE MEET; 6 REGRET FOUR TYPEWRITERS ORDER 0039 DAMAGED AGENTS INVESTIGATING PLEASE SEND IMMEDIATE REPLACEMENTS; 7 ARRIVING VICTORIA 1700 PLEASE MEET; 8 PLEASE CONFIRM ARRIVAL ORDER 6290; 9 PLEASE CONFIRM AGENT ARRIVING HEATHROW TUESDAY; 10 RECEIVED ORDER 87654.*

Aim: To introduce telex messages.

Discuss the first few sentences with SS to let them determine the sorts of words that can be left out of a message so that it still retains its meaning, eg: auxiliaries (*to be, have, do, will*); pronouns (*I, you, them, your, my* etc), long polite phrases which might be used in letters (four examples are given in the SB), some prepositions (eg *arriving* at *5 pm* on *Tuesday*). Do the exercise in class as pair work.

This might be an occasion when it is worth identifying and naming the parts of speech for SS: verbs (*am going, thinks*); nouns (*table, Simon*); pronouns (*he, mine*); articles (*the, a*); adjectives (*big, long*); adverbs (*tomorrow, occasionally*); prepositions (*to, at*); conjunctions (*and, then*).

UNIT THIRTEEN

Exercise 209 Letter of complaint

Sample letter:

```
Sales manager
Brighter Office Supplies Ltd
13 Mill Street
Harlow
Essex CM20 2JE

19 October 1992

Ref: Order 98534

Dear Sir

I am afraid that the order 98534 arrived damaged. A
chair seat was torn, a desk handle was broken and a
typewriter was dented. I would be grateful if you
could send immediate replacements.

I look forward to hearing from you.

Yours faithfully

Sam Worthington

Mr Sam Worthington
Manager
```

Aim: To understand a telex and to write a business letter.

Discuss in class what SS will write in the body of the letter before they do this exercise (possibly for h/w).

LANGUAGE DRILLS TAPESCRIPT

Drill 198 Do Exercise 198 before you do this drill. Say what is wrong with each object, like this:

P: What's wrong with the paper?
R: *It's torn.*

P: What's wrong with the cheque?
R: *It's not signed.*

Now you try.

P: What's wrong with the chair?
R: *It's broken.*
P: What's wrong with the plate?
R: *It's cracked.*

P: What's wrong with the letter?
R: *It's not finished.*
P: What's wrong with the car?
R: *It's dented.*

Aim: Comprehension; practice of past participles used as adjectives (passive present tense).

Drill 199 Listen to the sentences in Fred's speech and say them in the passive, like this:

COMPLAINTS

P: We opened a branch in Liverpool last May.
R: *Last May a branch was opened in Liverpool.*

Now you try.
P: We started a pension scheme two years ago.
R: *Two years ago a pension scheme was started.*
P: We sold a record number of desks in 1978.
R: *In 1978 a record number of desks was sold.*
P: We hired fifty more employees in January.
R: *In January fifty more employees were hired.*

P: We raised our prices in 1979.
R: *In 1979 our prices were raised.*
P: We gave three thousand pounds to charity last year.
R: *Last year three thousand pounds was given to charity.*

Aim: Practice of passive past simple (SS can do this drill with their books closed).
NB The dates are different in the updated SB.

Drill 200 Say these numbers, like this:

P: Six five nine oh
R: *Six thousand, five hundred and ninety.*

Now you try.
P: Nine six oh five
R: *Nine thousand, six hundred and five.*
P: Seven one two one
R: *Seven thousand, one hundred and twenty-one.*
P: One two one seven
R: *A thousand, two hundred and seventeen.*
P: Four four four four
R: *Four thousand, four hundred and forty-four.*

P: Eight oh three oh
R: *Eight thousand and thirty.*
P: Three oh oh eight
R: *Three thousand and eight.*
P: Eight three oh oh
R: *Eight thousand, three hundred.*

Aim: Number practice (SS can do this drill with their books closed).

Drill 201 Fill in the mathematical symbols to make these numbers into simple calculations, like this:

P: Two four eight
R: *Two times four equals eight.*

P: Nine three three
R: *Nine divided by three equals three.*

Now you try.
P: Four one five
R: *Four plus one equals five*
P: Six two four
R: *Six minus two equals four.*

P: Four four sixteen
R: *Four times four equals sixteen.*
P: Eighteen two sixteen
R: *Eighteen minus two equals sixteen.*

UNIT THIRTEEN

P: Twelve four three
R: *Twelve divided by four equals three.*
P: Nine three twelve.
R: *Nine plus three equals twelve.*
P: Five three fifteen.
R: *Five times three equals fifteen.*
P: Ten two five
R: *Ten divided by two equals five.*

Aim: Number practice in simple calculations (SS can do this drill with their books closed).

Drill 203

Talk about the post room procedure in the passive, like this:

P: The postman delivers the incoming post.
R: *The incoming post is delivered.*
P: Someone sorts the post into two categories.
R: *The post is sorted into two categories.*

Now you try.
P: Someone opens the business letters.
R: *The business letters are opened.*
P: Someone distributes the post to the different departments.
R: *The post is distributed to the different departments.*
P: In the afternoon someone collects the outgoing post.
R: *In the afternoon the outgoing post is collected.*
P: Someone sorts the outgoing post into four categories.
R: *The outgoing post is sorted into four categories.*
P: Someone wraps, labels and weighs the parcels.
R: *The parcels are wrapped, labelled and weighed.*
P: Someone franks all the post.
R: *All the post is franked.*
P: Someone takes the post to the postbox.
R: *The post is taken to the postbox.*
P: Someone distributes the internal post the next morning.
R: *The internal post is distributed the next morning.*

Aim: Practice of passives to describe procedures in the simple past (SS can do this drill with their books closed).

Drill 204

Look at the pictures and answer these questions, like this:

P: Who is 'We Mean Business' written by?
R: *Susan Norman*

Now you try.
P: Who is 'We Mean Business' published by?
R: *Longman*
P: Who is 'Funny Business' directed by?
R: *Andrew Branny*
P: Who is 'Funny Business' produced by?
R: *Jim Hill*
P: Who is 'Mind Your Own Business' sung by?
R: *Jimmy Grierson*
P: Who is 'Mind Your Own Business' arranged by?
R: *Pete Brown*
P: Who is 'Mind Your Own Business' conducted by?
R: *Chris Adey*
P: Where are Smudgitex photocopiers made?
R: *In Britain*
P: Who are Smudgitex photocopiers made by?
R: *Of-Op Ltd*

P: Who are Coconut Kisses made by?
R: *Zak's*
P: What are Coconut Kisses made with?
R: *Pure coconut*
P: Where are the blouses imported from?
R: *India*

P: Who are the blouses imported by?
R: *Jacksons*
P: What are the blouses made of?
R: *Silk*

Aim: Comprehension.

Drill 205 Say these sentences in the passive, like this:

P: Brazil exports coffee.
R: *Coffee is exported from Brazil.*

P: They grow coffee in Brazil.
R: *Coffee is grown in Brazil.*

Now you try.
P: They grow tea in Sri Lanka.
R: *Tea is grown in Sri Lanka.*
P: They produce butter in New Zealand.
R: *Butter is produced in New Zealand.*
P: They export tobacco from Cuba.
R: *Tobacco is exported from Cuba.*
P: They mine gold in South Africa.
R: *Gold is mined in South Africa.*

P: They export oil from Saudi Arabia.
R: *Oil is exported from Saudi Arabia.*
P: They grow wheat in North America.
R: *Wheat is grown in North America.*

Aim: Practice of passives and countries (SS can do this drill with their books closed).

Drill 207A Mary's situation is the same as Anne's. Comment on Anne's negative statements as Mary does:

P: I don't like using the telephone.
R: *Nor do I.*
P: I can't swim.
R: *Nor can I.*

Now you try.
P: I didn't go to work on Monday.
R: *Nor did I.*
P: I haven't been to Egypt.
R: *Nor have I.*
P: I don't cycle to work.
R: *Nor do I.*
P: I'm not going out to lunch today.
R: *Nor am I.*

P: I wasn't given a pay rise.
R: *Nor was I.*
P: I wouldn't like to leave BOS.
R: *Nor would I.*
P: I haven't got any more holiday this year.
R: *Nor have I.*
P: I'm not very busy.
R: *Nor am I.*

UNIT THIRTEEN

Aim: Practice of short responses with a variety of auxiliary and modal verbs (SS can do this drill with their books closed).

Drill 207B Helen's situation is different from Anne's. Comment on Anne's negative statements like Helen:

P: I don't like using the telephone.
R: *I do.*
P: I can't swim.
R: *I can.*

Now you try.
P: I didn't go to work on Monday.
R: *I did.*
P: I haven't been to Egypt.
R: *I have.*
P: I don't cycle to work.
R: *I do.*
P: I'm not going out to lunch today.
R: *I am.*
P: I wasn't given a pay rise.
R: *I was.*
P: I wouldn't like to leave BOS.
R: *I would.*

P: I haven't got any more holiday this year.
R: *I have.*
P: I'm not very busy.
R: *I am.*

Aim: Practice of short responses with a variety of modal and auxiliary verbs (SS can do this drill with their books closed)

WORKBOOK ANSWERS

Exercise 56 News article

1 the/an   2 soon/shortly/immediately   3 work   4 seen/noticed
5 secretary   6 fire   7 the/two/several   8 they   9 the
10 one/a   11 in/by   12 was   13 he   14 Ms/Miss/Anne
15 Brighter   16 I   17 and   18 about   19 way   20 I
21 the   22 the   23 then/afterwards   24 Mr (or a first name)   25 because   26 his   27 his/the
(Other words might be possible). This is a cloze test about a fire in a stationery shop involving practice of the passive.

Exercise 57 Post room puzzle

1 distribute   2 weigh   3 collect   4 deliver   5 label
6 sort   7 open   8 wrap   9 frank
This exercise practises post room vocabulary.

Exercise 58 Comparing situations

3 Nor did Mary. Helen did.   4 Nor has Mary. Helen has.
5 Nor does Mary. Helen does.   6. Nor is Mary. Helen is.
7 Nor was Mary. Helen was.   8 Nor would Mary. Helen would.   9 Nor has Mary. Helen has.   10 Nor is Mary. Helen is.

COMPLAINTS

Exercise 59 Problems

1 January 1st. On December 30th the young man was 18. His birthday was on December 31st. On January 1st he was 19. On December 31st that year he would be 20 and on December 31st the next year he would be 21.

2 The rich businessman gave them one of his factories. The eldest son then had half of eighteen (nine), the second son had a third of eighteen (six) and the youngest son had a ninth of eighteen (two). This adds up to seventeen, so the other businessman took his factory back.

In fact, although it is clever, this answer is not strictly accurate as the sons do not get the correct proportions of the original factories (half of eighteen is not the same as half of seventeen). The answer works because a half, a third and a ninth do not add up to one but to seventeen eighteenths.

This exercise consists of two mathematical problems in the form of mini-reading comprehension passages. Let SS consider the problem in pairs or small groups and think about them (possibly overnight) before you discuss the answers in class.

UNIT FOURTEEN
TELEPHONE MESSAGES

14

> *Business content*: Telephone messages
> *Structures*: Reported (indirect) speech
> Could/might be...
> Look like...
> Too + adjectives
> *Function*: Hypothesising
> *Pronunciation*: Homophones
> *Lexis*: Office equipment and stationery (*revision*)

TEACHING NOTES

Exercise 210   Comprehension

Answers: *1 Fred's   2 The bank manager   3 The garage and his wife   4 Because it has stopped ringing*
NB Contractions are used in the negative questions in the SB as the full forms sound very stilted to a native speaker. Mary has a slight Scottish accent on the tape.

SS should be able to understand this exercise before they study the unit. Introduce the uses of the verb *to want to* from this exercise: *I want to do it; I want him to do it.* Practise *want to* by asking SS to make as many sentences as they can from these words: *see – Mary – Fred – ? – to – you – not – go – want/s – what – it – do/does – go* eg *Mary wants Fred to do it. What does Fred want to see?*

To introduce ways of hypothesising

Put a number of objects each in its own sealed cloth or plastic bag, so that they can be felt but not seen. Choose indeterminate objects such as a handkerchief, a coloured pencil, an oddly-shaped rubber etc. Hand them round the class and let SS guess what the objects are. Teach them sentences to use: *It could be a... /It might be a... /I think it's a... /It feels like a...*

After this initial practice (and when the bags have been opened and the contents examined), point out that we can describe things by using our five senses: *It looks/feels/sounds/smells/tastes like...* (These are all verbs which are rarely used in the progressive tenses because they describe *states* and not *actions* or *activities*.)

To practise 'sounds like', ask SS to turn away or close their eyes while you drop a number of things (preferably unbreakable) on the floor. SS can guess from the sound what the objects are, using sentences such as: '*It sounds like a paper clip*', '*It could/might be a paper clip.*'

164

TELEPHONE MESSAGES

Exercise 211 Look like (LD A, B & C)

Answers: *There are no specific answers to this exercise, but see LDT for sample sentences.*

Aim: To practise the functional area of hypothesising.

Look at the pictures with the SS and elicit guesses as to what the objects are using the structures suggested in the SB. Introduce the idea that the pictures could be *part of* an object and not a whole object, then let them do the exercise orally in pairs before they look at the 'answer' pictures on the next page. For h/w they could write one or two sentences about each object.

Only a limited number of modal verbs are introduced in this book (*can, might, could, must, should*) with specific functions. Point them out to SS as they occur and warn them that their negative, past and future forms may be irregular or have different meanings.

Exercise 212 Answers to 211 (LD)

Answers: *See LDT*

Aim: To practise and reinforce the concept of *looks like*.

These are the objects which looked so unfamiliar in Exercise 211. It is important to make clear to SS that an object or a person can look like something or someone else without necessarily being it or him/her eg *He looks like his father. He does not look like a businessman, but he is.*

Note that with the plural objects you can use *it* (referring to the picture) or *they* (referring to the objects) eg *They didn't look like paper clips, but they were.*

Exercise 213 Too early (LD)

Answers: *See LDT*

Aim: To deduce the meaning of adjectives from context; to introduce *too*.

SS should be able to work out which adjective refers to which picture, so the exercise could be done for h/w. Teach the words *coat, jacket, dress, pair of trousers*, either from real articles of clothing worn by people in class, or from the pictures. When SS have done the exercise, check that they have understood the meaning of *too* by asking concept questions about each picture eg Picture 2 – *Do Helen and Mary want to go to the shop?* (Yes). *Can they go to the shop?* (No). *Why not?* (The shops closed at 5.30. It is now 6 o'clock. They are too late to go to the shop.)

UNIT FOURTEEN

Exercise 214 It doesn't fit (LD A, B, C & D)

Aim: To practise *too* in authentic dialogues.

Look at the notes on introducing dialogues on TB page xxv.

Exercise 215 Homophones

Answers: *right – write; there – their; know – no; won – one; too – two* (not *to*. This is usually pronounced /tə/ in context); *sea – see; weight – wait; here – hear; red – read* (past tense); *weigh – way*.

Aim: To help SS link spelling and pronunciation.

Most of the words have appeared in the book so SS can do the exercise without help in pairs or for h/w. When they have finished, check that they know the meaning of all the words and ask them to learn the words for h/w.

Exercise 216 Spelling

Answers: *1 right   2 won   3 hear   4 know   5 too   6 see/sea   7 red   8 weigh   9 wait   10 here   11 read   12 here   13 write   14 one   15 right way   16 their   17 too   18 one/two*

Aim: To test whether SS have learnt and understood the words in Exercise 215.

Do not play the tape more than twice. (See also WB Exercise 61)

Exercise 217 A telephone call (LD)

Answers: *See LDT*

Aim: To introduce and practise reported speech.

You need do no special presentation of reported speech apart from this exercise. Do the first four examples with the whole class and discuss the changes you need to make (eg *I → she/he* etc). The changes for reported speech depend on the situation, who is talking to whom and when. In this book all the examples follow the basic progression of tenses. Notice that the verb *say* (particularly when used to introduce reported speech) is not used in the progressive tenses except for rather special contexts which need not concern the SS. For their purposes, point out that '*say*' is used in the simple tenses.

NB   You can use *that* in all the sentences in reported speech in this book although it is natural to omit it, eg *She says she's your wife.* or *She says that she's your wife.* SS can do this exercise in pairs orally and write the 8 sentences for h/w.

Exercise 218 Reported speech (LD)

Answers: *See LDT*

TELEPHONE MESSAGES

Aim: To introduce and practise reported speech in the past simple tense.

SS should find it logical for things someone said in the past to be in the past tense. All the information the SS need is in the SB. After doing the exercise orally in pairs, they can write the 8 sentences for h/w.
NB Do not let SS say *He said me* ... The verb *say* does not take an object. We say *He said he wanted to see her*, or *He told me he wanted to see her*.

Exercise 219 Telephone messages (LD)

Answers: 1 *Mr Steven Cox* 2 *Mrs Sheila Baker* 3 *Anne* 4 *12.15* 5 *British Catering Ltd* 6 *To see Sheila next week about a large stationery order.* 7 *He wants Sheila to ring him back before 3.30.* 8 *Yes* (*urgent*) 9 *920 7689* 10 *No*

Aim: Comprehension of information presented in a common business format and practice of reported speech.

The exercise can be done for h/w or in pairs in class. The LD practises reported speech.
NB *Called to see you* means *visited*. *Will call again* might mean *visit* or *telephone*.

Exercise 220 Taking messages (LD)

Sample telephone messages:

MESSAGE FOR Mrs Sheila Baker		WHILE YOU WERE OUT Mr David Rogers	
of Rogers & Co		TEL NO 854524	
TELEPHONED	✓	WANTS TO SEE YOU	PLEASE RING ✓
WILL CALL AGAIN		CALLED TO SEE YOU	URGENT ✓

MESSAGE *Please ring David Rogers about their order no 0804 before 5 o'clock*

TIME *12.30 pm* DATE *16 Dec* RECEIVED BY *Anne*

UNIT FOURTEEN

MESSAGE FOR M**rs Sheila Baker** WHILE YOU WERE OUT M**s Fiona Donaldson**
of **Of-Op** .... TEL NO **59761**

TELEPHONED	✓	WANTS TO SEE YOU	✓	PLEASE RING	✓
WILL CALL AGAIN		CALLED TO SEE YOU		URGENT	

MESSAGE **Fiona Donaldson wants to see you one day next week about some new office furniture**

TIME **12·45 pm**   DATE **16 Dec**   RECEIVED BY **Anne**

MESSAGE FOR M**rs Sheila Baker** WHILE YOU WERE OUT M**r Adam Haines**
of .... TEL NO ....

TELEPHONED	✓	WANTS TO SEE YOU		PLEASE RING	
WILL CALL AGAIN	✓	CALLED TO SEE YOU		URGENT	

MESSAGE **It was a personal call. It wasn't urgent.**

TIME **1 pm**   DATE **16 Dec**   RECEIVED BY **Anne**

Aim: To improve listening comprehension and the business skill of taking telephone messages.

TELEPHONE MESSAGES

Play the tape as often as necessary for SS to fill in message forms they have prepared. The LD practises turning reported speech into direct speech. The examples are all taken from this exercise. (See also WB Exercise 63)

Exercise 221 A telephone conversation

Sample dialogue:

ANNE: *Good morning, sales department.*
STEVEN: *Good morning. Can I speak to Sheila Baker please?*
ANNE: *I'm afraid she isn't in the office at the moment. Can I take a message?*
STEVEN: *Yes. Can you tell her Steven Cox rang, of British Catering Ltd. I want to see her next week about a large stationery order. She knows all about it. It's urgent, but I'm leaving the office at 3.30 this afternoon.*
ANNE: *Right. I'll ask her to ring you before 3.30. Has she got your telephone number?*
STEVEN: *It's 920 7689.*
ANNE: *920 7689. I'll give her the message. Goodbye.*
STEVEN: *'Bye.*

Aim: To examine in detail the language of leaving and taking a telephone message.

Play the tape for Exercise 220 again and ask SS to take down as a dictation the conversation between Anne and David Rogers. This exercise then consists of substituting the information from Steven Cox's message. It can be done for h/w.
NB You may have to distinguish between the verbs *say* and *tell* if you have not already done so (see note on Exercise 218).

These telephone messages could be used as the basis of a roleplay exercise to re-enact the conversations (see TB page xxvi).

Exercise 222 Roleplay

Aim: Fluency, creativity and revision.

(Dialogue 1, see Unit 13; 2 see Unit 6; 3 see Unit 5.) See notes on roleplay on TB page xxvi.

LANGUAGE DRILLS TAPESCRIPT

Drill 211A Say what things could be, like this:

P: A typewriter
R: *It could be a typewriter.*

Now you try.
P: A paper clip
R: *It could be a paper clip.*
P: A roll of sellotape
R: *It could be a roll of sellotape.*

P: A ruler
R: *It could be a ruler.*
P: A box of drawing pins
R: *It could be a box of drawing pins.*

UNIT FOURTEEN

Aim: Practice of *could be* for hypothesising (SS can do this drill with their books closed).

Drill 211B Say what things might be part of, like this:

P: A typewriter
R: *It might be part of a typewriter.*

Now you try.
P: A calculator
R: *It might be part of a calculator.*
P: A photocopier
R: *It might be part of a photocopier.*

P: A filing cabinet
R: *It might be part of a filing cabinet.*
P: A desk
R: *It might be part of a desk.*

Aim: Practice of *might be* for hypothesising (SS can do this drill with their books closed).

Drill 211C Say what things look like, like this:

P: A typewriter
R: *It looks like part of a typewriter.*

Now you try.
P: A ruler
R: *It looks like part of a ruler.*
P: A paper clip
R: *It looks like part of a paper clip.*
P: A telephone
R: *It looks like part of a telephone.*

P: A wastepaper bin
R: *It looks like part of a wastepaper bin.*

Aim: Practice of *looks like* (SS can do this drill with their books closed).

Drill 212 Talk about the pictures, like this:

P: A typewriter
R: *It didn't look like a typewriter, but it was.*

Now you try.
P: A calculator
R: *It didn't look like a calculator, but it was.*
P: A stapler
R: *It didn't look like a stapler, but it was.*
P: A chair
R: *It didn't look like a chair, but it was.*

P: A lamp
R: *It didn't look like a lamp, but it was.*
P: A telephone
R: *It didn't look like a telephone, but it was.*

Aim: Reinforcement of the concept of *look like* (SS can do this drill with their books closed).

TELEPHONE MESSAGES

Drill 213 Say what the people in the pictures are saying, using these adjectives, like this:

P: Picture 1 Early
R: *We're too early.*

Now you try.
P: Picture 2 Late
R: *We're too late.*
P: Picture 3 Dangerous
R: *It's too dangerous.*
P: Picture 4 Expensive
R: *They're too expensive.*
P: Picture 5 Big
R: *It's too big.*

P: Picture 6 Short
R: *It's too short.*
P: Picture 7 Small
R: *It's too small.*
P: Picture 8 Long
R: *They're too long.*

Aim: Practice of *too* + adjective.

Drills 214A, B, C & D

(See dialogues in SB.)
A: Mary's coat is too big, but she buys it.
B: Helen does not buy the dress because it is too short.
C: Howard's jacket is too small, but he buys it.
D: Simon does not buy the trousers because they are too long.

Aim: Dialogue practice using *too* + adjective (SS should do each drill a second time with their books closed).
NB The first dialogue is recorded in full before SS take the parts so it can be used for presentation.

Drill 217 Tell Fred what the person on the phone says and tell the person on the phone what Fred says, like this:

P: I'm his wife.
R: *She says she's your wife.*
P: I'm leaving work in half an hour.
R: *He says he's leaving work in half an hour.*

Now you try.
P: It's urgent.
R: *She says it's urgent.*
P: I'll ring her back.
R: *He says he'll ring you back.*
P: He can't ring me back.
R: *She says you can't ring her back.*
P: I'm in a phone box.
R: *She says she's in a phone box.*
P: I'm very busy.
R: *He says he's very busy.*

P: The football match starts in fifteen minutes.
R: *She says the football match starts in fifteen minutes.*
P: I'll leave immediately.
R: *He says he'll leave immediately.*

Aim: Practice of reported speech in the present (SS can do this drill with their books closed).

171

UNIT FOURTEEN

Drill 218

Tell someone about the conversation you had in Exercise 217 using the past simple tense, like this:

P: I'm his wife.
R: *She said she was his wife.*
P: I'm leaving work in half an hour.
R: *He said he was leaving work in half an hour.*

Now you try.
P: It's urgent.
R: *She said it was urgent.*
P: I'll ring her back.
R: *He said he would ring her back.*
P: He can't ring me back.
R: *She said he couldn't ring her back.*
P: I'm in a phone box.
R: *She said she was in a phone box.*
P: I'm very busy.
R: *He said he was very busy.*

P: The football match starts in fifteen minutes.
R: *She said the football match started in fifteen minutes.*
P: I'll leave immediately.
R: *He said he would leave immediately.*

Aim: Practice of reported speech in the past (SS can do this drill with their books closed).

Drill 219

Say these sentences in reported speech in the past tense, like this:

P: I want to speak to Sheila about an order.
R: *He said he wanted to speak to Sheila about an order.*

Now you try.
P: I'm leaving the office at about five o'clock.
R: *He said he was leaving the office at about five o'clock.*
P: It's quite urgent.
R: *He said it was quite urgent.*
P: I want to see Sheila about some office furniture.
R: *She said she wanted to see Sheila about some office furniture.*

P: My telephone number is eight five four two.
R: *She said her telephone number was eight five four two.*
P: I'll ring again.
R: *He said he would ring again.*
P: It's a personal call.
R: *He said it was a personal call.*
P: It's not urgent.
R: *He said it wasn't urgent.*

Aim: Further practice of reported speech in the past (SS can do this drill with their books closed).

Drill 220

Listen to these sentences in reported speech and say what the person said in direct speech, like this:

P: He said he wanted to see her.
R: *I want to see her.*

TELEPHONE MESSAGES

Now you try.
P: He said it was about some office furniture.
R: *It's about some office furniture.*
P: He said she knew all about it.
R: *She knows all about it.*
P: He said it was urgent.
R: *It's urgent.*
P: He said he was leaving the office at three o'clock.
R: *I'm leaving the office at three o'clock.*
P: He said he would ring again.
R: *I'll ring again.*

Aim: Comprehension of reported speech (SS can do this drill with their books closed).

WORKBOOK ANSWERS

Exercise 60 To do/doing

The remaining words are: *2 ringing   3 go   4 to hearing   5 work   6 to ring   7 to go   8 doing   9 to earn   10 see*
This is a revision exercise to distinguish structures which take the infinitive or *-ing*, with or without *to*.

Exercise 61 Rhyming words

1 weigh – b day   2 do – f through   3 car – a are   4 know – g go   5 chair – c wear   6 floor – i your   7 near – h here   8 I – d my   9 were – e her This exercise helps SS link sounds and spellings.

Exercise 62 Word puzzle

1 add   2 and   3 any   4 bad   5 bank   6 boring   7 box   8 coat   9 desk   10 know   11 letter   12 long   13 look   14 make   15 me   16 message   17 no   18 now   19 old   20 or   21 paper   22 pencil   23 ring   24 say   25 see   26 talk   27 tape   28 telephone   29 too The words in this puzzle are on no particular theme. SS might find other words in the puzzle.

Exercise 63 Reported speech

2 I like typing   3 I don't/He doesn't want to go.   4 She is going to visit me/him.   5 Helen's not having lunch today.   6 They/We are having a meeting. This exercise practises turning reported into direct speech. The variations possible depend on what or who the original speaker was referring to. Reported speech can frequently be ambiguous when you do not know the original context.

UNIT FIFTEEN
PLANS

15

> Business content: Meetings, minutes and agenda
> Structures: *Going to* future
> Reported speech (*continued*)
> Function: Discussing plans
> Lexis: Meetings

TEACHING NOTES

Exercise 223 Comprehension

Answers: *1 New items of stationery 2 The Middlesex branch 3 We do not know*

Aim: Comprehension and introduction of *going to*.

Use this exercise to introduce the concept of *going to* (ie intention; plans which are not definite). As you work through the questions, ask the SS whether Fred is talking about the present, the past or the future (the future). Then ask whether the plans are definite or not (not). They can then write a sentence using *going to* + infinitive taken from the tape and they are ready to practise the structure in the next exercise.

Exercise 224 Daydreams (LD)

Answers: *See LDT*

Aim: To practise *going to*.

Teach any vocabulary the SS do not know or let them decide in pairs which note refers to which picture. When they have done the exercise orally, they can write seven sentences for h/w. *A lot of* is slightly more formal than *lots of* (which could also be said in this exercise).

You could teach the three 'comparative' verbs in this unit together (see Exercise 229): *improve*, *enlarge* and *expand*.
NB The author recognises the possible sexist interpretation of this exercise, but also recognises that such people as Helen do exist.

Exercise 225 Dislikes (LD)

Answers: *See LDT*

Aim: To practice the negative of *going to* with polite responses.

SS should know all the vocabulary related to these pictures. Practise the response: *Oh aren't you?* (which indicates polite interest) with a fall-rise intonation (the same intonation as the question tag in LD 227). SS could also practise the pattern

PLANS

Oh are you? with Exercise 224. SS could write six sentences for h/w. (See also WB Exercise 64)

Exercise 226 Plans

Aim: Creative practice of the *going to* future (and possibly the present progressive future).

You may have to contrast the various future forms presented in this book (see SB page 127) before SS do this exercise. SS should use the present progressive to talk about definite arrangements they have for the future. Note that English people rarely use *going to* with the verbs *go* or *come*. They are more likely to use the present progressive future instead.

Exercise 227 Town planning (LD)

Answers: 1–c 2–8 3 see map below 4–a 5–10
6–a 7–I 8–E 9–b 10–P

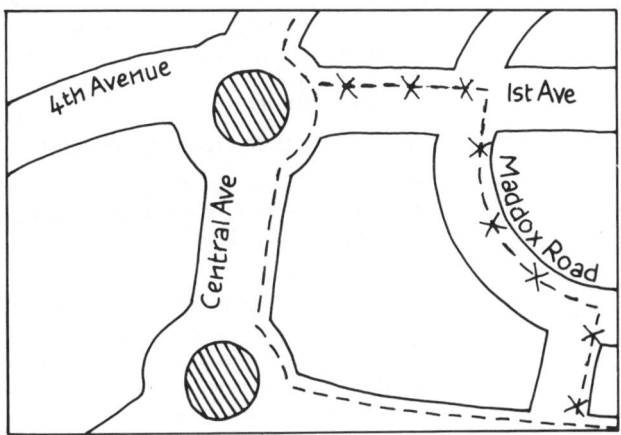

Aim: Listening comprehension.

Let SS listen to the tape as many times as necessary for them to answer the questions. Pre-teach *north* and *south* (and possibly *east* and *west* for completeness). The LD gives practice in forming question tags with sentences taken from this exercise.

SS could follow up this exercise by writing a short account of the changes which are going to take place in Harlow. SS could be encouraged to use passives (*The station is going to be closed*) and reported speech (*Simon/The planners said they were going to close the station.*)

Exercise 228 Meeting word puzzle

Answers: 1 *minutes* 2 *open* 3 *item* 4 *take* 5 *chair*
6 *present* 7 *agenda* 8 *close* Hidden word: *meetings*

Aim: To deduce the meaning of words from context.

UNIT FIFTEEN

Ask SS to do this exercise in pairs as a way of teaching themselves the vocabulary. You can ask them to learn it for h/w and in another lesson check that they have understood and remembered the words.

Exercise 229   **The agenda (LD A & B)**

Answers: *See LDT*

Aim: To practise the question form of *going to*.

Write a sentence containing *going to* on the board and see if SS can work out the question for themselves. You will need to teach any vocabulary the SS do not know and *I think so*. Note that in the negative it is possible to say *I think not*, but more usual to say *I don't think so*.

Exercise 230   **The minutes**

Answers: 1 meeting   2 director's   3 on   4 the   5 were   6 in   7 to   8 are/were   9 floor   10 said   11 the   12 enlarge   13 in   14 in   15 is   16 closing   17 branch/office   18 was   19 staff/workers/people/employees   20 at

Aim: To check SS' reading comprehension.

SS can do this exercise in pairs, in class under test conditions or for h/w. By this stage in the book, their reading level should be adequate for them to get at least 15 words correct.

You could look at the agenda and minutes with SS when they have done this exercise to see whether Mary was right in her predictions about what was going to happen (see Exercise 229) and make sentences such as *She thought they were going to ... and they did/but they did not. She did not think they were going to ... and they did not/but they did.*

Additional activity

Hold a small class meeting (eg about people coming to class late, not doing their h/w etc) and make recommendations for action. Ask SS to write an agenda. Have a chairman, but everyone should be responsible for taking their own notes which can be written up in the form of minutes.

Exercise 231   **Reported speech (LD)**

Answers: *See LDT*

Aim: Further practice of reported speech.

In this exercise SS work from what is reported to what was actually said.

Exercise 232   **News article**

Sample:

CHANGES AT BOS
There are going to be some changes at Brighter Office Supplies

Ltd, a local office equipment and stationery company. BOS has branches all over the country, but it is going to close its Middlesex branch shortly. Mr Fred McLean, BOS's managing director, said the Middlesex branch was losing money, but the company would offer jobs at the Harlow head office to the Middlesex staff. Mr McLean also said BOS were going to sell new items of stationery, but he did not give any details.

Aim: Creative writing.

The article can be written for h/w.

LANGUAGE DRILLS TAPESCRIPT

Drill 224 Listen to Helen daydreaming and say what she plans to do with her life, like this:

P: Improve my typing
R: *She's going to improve her typing.*

Now you try.
P: Work for a handsome boss
R: *She's going to work for a handsome boss.*
P: Earn more money
R: *She's going to earn more money.*
P: Travel abroad
R: *She's going to travel abroad.*
P: Marry my boss
R: *She's going to marry her boss.*
P: Have a lot of children
R: *She's going to have a lot of children.*
P: Do a lot of housework
R: *She's going to do a lot of housework.*

Aim: Practice of *going to* future (SS can do this drill with their books closed).

Drill 225 Say what Helen's not going to do, like this:

P: Open the post
R: *She's not going to open the post.*

Now you try.
P: Make coffee
R: *She's not going to make coffee.*
P: Type
R: *She's not going to type.*
P: Send telexes
R: *She's not going to send telexes.*
P: Do photocopying
R: *She's not going to do photocopying.*
P: Take shorthand
R: *She's not going to take shorthand.*

Aim: Practice of *going to* negative sentences (SS can do this drill with their books closed).

Drill 227 Express surprise at the changes that are planned for Harlow, like this:

P: They're going to make Rose Hill one way.
R: *They're not going to make Rose Hill one way, are they?*
P: The bus route is going to change.
R: *The bus route isn't going to change, is it?*

UNIT FIFTEEN

Now you try. Listen carefully to the intonation of the question tag and try to copy it exactly.

P: The station is going to close.
R: *The station isn't going to close, is it?*
P: They're going to move the supermarket.
R: *They're not going to move the supermarket, are they?*
P: They're going to knock down the old cinema.
R: *They're not going to knock down the old cinema, are they?*

P: They're going to open a new cinema.
R: *They're not going to open a new cinema, are they?*
P: They're going to build a new roundabout.
R: *They're not going to build a new roundabout, are they?*
P: It's going to happen next year.
R: *It's not going to happen next year, is it?*

Aim: Practice of question tags with *going to* (SS can do this drill with their books closed).
NB In the updated SB, the post office not the station is going to close.

Drill 229A

Look at the agenda for a meeting. Tell Simon what you think is going to happen at the meeting. If Mary has written a tick, answer like this:

P: Are they going to approve the minutes of the last meeting?
R: *Yes I think so.*

If Mary has written a cross, answer like this:
P: Are they going to approve the minutes of the last meeting?
R: *No I don't think so.*

Now you try with the other items on the agenda.

P: Are they going to redecorate the building?
R: *Yes I think so.*
P: Are they going to enlarge the office space?
R: *No I don't think so.*
P: Are they going to expand the business?
R: *Yes I think so.*

P: Are they going to hire more staff?
R: *Yes I think so.*
P: Are they going to export to Italy?
R: *No I don't think so.*
P: Are they going to close the Middlesex branch?
R: *No I don't think so.*

Aim: Comprehension; practice of short answers expressing opinion.

Drill 229B

Ask questions about the agenda for a meeting, like Simon:

P: Approving the minutes of the last meeting
R: *Are they going to approve the minutes of the last meeting?*

Now you try.
P: Redecorating the building
R: *Are they going to redecorate the building?*
P: Enlarging the office space
R: *Are they going to enlarge the office space?*
P: Expanding the business
R: *Are they going to expand the business?*
P: Hiring more staff
R: *Are they going to hire more staff?*
P: Exporting to Italy
R: *Are they going to export to Italy?*
P: Closing the Middlesex branch
R: *Are they going to close the Middlesex branch?*

Aim: Question practice with *going to* (SS can do this drill with their books closed).

Drill 231   Listen to these sentences in reported speech and say what people actually said, like this:

P: Mr McLean said it was going to take a week.
R: *It's going to take a week.*

Now you try.
P: He said they were going to start in January.
R: *We're going to start in January.*
P: Mr Hall said it was too expensive.
R: *It's too expensive.*
P: Mrs Baker said it wasn't necessary.
R: *It's not necessary.*
P: Mrs Baker said there was a new market in Italy.
R: *There's a new market in Italy.*
P: She said Lorenzo Magnani would be in charge.
R: *Lorenzo Magnani will be in charge.*
P: Mr McLean said they were closing the Middlesex branch.
R: *We're closing the Middlesex branch.*
P: He said it was losing money.
R: *It's losing money.*
P: Mr Spencer said BOS needed more staff at their main office.
R: *We need more staff at our main office.*
P: Mr McLean said they would offer jobs to the Middlesex staff.
R: *We'll offer jobs to the Middlesex staff.*

Aim: Further practice of reported speech (SS can do this drill with their books closed).

WORKBOOK ANSWERS

Exercise 64   Short responses

3 *Oh will you?*   4 *Oh have you?*   5 *Oh must you?*   6 *Oh can't you?*   7 *Oh do you?*   8 *Oh were you?*   9 *Oh won't you?*   10 *Oh haven't you?* (NB *never* makes this sentence negative.) This exercise practises writing polite responses with a variety of modal and auxiliary verbs.

UNIT FIFTEEN

Exercise 65 Going to/present progressive

3 I am not coming to work tomorrow.   4 I am going to get a job.   5 They are going to have a meeting.   6 What is he going to do? This exercise contrasts two future forms.

Exercise 66 Word stress

2 *photocopy* Oooo – c *supermarket* Oooo   3 *roundabout* Ooo – h *anywhere* Ooo
4 *around* oO – b *precise* oO   5 *apostrophe* oOoo – g *redecorate* oOoo   6 *agenda* oOo – a *direction* oOo   7 *housework* Oo – d *handsome* Oo   8 *understand* ooO – e *personnel* ooO

This exercise revises and provides further practice in recognising word stress. (See also SB Exercises 96–99 and WB Exercise 40)

Exercise 67 The news

1 headline   2 newspaper   3 journalist   4 reporter   5 editor   6 article This exercise focuses on vocabulary to do with newspapers.

Exercise 68 A worker's quiz

A 8,760   B 2,920   C 5,840   D 2,496   E 3,344   F 365   G 2,979   H 504   I 2,475   J 1,825   K 650   L 365   M 285   N 84   O 201   P 192   Q 9   R 0

This is a light-hearted quiz to practise reading comprehension. Because large numbers are are involved and students are liable to make mistakes, encourage them to help and correct each other in English for extra practice of numbers.

CONSOLIDATION UNIT C
YOUR NEWS AND NEWS EXTRACTS

TEACHING NOTES

Exercise 233 Headline grammar

Answers: 1–a, b, c, d, i 2–e, f, k 3–h, j 4–g, l

Aim: Deciphering newspaper headlines.

Take the headlines from the book (or cut out of British newspapers headlines which conform to the four rules given in the SB) and write them on the board. Ask SS to arrange them into categories (they decide what the categories are) and see if they can decide on the 'grammatical rules' for themselves. You can then talk about the meaning of the headlines and whether they refer to actions or facts in the past, present or future. Before SS look at the articles on SB page 129 they could speculate from the headlines what they expect the articles to be about (*It might/could be about . . .*).

Exercise 234 Matching headlines

The answers to this exercise are a matter of opinion.

Suggestions are: 1–d 2–b/i 3–f/g 4–c/h 5–a/l 6–e/j

Aim: To encourage skim reading.

SS need have only a general impression of what the articles are about in order to do this exercise. The class could come to an agreement about which headline is suitable for which article in a general discussion or you could organise a pyramid activity to achieve the same result (see TB Exercise 106).

Additional activity

Cut a number of different articles out of an English newspaper, cut the headline off each and ask SS to match the headlines with the articles.

Exercise 235 Wrong order

Answer:

FOCUS ON EUROPE
The first European Community was the ECSC (the European Coal and Steel Community) which was founded in 1952. The six founder countries were Belgium, France, the Netherlands, Germany, Italy and Luxembourg. Steel production increased steadily after 1952, but oil began to take over the market from coal.

The first talks about greater economic integration in Europe were held in Sicily in 1955. On 25th March 1957, the six founder members of the ECSC signed the Treaty of Rome and founded the EEC (the European Economic Community, also called the Common

CONSOLIDATION UNIT C

Market). The intention was to make trading easier and for people to be able to travel freely between the member countries. Britain, Ireland and Denmark joined what is now known as the EC (the European Community) on 1st January 1973 and Greece followed in 1981. Since then other European countries have joined and are continuing to join and more and more aspects of life are being controlled from the central European parliament in Brussels.

Aim: Reading comprehension and sequencing sentences.

Give this exercise to SS to do in pairs without any preparation.
NB Note the use of commas in the list of countries in line 3. If this sentence is read aloud, there is a rising intonation on all the countries in the list except the last one when the voice should fall (see Exercise 136).

Exercise 236 Missing words

Answers: Prices are going *down* in the... and supermarkets *are* cutting... is 10% (or *per cent*) higher... many prices *are* lower... money than last *year* too.

Aim: Reading comprehension and to test SS' knowledge of sentence structure.

No preparation necessary.

Exercise 237 Bad printing

Answers: 1 *director* 2 *factory* 3 *yesterday* 4 *because* 5 *office* 6 *taken* 7 *friend* 8 *from*

Aim: Reading comprehension and to test SS' knowledge of sentence structure.

No preparation necessary.

Exercise 238 Reported speech

Answers: Article 3: He said he was going home./*I'm going home*. He said he didn't feel well./*I don't feel well*. Article 4: She said she didn't like her boss./*I don't like my boss*. Article 5: Officials say next year's figures will be higher./*Next year's figures will be higher*. Article 6: Mr Stubbs says the cigarette was his. /*The cigarette was mine*.

Aim: To encourage scanning; to practise reported speech.

Exercise 239 News quiz

Aim: To encourage scanning; question practise.

SS must write one question for each article on SB page 129. It is best done as classwork in pairs or small groups, although questions can be written by individuals for h/w, exchanged in class and answered either in class or for h/w (in which case SS should also be on the lookout for mistakes in questions they are given).

CONSOLIDATION UNIT C

Additional activity

Make up your own news quiz using a British newspaper. Ask one question per page (but not necessarily one question for every page). You need enough copies of the paper for one between three or four SS (the same paper can be used again for other activities.) The quiz can be written at any language level – elementary SS will be directed to very obvious information to do with headlines or pictures, while advanced SS could search for some specific information in the text of an article.

Exercise 240 Radio news

Answers: *1–b   2–c   3–a   4–a   5–a*

Aim: To distinguish the main point of a news item in furtherance of note-taking skills.

Allow SS to decide on their answers in small groups and then discuss the answers with the whole class. If the class decide that one of the answers is better than the answer suggested and they can support this with reasons, it is a good idea to accept that answer.

Exercise 241 Headlines

Suggestions: *SECOND STRIKE AT WHITAKER'S; EMPLOYEES NOT TO SHARE RECORD PROFIT; FUNERAL OF SIR ALAN SMITH; LONDON'S LOWEST RECORDED TEMPERATURE; WORK FOR A RADIO PROGRAMME*

Aim: To distinguish the main point of news items and to practise headline (telex) writing.

These answers are based on the answers to Exercise 241. They are only suggestions and the class might come up with headlines they like better. This exercise is best done in groups or as a pyramid activity (see TB Exercise 106).

Exercise 242 A family tree

Answers: *Sir Alan Smith had three children. Two were boys and one was a girl (you can only have an 'elder' of two). The elder son is single, but we do not know whether the other two children are married. Sir Alan had two grandchildren. They were both girls. The possibilities of the family tree are:*
1 *Sir Alan's daughter might be older or younger than his second son.*
2 *Sir Alan's second son could be married or single. His daughter might be married or single.*
3 *Both the granddaughters could be the children of the second son or of the daughter, or the son and the daughter could have one child each.*

CONSOLIDATION UNIT C

Aim: Revision of *might/could be*.

This exercise is designed to be discussed in class. If you did not introduce the family vocabulary suggested in the additional activities in Consolidation Unit A you will need to do so before SS do this exercise.

Exercise 243 A radio programme

Aim: Creativity and fluency.

This exercise is intended as a class project. Either the whole class produces a radio programme together or the SS work in groups in which each produce their own programme.

Discuss the project before the SS begin and decide on five topics which everyone will have in their programme (eg somebody dying, a strike, an item about the weather etc). Elicit ways in which more than one person can speak in the programme to add interest (eg interviews, specialist reporters, reporters 'on the spot') and then set a deadline (eg 30 minutes) after which time SS must 'go on the air' (preferably speaking into a cassette recorder). Their programmes can be shorter than five minutes, but not longer. If you tape the 'programmes' SS will enjoy listening to them afterwards (beware stopping the tape too often to correct mistakes as this can be de-motivating – see TB page xxvii).

There are no language drills for the Consolidation Units.

WORKBOOK ANSWERS – TEST C

Allow SS 20 minutes to do this test.

Part one   Question formation

1 Where is tea grown?   2 Has she typed the letter yet? 3 How long is it going to take?   4 When did they close the Newcastle branch?   5 Whose typewriter is the oldest?

Mark this section out of ten. Give two marks for each sentence and subtract half a mark for each mistake, up to a maximum of two marks per sentence.

Part two   Reported speech

1 We/They are leaving.   2 I/She will ring him.   3 He goes/ You go to work by bus.   4 She/You can't/cannot do it.   5 It is in my/her office. Although variations are possible, SS should only write one sentence for each question.

Give two marks per sentence. Subtract half a mark for each mistake up to a maximum of two marks per sentence.

Part three   Past participles

1 written   2 broken   3 sent   4 exported   5 seen

Give one mark for each correct answer.

CONSOLIDATION UNIT C

Part four Short responses

1 So do I   *2 Nor can I*   *3 So must I*   *4 Nor am I*   *5 So have I* Give one mark for each correct answer.

Part five Figures

1 twenty-two and a half per cent   *2 seven hundred and twenty-five pounds*   *3 six thousand, two hundred and ninety-four dollars*   *4 three hundred and sixty degrees*   *5 eight million*
Give one mark for each correct answer. Subtract half a mark if there is only one mistake in a phrase.

Part six Comparatives

1 more expensive   *2 bigger*   *3 more intelligent*   *4 less*   *5 easier*
Give one mark for each correct answer.

This test is marked out of 40. To find a percentage mark, multiply each total by 4/10 (or 2/5).

TEST D

Allow fifteen minutes for this test which consists of multiple choice sentence completion.

Part one   *1–c*   *2–d*   *3–b*   *4–b*   *5–a*   *6–c*   *7–a*   *8–a*   *9–c*   *10–a*

Part two   *11–a*   *12–c*   *13–c*   *14–b*   *15–a*

Allow one mark for each correct answer. The test is marked out of fifteen.

Final note

Thank you for choosing *We Mean Business*.
We hope you have found it effective and enjoyable to use.